Ancient Paquimé and the Casas Grandes World

Amerind Studies in Anthropology

Series Editor **John A. Ware**

Ancient Paquimé and the Casas Grandes World

Edited by **Paul E. Minnis**
and **Michael E. Whalen**

The University of
Arizona Press

TUCSON

The University of Arizona Press
www.uapress.arizona.edu

We respectfully acknowledge the University of Arizona is on the land and territories of Indigenous peoples. Today, Arizona is home to twenty-two federally recognized tribes, with Tucson being home to the O'odham and the Yaqui. Committed to diversity and inclusion, the University strives to build sustainable relationships with sovereign Native Nations and Indigenous communities through education offerings, partnerships, and community service.

© 2015 The Arizona Board of Regents
All rights reserved. Published 2015
First paperback edition published 2025

ISBN-13: 978-0-8165-3131-8 (cloth)
ISBN-13: 978-0-8165-5596-3 (paper)
ISBN-13: 978-0-8165-0220-2 (ebook)

Cover designed by Miriam Warren
Cover photo © Adriel Heisey

Publication of this book was made possible by the Department of Anthropology, the College of Arts and Sciences, and the Office of Research and Sponsored Programs at the University of Tulsa.

Library of Congress Cataloging-in-Publication Data
Ancient Paquimé and the Casas Grandes world / edited by Paul E. Minnis and Michael E. Whalen.
    pages cm — (Amerind series in anthropology)
  Includes bibliographical references and index.
  ISBN 978-0-8165-3131-8 (hardcover : alk. paper)
  1. Casas Grandes culture. 2. Casas Grandes Site (Mexico)   I. Minnis, Paul E., editor. II. Whalen, Michael E., editor.   III. Series: Amerind series in anthropology.
  E99.C23A53 2015
  972'.16—dc23
                    2014030797

Printed in the United States of America
♾ This paper meets the requirements of ANSI/NISO Z39.48-1992 (Permanence of Paper).

*Dedicated to the members and supporters
of the Joint Casas Grandes Expedition*

*Especially to Charles C. Di Peso
and
Eduardo Contreras Sánchez*

Charles C. Di Peso (left) and Eduardo Contreras Sánchez (right) (Courtesy of the Amerind Foundation).

CONTENTS

Foreword by John A. Ware — ix

Introduction: The Joint Casas Grandes Expedition in Historical Context — 3
Paul E. Minnis and Michael E. Whalen

1. Beginnings: The Viejo Period — 17
Jane H. Kelley and Michael T. Searcy

2. Ecology and Food Economy — 41
Paul E. Minnis and Michael E. Whalen

3. Organization of Production at Paquimé — 58
Gordon F. M. Rakita and Rafael Cruz

4. Religion and Cosmology in the Casas Grandes World — 83
Christine S. VanPool and Todd L. VanPool

5. Settlement Patterns of the Casas Grandes Area — 103
Michael E. Whalen and Todd Pitezel

6. Society and Polity in the Wider Casas Grandes Region — 126
John E. Douglas and A. C. MacWilliams

7. The End of Paquimé and the Casas Grandes Culture — 148
David A. Phillips, Jr., and Eduardo Gamboa

8. Paquimé: A Revision of Its Relationships to the South and West — 172
José Luis Punzo and M. Elisa Villalpando

9. Ancient Paquimé: A View from the North — 192
Linda S. Cordell

References Cited — 209
Contributors — 239
Index — 245

FOREWORD

In the late 1950s, the Amerind Foundation's young director, Dr. Charles C. Di Peso, had just completed a decade-long series of excavation projects in southern Arizona and was looking forward to a sabbatical in Italy where he planned to spend his leisure time tracing his family roots. Amerind's founder, William Shirley Fulton, had other plans. He asked Charlie to postpone his vacation a year or two until after their planned excavations at Casas Grandes were wrapped up. Di Peso spent most of the next three years in northern Chihuahua directing the Joint Casas Grandes Expedition (JCGE), and, on his return to Dragoon, he devoted the next 13 years to analyzing, crafting, and publishing the results of the work. Italy was forgotten in the swirl of activities that formed around one of the largest archaeological projects ever attempted in the U.S.-Mexico borderlands.

Charlie Di Peso's prodigious research efforts in the borderlands, capped by the JCGE and its massive eight-volume excavation report, which J. Charles Kelley once referred to Charlie's beautifully illustrated Casas Grandes report as the "Codex Di Peso," forms a legacy that includes a remarkably broad vision of Southwest prehistory backed by painstaking research and meticulous documentation (Di Peso 1974, vols. 1–3; Di Peso, Rinaldo, and Fenner 1974, vols. 4–8). Few archaeologists manage to publish all the research they do, but Di Peso came close. And he wrote without jargon for a broad audience, not just the people with clusters of capital letters after their names, because he believed that research and education must go hand in hand. In addition to the many colored illustrations, Di Peso insisted on including vast quantities of data so that his colleagues in archaeology would be inspired to pursue their own research using his data. The final five volumes of his Casas Grandes opus are packed with data tables, statistics, maps, and figures that have inspired North American and Mexican researchers for four decades.

Charlie Di Peso was only 62 when he died in 1982, but his legacy as one of the principal theorists of Southwest archaeology already had been established. A member of one of the first cohorts of graduate students trained at the University of Arizona under Emil Haury and Edward Spicer—who viewed the Southwest as part of a much larger region that included most of northwest Mexico—Di Peso would devote his considerable research energies to addressing the implications of this wider region, which he called the *Gran Chichimeca* (a typical Di Peso flourish!). The narrative he embraced very early and refined over the years described waves of migrants, raiders, and traders coming from the central highlands and west coast of Mexico to interact with, influence, and ultimately control the indigenous people of Mexico's northwestern frontier. People from the south brought new technologies, political organizations, and religions, and took home turquoise—the God-stone of the Toltecs. What Di Peso found at Casas Grandes helped him fill in the details of this "archaeohistorical" narrative: a Mesoamerican outpost established in the eleventh century whose merchant rulers used mercantile coercion to control a vast northern region rich in turquoise and other commodities.

Six years after Di Peso's death, the Amerind Foundation sponsored a retrospective seminar to examine his legacy and work (Woosley and Ravesloot 1993). All the papers in that seminar praised Di Peso's vision, but many were critical of his interpretations; other papers brought new data to light that expanded and complicated the Di Peso narrative. The present volume goes much further by summarizing nearly 30 years of research conducted in northern Chihuahua and adjacent areas since the Di Peso retrospective. In those 30 years, there has been something of a renaissance of archaeological research on the Casas Grandes world, all of it inspired by Di Peso's pioneering work. A world-class museum (Museo de las Culturas del Norte) was opened adjacent to the site in 1996, and Casas Grandes was designated a UNESCO World Heritage Site in 1998, and a new generation of Mexican, U.S., and Canadian archaeologists began collaborations that have advanced our understanding of the regional character and historical context of Casas Grandes society. Charlie would be very pleased!

The editors of the current volume are perhaps better equipped than anyone else to reflect on and synthesize the recent research in northern Chihuahua. Paul Minnis, from the University of Oklahoma, and Michael Whalen, from the University of Tulsa, came to Chihuahua in the late 1980s to work with archaeologists from Mexico's Instituto Nacional de Antropología e Historia in order to study the larger region around Casas Grandes (known locally as Paquimé). Surveying northwest Chihuahua, Minnis, Whalen, and colleagues documented a long developmental sequence starting with the earliest hunters and gatherers 12,000 years ago, progressing from there to the first scattered farming villages around AD 200, and finally to the fluorescence of Paquimé—a deeply stratified community with evidence of organized labor, craft production, and a complex ritual-political system—that influenced a large swatch of the U.S.-Mexico Borderlands in the thirteenth and fourteenth centuries. Many of the authors of the present work came to Chihuahua as students to work for Minnis and Whalen and have gone from there to pursue careers in archaeology.

The present volume had its genesis in 2007 at the annual meeting of the Society for American Archaeology (SAA) in Austin, Texas, where Paul, Mike, and I sat down to discuss the need for an advanced seminar on recent work in Chihuahua. From that meeting came a symposium the following year at the SAAs in Vancouver, where many of the present chapter authors participated. Our plan at the time was to bring the participants to the Amerind Foundation in Dragoon for a multi-day seminar in 2008, the year following the Vancouver meetings, but other commitments intervened, and I was unable to carve out time and resources for the Amerind seminar until the fall of 2012. In retrospect, that decision produced a happy coincidence, as 2012 marked the 75th anniversary of the Amerind Foundation, and this edited volume from the seminar that year will be published close to, if not precisely on, the fortieth anniversary of the publication of Di Peso's magnum opus.

The work of the present authors in northwest Mexico has added greatly to our knowledge of the Northwest/Southwest (NW/SW), and their work continues to challenge many of the interpretations of the JCGE, as readers will see in the chapters that follow. That, of course, is the nature of scholarship in science and history. We respect those who came before, but we reserve our most abiding respect for historical facts. As new facts come to light, interpretations inevitably change. Thirty years hence (or much sooner, since the pace of archaeological research seems to be constantly accelerating), the research and interpretations presented here will be reviewed, new facts will be brought to bear, and old theories will be challenged and discarded as new theories are advanced. And, who knows, some previously discarded theories may be resurrected in light of the new facts! It is my hope that the Amerind Foundation will continue to play an important role in ongoing research in northwest Mexico, and that the legacy of Charlie Di Peso will continue to inspire creative research on the deep history of the U.S.-Mexico Borderlands.

—John A. Ware, Editor
Amerind Series in Anthropology

Ancient Paquimé and the Casas Grandes World

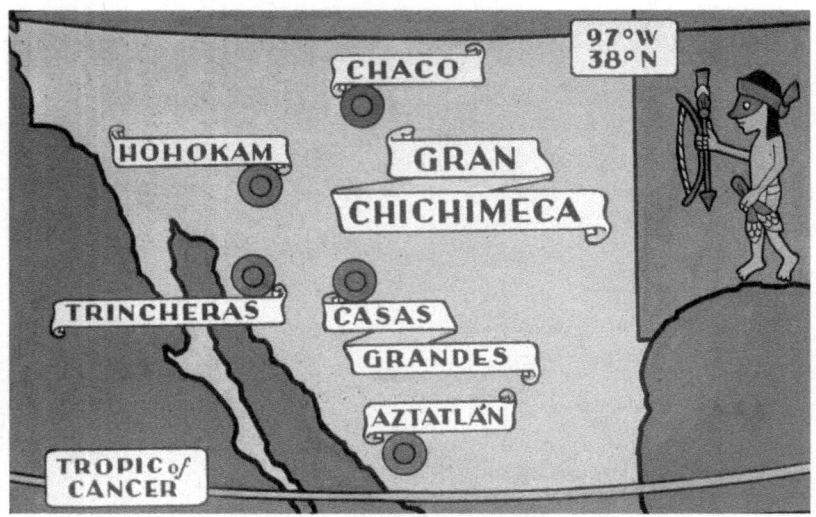

An original Joint Casas Grandes Expedition illustration of Paquimé (Casas Grandes) in the U.S. Southwest and northern Mexico (Courtesy of the Amerind Foundation).

Introduction

The Joint Casas Grandes Expedition in Historical Context

Paul E. Minnis and Michael E. Whalen

Casas Grandes (Paquimé) has been long recognized as one of the premier pre-Hispanic communities in northwest Mexico-U.S. Southwest (NW/SW). Despite its importance, the history of research of the region has not only varied greatly through time, but has lagged behind many adjacent areas.

The first European explorers in the region noted the site—one of the first archaeological sites in what is now the NW/SW described by Europeans—in the mid-1560s. Balthazar de Obregón, the chronicler of the Ibarra Expedition, described Paquimé perhaps a short time after its abandonment:

> There are many houses of great size, strength, and height. They are 6–7 stories with towers and walls like fortresses for protection and defense against the enemies who undoubtedly used to make war on its inhabitants. The houses contain large and magnificent patios paved with enormous and beautiful stones resembling jasper. There are knife-shaped (cut?) stones which support the wonderful and big pillars of heavy timbers brought from far away. The walls of the houses were whitewashed and painted in many colors and shades with pictures of the buildings. The structures had some kind of adobe walls. However, it was mixed and interspersed with stone and wood, this combination being stronger and more durable than boards. (Hammond and Rey 1928, 206)

Unfortunately, Paquimé was largely ignored for the following half-millennia until 1958 when the Joint Casas Grandes Expedition (JCGE) began. The JCGE changed forever the place of the Casas Grandes region in archaeological research. The Amerind Foundation was one of the two principal institutions of the JCGE, and this project is one of the signature contributions of the Amerind Foundation. As such, we hope that this volume is a fitting tribute to the institution and its staff during the Amerind's 75th anniversary and the fortieth anniversary of the publication of its monumental, eight-volume report.

Early Interest in Casas Grandes: 1567–1959

For 500 years after Obregón's visit, a small number of scholars, adventurers, and others visited northwest Chihuahua and Paquimé. However, there was almost no research except for some initial reconnaissance survey. Some well-known foreign explorers, such as Bartlett (1854), Bandelier (1890), and Lumholtz (1902) visited and described the ruins as did lesser known figures such as Blackiston (1905, 1906a, 1906b, 1908, 1909). Mexican scholars also presented descriptions, including Noguera (1930) and Robles (1929).

The beginning of modern archaeology in Chihuahua arguably are found in reconnaissance surveys by Brand (1933, 1935, 1936, 1943) and E. B. Sayles (1936). Donald Brand's primary research was conducted for his doctoral dissertation in geography at the University of California, Berkeley. Sayles's research was part of a wider effort by the Gila Pueblo, a private research foundation in Globe, Arizona, to document the regional variation of archaeological traditions throughout the NW/SW. Brand and Sayles described hundreds of archeological sites and conducted a little excavation. Robert Lister (1946, 1953, 1958) excavated cave sites in the Sierra Madre, just west of Casas Grandes, and Henry Carey (1931) tested sites in the Casas Grandes region. This limited amount of research prior to 1959 began building a foundation defining Chihuahuan archaeology by highlighting the interesting nature of pre-Hispanic heritage. Given the small number of researchers, it was only a skeletal foundation.

The paucity of scientific attention is especially glaring when northwest Chihuahua is contrasted with two adjacent areas that are two of the most intensively investigated regions in the world. With Mesoamerica's spectacular ruins that have attracted attention for centuries, it is not surprising that Mexican archaeologists have focused in these areas of the country. To the north, the U.S. Southwest has long fascinated a large number of archaeologists because of its pre-Hispanic remains. For over more than a century, many archaeologists have investigated hundreds of archaeological locations in the U.S. Southwest. Perhaps this can be illustrated by Chaco Canyon, a general analogy to Casas Grandes, because both were major and influential centers in the pre-Hispanic NW/SW. The bibliography of a recent summary of Chacoan archaeology (Lekson 2006) enumerates about 125 archaeologists who have published on Chaco. In contrast, very few North American archaeologists have ventured south of the border to Chihuahua (or other borderland states). Most of those who have done so did not make these areas their professional foci, so research continued in fits and starts. Likewise, Mexican archeologists largely ignored the northern-most part of their country.

This lack of research is unfortunate for two major reasons. First, it delayed an understanding of the unique pre-Hispanic history of the region. As importantly, there were pre-Hispanic relationships between Mexico and the U.S. Southwest. Understanding the prehistory of northwest Mexico, the intervening region between the Southwest and Mesoamerica, including West Mexico, is essential for detailing the nature, scope, and scale of the relationships between the three areas. These deficiencies were recognized and addressed by an archaeological project of unprecedented scale and complexity.

The Joint Casas Grandes Expedition

The watershed for Chihuahuan archaeology was the JCGE, which conducted fieldwork from 1958 to 1961. Charles C. Di Peso and William Shirley Fulton, founder and patron of the Amerind Foundation, first conceived the JCGE in collaboration with the Instituto Nacional de Antropología e Historia (INAH), and the JCGE still remains after many decades the largest internationally collaborative archaeological project in the NW/SW. Di Peso was responsible for the excavations, analyses, and publication of the results. As the representative of INAH, Eduardo Contreras Sánchez, mapped the site and oversaw the herculean task of stabilization and reconstruction of the excavated structures. John Rinaldo and Gloria Fenner were the primary collaborators and coauthors during analyses and preparation of the publications. Needless to say, many others, from photographers, analytic specialists, office staff, support staff, and local excavation crew members were needed to bring to completion this massive project (see Di Peso 1974:1, 20–47 for a discussion of the project organization, history, and staffing). Contreras (1982, 1985, 1986) authored several monographs in Spanish on the site, although they are not as well known as JCGE's major publication, *Casas Grandes: A Fallen Trading Center of the Gran Chichimeca* (Di Peso 1974, vols. 1–3; Di Peso, Rinaldo, and Fenner 1974, vols. 4–8). Along with the Snaketown project (Gladwin et al. 1936), the JCGE was one of the two largest and best-organized archeological projects of its day in the NW/SW, and it remains one of the most important classics in archaeology of the region (Figures I.1 and I.2).

Here we very briefly summarize JCGE's excavation at Paquimé as a guide for those unfamiliar with its characteristics. The focus of the

Figure I.1. Aerial view of Paquimé before excavation, looking south (Courtesy of the Amerind Foundation).

Introduction

Figure I.2. Aerial view of Paquimé excavations, looking south (Courtesy of the Amerind Foundation).

JCGE was the Medio Period, which Di Peso dated to AD 1060–1340, dates now universally recognized as beginning too early. Rather, the Medio now begins AD 1150/1200 and continues until the mid-to-late 1400s. During this period, Paquimé was a vibrant community influencing if not controlling hundreds of outlying communities. It is argued to have been heavily invested in long-distance trade. Di Peso believed that Paquimé was then destroyed in an epic attack that ended its role as a central community in the southern NW/SW. The authors of the following chapters discuss various aspects of this narrative in light of current research.

Excavation at Paquimé proceeded from west to east revealing isolated adobe-walled room blocks, multistory room blocks, a complex water distribution system, ball courts, platform and effigy mounds, large earthen ovens, and other features. A crew of local workers did the basic excavation under the supervision of the archaeologists, and overburden was removed by mechanical equipment. As was common for that time, few deposits were fine screened, and most screening was through a wide mesh. This efficient methodology uncovered large areas. From the perspective of current field techniques, the very limited fine screening resulted in the recovery of few very small artifacts, so some analytic comparisons with artifact assemblages from modern projects can be difficult. Much of Paquimé remains unexcavated.

Di Peso describes Paquimé as U-shaped with a large central plaza. The intensive excavations concentrated on the western portion of this community organization with only testing on the eastern side of the site. Others (Whalen, Mac Williams, and Pitezel 2010) argue that there are no multistoried, eastern room blocks, and they suggest that there were closer to 1,100 rooms rather than the about 2,300 suggested by Di Peso (1974, vols. 1–3). This would then reduce the estimated population of Paquimé from about 5,000 at its height closer to 2,000.

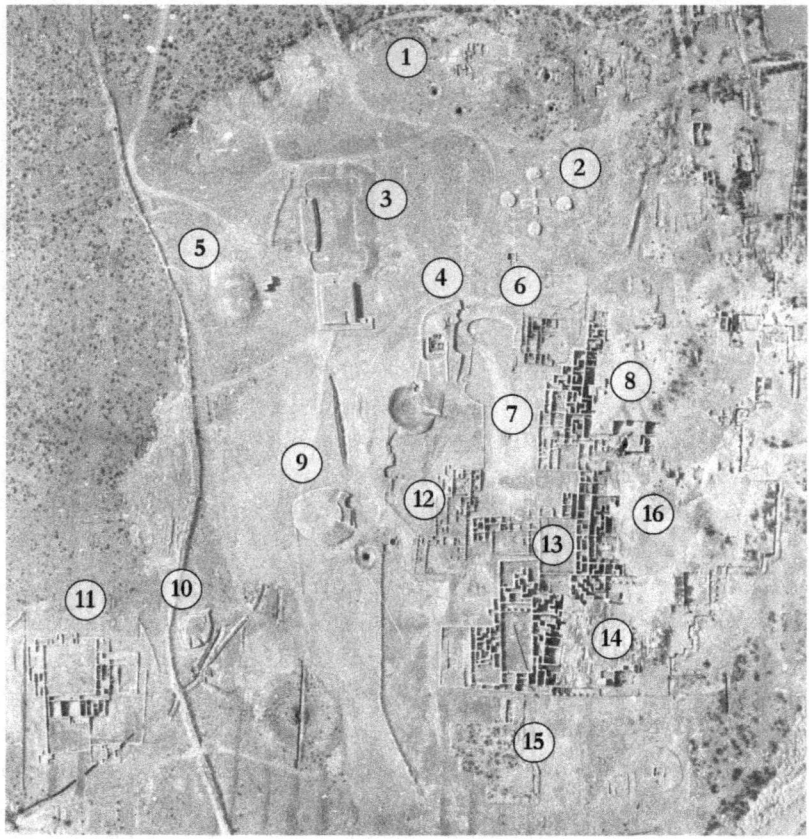

Figure I.3. Major excavation units of the Joint Casas Grandes Expedition (Courtesy of the Amerind Foundation).

Excavation areas were divided into "units" which were either discreet features, such as ball courts or mounds, or clusters of rooms within room blocks. Below is a summary of the units (see Figure I.3). Exceptionally detailed descriptions of these units are present in Di Peso (1974, vols. 1–3) and Di Peso, Rinaldo, and Fenner (1974, vols. 4–8).

A Short Description of Paquimé

Paquime is a remarkable community, much of which was revealed by JCGE's research. Below are very brief descriptions of JCGE's major excavation units.

UNIT 1: MOUND OF THE PIT OVENS. Located at the north end of the site, this unit consists of 2 room blocks with about 10 rooms and 4 exceptionally large earthen ovens surround a mound composed in part of cooking debris from the ovens.

UNIT 2: MOUND OF THE CROSS. A low cross shaped feature slightly less than 40 m in length with a low circular mound at the end of each cross arm. This feature may mark specific sunrises.

UNIT 3: BALL COURT I. This is the largest ball court at Paquimé and probably in the Casas Grandes region. Its flat field is about 19 × 50 m that is flanked on one side by a low rectangular mound and a taller square mound on its southern end.

UNIT 4: MOUND OF THE OFFERINGS. This eccentrically shaped mound is at the northwestern corner of the main plaza near a reservoir. Embedded within the main mound features are three small tombs. One held a finely made, ground stone altar, and the other two contained very special secondary burials. An unusual set of adobe walled enclosures are present in an enclosed plaza within the southern portion of this unit.

UNIT 5: MOUND 1–5. This is a mound south of Ball Court I. It was most likely an incomplete ceremonial mound, a stockpile of construction material, or a trash deposit.

UNIT 6: HOUSE-CLUSTER. This is a one- and two-story, adobe-walled room block with approximately 30 rooms of different periods surrounding an enclosed plaza. Viejo period pithouses were present.

UNIT 7: RETAINING WALL AND ROOM. The western edge of the main plaza is demarcated by a low stone wall with a small embedded room having a *jacal* front wall facing the plaza.

UNIT 8: HOUSE OF THE WELL. This unit is one of the largest multi-storied room blocks at Paquimé with about 75 excavated rooms and multiple enclosed plazas. It is named after the walk-in well, a water shrine below one of the plazas. In addition to the many domestic rooms, several rooms contained vast quantities of goods, such as shell, unworked minerals, and whole vessels.

UNIT 9: MOUND OF THE HEROES. A large, roughly circular mound, 55 × 40 m, dominates this unit. It is next to what is likely the largest earthen pit oven in the NW/SW and other features interpreted by Di Peso as pithouses.

UNIT 10: MOUND OF THE BIRD. This large earthen mound, approximately 24 × 17 m, is shaped like a decapitated bird.

UNIT 11: HOUSE OF THE SERPENT. This complex is located at the far western portion of the site. It is a single-story room block with approximately 30 rooms and 4 walled plazas. Just to the west is a low mound shaped as a feathered/horned effigy about 115 m long.

UNIT 12: HOUSE OF THE MACAWS. This set of single-story high rooms is named for the plaza with the best-preserved macaw pens and with numerous macaw burials. About 35 rooms surround three to five plazas.

UNIT 13: HOUSE OF THE DEAD. This unit of 19 excavated rooms and 2 plazas yielded an unusually large number of burials. One of the plazas had a large number of turkey pens and turkey burials. One room contained a unique subfloor burial chamber interpreted as the internment of a very special person.

UNIT 14: HOUSE OF THE PILLARS. This unit is one of the large, multistoried set of room blocks with around up to 6 plazas and what is interpreted as a small ball court enclosed in one of the plazas. Several rooms in this unit have notably eccentric shapes that likely indicate other than domestic use. One of the site's most impressive colonnades faces south from this unit.

UNIT 15: HOUSE-CLUSTER. This largely unexcavated unit was estimated to have had about 30 one-story rooms and at least one plaza. Two rooms were excavated by the JCGE.

UNIT 16: HOUSE OF THE SKULLS. Named for "trophy" skulls found in a cruciform room, this unit is one of the large multistoried sets of room blocks and has at least two plazas. Thirty-nine rooms were excavated.

UNIT 17: BALL COURT II. This large ball court at the southern end of the site is much like Ball Court I but has been partially destroyed by an arroyo.

Introduction

UNIT 18. This unit at the south end of the site had a small room block and a rectangular room on a platform, a unique architectural feature at Paquimé.

UNITS 19–23: HOUSE-CLUSTERS AND NORTH-HOUSE. These units are largely unexcavated room blocks.

WATER SYSTEM. The water distribution system at Paquimé is truly remarkable; nothing like it existed in the pre-Hispanic NW/SW. A canal (5 km long) brought water from the dependable Ojo Varaleño north of the site to a reservoir that diverted water into canals snaking throughout the room blocks. The system was changed, and a new reservoir constructed. A series of drainage canals removed water from the adobe room blocks.

JCGE's Research at Other Sites

While most work at Paquimé focused on the community's apogee in the Medio Period (AD 1150/1200–late 1400s), the JCGE also excavated earlier and later sites. The Convento site, just north of Paquimé, includes the ruins of the church of San Antonio de Padua, which dates to the early seventeenth century (Figure I.4). While testing this historic site,

Figure I.4. The Convento site, the colonial Spanish church and much earlier Viejo Period village (Courtesy of the Amerind Foundation).

the project discovered a village of semisubterranean structures dating to the Viejo Period, the time predating the Medio Period. This pithouse village forms the foundation for our understanding of the Viejo Period. Finally, the JCGE did other very limited excavations and reconnaissance surveys that emphasized Medio Period sites.

Di Peso's Interpretive Framework and Outreach

The project not only pioneered the collection of data about the prehistory of northwest Chihuahua, but it also introduced an interpretation that was new and novel in two ways. First, Di Peso used an interpretive approach he called archaeohistory, a highly detailed historical account of the rise and fall of Paquimé. While we have criticized this approach (Whalen and Minnis 2001; see also Cordell, this volume), it did provide an easily accessible narrative for all readers. Second, he saw the development of Paquimé as a result of direct trade between Mesoamerica and the NW/SW. In fact, he suggested that long-distance traders from Mesoamerica (like the Aztec *pochteca* or *puchteca*) organized and controlled Paquimé as a trading center. Moreover, he phrased the discussion of religion and economy in a way traditionally conceived for polities with powerful leaders and complex economies with many craft specialists. This interpretation contrasted sharply with the dominant view among North American archaeologists at the time, who argued that developments in the NW/SW were largely local and that economic production was less organized.

Finally, the JCGE was a pioneer in public outreach. The eight volumes published on the site are arranged for different audiences. The first three volumes are well-illustrated overviews that both professionals and the public could read. The last five volumes are dense data presentations for professionals. In addition, the illustrator for the project report, Alice Wesche, produced a delightful children's book about ancient Paquimé (Wesche 1981). The Amerind Foundation also prepared a filmstrip useable in schools. Di Peso was a prolific and popular lecturer to nonprofessional groups. Perhaps most important of all, the JCGE increased the interest and pride in Paquimé among the people of Chihuahua that also set the foundation for archaeological tourism in the region.

Paquimé in Current Context

The JCGE ended fieldwork in 1961, and attention shifted to analyses and publication that was available 13 years after the fieldwork ended. Di Peso and his staff moved on to other projects north of the international border. Eduardo Contreras continued to do some limited reconnaissance in the area, a commitment to the Casas Grandes region recognized by the naming of the public library in Nuevo Casas Grandes after him. For the 25–30 years following the end of the JCGE's fieldwork, Chihuahuan archaeology went into a period of inactivity. It was not until the 1980s that INAH appointed its first residential archaeologist in Chihuahua, Eduardo Guevara. Guevara (1984, 1986, 1988) conducted an important project at a major cliff dwelling site, Cuarenta Casas, in the Sierra Madre to the southwest of Paquimé and a few smaller INAH projects in Chihuahua.

Starting in the 1980s, there was a renaissance of research in Chihuahua, sparked by substantially more investment by INAH in Chihuahua. This permitted the hiring of more archaeologists, the opening of other archaeological sites to the public, and the construction of a world-class museum at Paquimé. These efforts ultimately culminated in the designation of Paquimé as a UNESCO World Heritage site. As well, more non-Mexican archaeologists have devoted significant efforts to research. These include project directors from three counties: Mexico, Canada, and the United States.

It is worth noting here that, despite its far smaller size, the archaeological community in Chihuahua is more cosmopolitan than that north of the border. Nearly all or all project directors north of the border in the U.S. Southwest are North Americans; a very small number of these are Native Americans. Thus, there is insularity in Southwestern archaeology that is not often acknowledged and is in contrast to the situation south of the border. One problem, however, is the fact that the majority of the archaeological literature on Chihuahuan archaeology is in English which can disenfranchise non-Native speakers of English. Also, it would serve all North American archaeologists working in the NW/SW to understand archaeology in Mexico. A good place to start is "The Practice of Archaeology in Mexico," a 2007 special issue of the *SAA Archaeological Record* (vol. 7 no. 5), which has excellent discussions of archaeological research and the archaeological community in Mexico.

The Chihuahuan research renaissance just described includes not only more archaeologists and resources but also a wider-than-ever range of regions and time periods. Major recent projects have focused on a wide range of topics from the Late Archaic, through the Viejo and Medio Periods, and then into historic times. Similarly, research includes excavation and survey around Paquimé, survey and excavation in central and southern Chihuahua, research and conservation in the Sierra Madre, and archaeological study in the plains and dunes of eastern Chihuahua. Fortunately, the authors of the chapters in this volume reflect this topical, geographic, and chronological diversity, and they bring their considerable expertise to their chapters.

The renaissance of Chihuahuan archaeology has resulted in many new publications, many of which are referenced in these chapters. In addition, summaries and edited volumes about the pre-Hispanic heritage of Chihuahua include Phillips (1980), Guevara (1985), Schaafsma and Riley (1999), Minnis and Whalen (2001), Newell and Gallaga (2001), and Mendiola (2008).

Where We Need to Go

We can only hope that the research renaissance continues. There are reasons to expect so. A Chihuahuan branch of the Escuela Nacional de Antropología e Historia has added an academic major in archaeology. More students—Mexican and North American—are beginning to work in Chihuahua. There seems to be greater recognition of the value of Chihuahuan archaeology by the Mexico archaeological community and elsewhere.

There is so much to learn about Paquimé, the Chihuahuan tradition, and the prehistory of north and central Chihuahua. In recognition of this, seminar participants discussed critical archaeological imperatives. Below is our compilation of critical issues in rank order:

1. Viejo Period and Viejo-to-Medio transition
2. Improved chronological control
3. More fieldwork, survey, and excavation
4. The end of Paquimé
5. Examination of exchange patterns and ceramic sourcing
6. Settlement patterns and regional comparisons

This is not a list of all-important research topics but rather what we believe to be especially critical at this time. It is clear from this list that the beginning and end of the Medio Period deserve much more attention. Di Peso's (1974, vols. 1–3) interpretation and a more recent explanation proposed by Lekson (1999) argue that outsiders were the stimulus for the florescence during the Medio Period. They tended to view the pre-Medio occupation in the Paquimé region as a cultural backwater that was then organized by outsiders with Medio Period Paquimé as the result. In Di Peso's scenario, the outsiders were pochteca from Mesoamerica, and in Lekson's scenario, they were Chacoan elites. In contrast, we (Minnis 1984, 1989a; Whalen and Minnis 2009a) emphasize the importance of intraregional relationships in the development of Paquimé, a far more substantial Viejo Period population, and largely local causes for Paquimé's development. Clearly, the nature and size of pre-Medio communities is a research priority as Kelley and Searcy consider in their chapter. Similarly, the causes and circumstances of Paquime's end merit archaeological attention as Phillips and Gamboa make clear in their chapter. The other issues involve the nature of Medio Period Paquimé and its relationships with adjacent and distant communities. Most chapters (Minnis and Whalen, Whalen and Pitezel, Rakita and Cruz, VanPool and VanPool, Punzo and Villalpando, and Cordell) discuss what we know about the Medio Period in the International Four Corners and beyond.

The current renaissance in Chihuahuan archaeology still pales in comparison to the adjacent areas of Mesoamerica and the U.S. Southwest. The number of scholars and resources devoted to Chihuahua is quite limited. Therefore, more excavation and survey are needed in the many areas in Chihuahua that are still grossly understudied. Furthermore, field research is needed to identify and protect endangered archaeological sites.

More fieldwork is not the only research avenue, however. Extant artifact collections, especially from the JCGE, are massive and diverse. Unfortunately, the technical analyses of these artifact categories have not reached their full potential. In recognition of this need, the seminar participants listed more technical analyses as a research priority, especially techniques not available at the time of the JCGE.

Concluding Thought

Paquimé still fascinates us, and it has fascinated people for over 500 years. Fortunately, this volume comes at a time when data have accumulated, so that we can see in more detail than ever what needs to be known and how to achieve these goals. We all share an optimism that the progress we see in the study of Paquimé and the prehistory of Chihuahuan tradition will continue. And we all recognize that whatever our contributions, they are founded on a remarkable project directed by remarkable and unusually dedicated scholars and staffed by a remarkable group of people. The Joint Casas Grandes Expedition was one of the major accomplishments of the Amerind Foundation during its 75 years. As such, we are pleased that this volume is an acknowledgment—an inadequate one to be sure—of the significance of the work that has gone before.

A Note on Nomenclature

Casas Grandes or Paquimé? There is a trend to call the actual site Paquimé rather than Casas Grandes in order to differentiate it from the Casas Grandes region, Casas Grandes tradition, historic town of Casas Grandes, and Rio Casas Grandes. As this volume is tribute to the JCGE, it is only fitting for the chapter authors to use either name for the site. We do not think that this will cause much, if any, confusion.

Acknowledgments

A volume conceived as a tribute to the pioneers of Chihuahuan archaeology that also summarizes a large corpus of research owes intellectual debts to many people. The first to be recognized are William Shirley Fulton, Charles Di Peso, Eduardo Contreras Sánchez, their staff and collaborators, the Amerind Foundation, and INAH. The seminar could not have succeeded without the efforts of John Ware, Barbara Hanson, and the seminar staff at the Amerind Foundation. Thanks to Ron Bridgemon for production help. Valuable comments by two anonymous reviewers are much appreciated. The University of Arizona Press did an excellent job producing this volume.

Beginnings

The Viejo Period

Jane H. Kelley and Michael T. Searcy

The history of the Medio Period is marked by population growth, aggregation, ideological shifts, and the building of the large, central polity of Paquimé (Casas Grandes). But before this colossal social transformation took place, people in northwest Chihuahua lived a lifestyle that had persisted for at least 400 years, which is known as the Viejo Period. This period is far from the beginning of human occupation in this area; Paleo points, extensive Archaic remains, the early agricultural site of Cerro Juanaqueña (Hard and Roney 1998), and an early pithouse period preceded Paquimé and can be seen as more distant precursors of the Chihuahua culture. Di Peso's (1974, vols. 1–3) postulated Plainware Period has yet to be isolated, but may exist. However, the Viejo Period is certainly the beginning of a lifestyle of increased sedentism associated with more intensive maize agriculture and life in hamlets and small villages. This way of living produced a social milieu that formed a foundation for transition to the Medio Period.

The Viejo Period is now thought to have covered all or much of the area known as the Chihuahua culture, to have been characterized by small pithouse communities scattered over locations with water and arable land, and is associated with a brown ware pottery tradition. Evidence for the Viejo Period is clear for what we call the northern and southern zones of the area.[1] We are not discussing the Sierra Madre Occidental beyond the information provided by Douglas and Quijada (2003) because we know of no other Viejo Period evidence from that area; nor do we discuss the Bootheel of New Mexico and the partly contemporary Mimbres culture of southern New Mexico and northern Chihuahua beyond noting the relevance of the Viejo Period to understanding the history of agriculture within the larger pre-Hispanic northwest Mexico and U.S. Southwest (NW/SW).

While these other areas are not addressed in this chapter, it is interesting to note the broader context within which the Viejo Period people lived. Within this span of about 500 years, people practicing the Hohokam and Mimbres traditions were manufacturing pottery with similar designs and color schemes as those in northwest Chihuahua; the Hohokam were engaged in shell trade from the west Mexican coast; and the Ancestral Puebloans to the north were making the transition from pithouse to pueblo dwellings. While isolated on what is considered the fringe of the NW/SW, people in the Casas Grandes area at this time were very much connected to the larger structural spheres perpetuated throughout the rest of the NW/SW and beyond.

In light of these regional interactions and changes, Casas Grandes communities experienced similar transitions and structural changes. During the succeeding Medio Period, adobe room blocks replaced pithouses; the pottery inventory became more diversified; and most importantly, some of that pottery carried a great deal of symbolic content in part of the culture area, which has been useful in interpreting the period. This is the period in which the inner core of the Chihuahua culture developed the complexity that has intrigued archaeologists for many decades. The nature of this change and the catalysts that prompted such a massive structural transformation is debated among some archaeologists. Countering the idea of a locally spurred population growth as suggested by Whalen and Minnis (2001, 106), Lekson (2008, 320) proposes that the Viejo Period was underpopulated and perhaps too small to be solely responsible for the Medio Period florescence. Lekson (1999), Moulard (2005), and Searcy (2011) have suggested that evidence exists pointing to the migration of people from the Mimbres region. We do not address these debates here because we first need a firm foundation of what the data actually are, and while they are indeed sparse (Lekson 2008, 176, 319–20; Pitezel and Searcy 2013) and in no way comparable to the information that has been amassed north of the international border, the insufficiency of our current knowledge of the Viejo Period should be addressed before we postulate what caused the cultural transformation in the twelfth and thirteenth centuries.

The most obvious fact about Viejo Period archaeology is that there is a paucity of data in comparison to the Medio Period, which lasted less than half as long. While this situation is currently shifting with new scholars working to fill the void, it is important to remember that our current interpretations of the Viejo people are based on a few studies by a handful of archaeologists over the last 50 years. The Viejo is certainly the lesser known of the two major Chihuahua culture periods.

Viejo Period research has been slow to take off for a number of reasons. Foremost is the amount of attention focused on the larger, more numerous Medio Period sites, especially Paquimé. This is a classic example of people being drawn to the flashy first. In their discussion of the beginning of Chaco, Wilshusen and Van Dyke (2006, 211–12) echo this dilemma in regard to the origin of occupation at and around Chaco Canyon. They also point out that the inception of the Chaco system was likely associated with region-wide changes, which included migration and the development of corporate or religious power structures (Wilshusen and Van Dyke 2006, 246–47). We echo their sentiment; it is extremely important to look at areas outside of primary centers to fully understand the developmental processes leading to those centers. We further argue that 400 or more years of successful adaptation is well worth studying in its own right. It is probably also significant that Di Peso's (1974, vols. 1–3) definition of the Viejo Period near the central site of Paquimé was more satisfying to archaeologists, contained less controversial assertions, fit more easily into the worldviews of NW/SW archaeology, and so needed less investigation and revision than did his views of the Medio Period.

We present a perspective that provides a broader view of Viejo Period occupation in northwest Chihuahua within the limits of available knowledge. Initial work by Charles Di Peso makes up the majority of information for the Viejo Period in the northern zone of the Chihuahua culture. Lister (1946) reported pre-Medio components in the Sierra Madre, which he called Mogollon and which reanalysis might place in the Viejo Period. Di Peso had Viejo Period sherds from Tres Rios. Recent additions to inventories of site locations by Phelps (1998) and Whalen and Minnis (2001) have enlarged the discussions for the northern zone, as has Douglas (1992, 1996, 2000). Recent excavations by Kelley and colleagues (2012), Stewart, MacWilliams, and Kelley (2004), and Stewart et al. (2005) in the southern zone have brought to light the variability in Viejo Period architecture and material culture leading to suggestions of divergence between the northern and southern zones by the end of the Viejo Period.

Chronology

Di Peso (1974, vol. 1) initially developed three phases within the Viejo Period: Convento (AD 700±50–900), Pilón (AD 900–950), and Perros Bravos (AD 950–1060). A number of critiques of Di Peso's chronology emerged; most focused on the Medio Period (e.g., see LeBlanc 1980; Lekson 1984; Stewart 1984). Dean and Ravesloot (1993) offered the definitive revision that provided a temporal framework subsequently supported by a growing body of radiocarbon dates. Except for dates on the Viejo Period obtained by the Proyecto Arqueológico Chihuahua (PAC) (Stewart, MacWilliams, and Kelley 2004; Stewart et al. 2005), the most recent dates pertain to the Medio Period (Casserino 2009; Whalen and Minnis 2009a).

In the southern zone, Viejo Period radiocarbon dates span ca. AD 800–1250, with other dates not associated with architecture in the AD 600s and 700s (Kelley, Garvin, and Cunningham 2012; Stewart, MacWilliams, and Kelley 2004; Stewart et al. 2005). Since radiocarbon dating lacks the precision of dendrochronological dates, the complete sequence is now more loosely construed, and the Medio Period is seen as beginning between AD 1200 and 1250 or later (Stewart, MacWilliams, and Kelley 2004; Stewart et al. 2005; Whalen and Minnis 2009a). The Viejo Period is consistently seen as preceding the Medio Period, and as the date of the beginning of the Medio Period has changed, so have estimates of the end of the Viejo Period; its beginnings are still murky.

Di Peso's breakdown of the Viejo Period phases rested almost exclusively on house types, with the Convento phase represented by houses-in-pits, the Pilón phase by pithouses, and the Perros Bravos phase by adobe room blocks. The associated pottery, which was particularly sparse for the houses-in-pits, did not correlate neatly with this categorization and was the source of many earlier chronological critiques (see also Douglas 2000). The two radiocarbon dates from the Convento site have been shown to be severely flawed (Stewart et al. 2005, 172). In addition, the Pilón phase dates have been determined solely by the

Beginnings

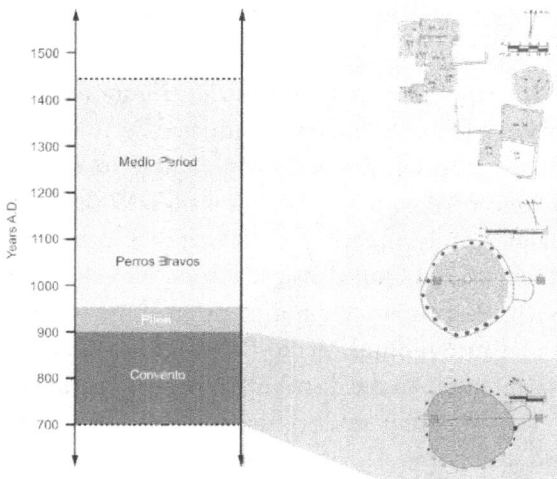

Figure 1.1. Viejo Period chronology and associated architecture types as described by the JCGE (Adapted from Di Peso, Rinaldo, and Fenner 1974:4, 153, 161, 179).

purported end of the Convento phase and beginning of the Perros Bravos phase. We suspect that the cultural stratigraphy at the Convento site was quite complex, as can be seen in descriptions of individual houses in the Joint Casas Grandes Expedition (JCGE) report. We do not second guess Di Peso's interpretations now, except to say his phases with their orderly architectural progression has not been duplicated in other places at this time. We use his Viejo Period phase designations for this chapter because they have yet to be revised.

At the moment, the best temporal subdivision of the southern Viejo Period is early and late. "Late" is characterized by the presence of Mimbres Black-on-white and the introduction of the earliest local polychromes to ceramic assemblages. Since so many of the houses at the Convento site contained Mimbres pottery, we are tempted to see most of, or even the entire sequence at that site, as late Viejo. As pottery seriation is improved and more radiocarbon dates become available in the northern and southern zones, internal Viejo Period chronology will be refined.

Settings and Site Distributions

For all regions, there is a scarcity of good distributional data for either Viejo or Medio period sites. Surveys conducted by Whalen and Minnis (2001), work by Cruz and Maxwell (1999), and Cruz et al. (2004) have mostly been concerned with Medio Period sites. With the exception of the Whalen and Minnis surveys (2001), Phelps's documentation of sites (1998), and Douglas and Quijada's (2003, 2004a) work in adjacent areas of Sonora, Viejo sites are usually not mentioned; however, we are confident that the distribution of Medio Period sites will eventually prove to be an excellent guide to the distribution of Viejo period sites because location selection in both periods is fundamentally based on availability of arable land and water. The close spacing of the Convento and Los Reyes Viejo period sites along the Rio Casas Grandes encourages us to anticipate that other Viejo Period sites are nearby; Phelps (1998) located a number of small sites with Mimbres Black-on-white on the terminal stretches of the Santa María and Casas Grandes rivers and in the Samalayuca dune area to the east, further suggesting that Viejo Period sites and/or sites with Mimbres Black-on-white are fairly numerous in the northern zone.

Whalen and Minnis (2001, 103) note that northern Viejo sites exist from the Sierra Madre to the eastern desert lowlands and along the main rivers. Di Peso (1974:1, 155) noted sites of this period on the eastern flanks of the Sierra Madre, as well as along the Rio Casas Grandes. Whalen and Minnis found fewer Viejo sites in upland areas along secondary drainages than along primary drainages, and those few upland sites had low artifact density, low artifact diversity, and simple stone foundations. More numerous and more complex Viejo Period sites were found along the major drainages where arable land and water were found. These include Viejo Period sites recently identified by Michael Searcy and Todd Pitezel along the Rio Palanganas near Mata Ortiz.

Chihuahua culture sites in the northern zone occur mostly in the Semi-desert Grassland biotic zones (Brown 1982), at roughly 10–15 km or more from the higher biotic zones. The three geographical regions of the southern zone (the Babícora region, the upper Santa María valley, and the Santa Clara valley) occupy upland basins with basal elevations of ca. 1,900 to 2,100 meters. Plains and Great Basin Grassland biotic communities occupy these basin/valley floors, which are immediately adjacent to the Madrean Evergreen Woodland biotic communities that begin at the valley/basin margins (Brown 1982; Brown and Lowe 1994). Petran Montane Conifer Forest occurs immediately west of the Babícora Basin, and in higher elevations in the sierras between the three regions. Thus, resources from higher elevations and higher biotic zones are close to sites in the southern zone.

The observed site distribution appears to hold true for the Viejo and Medio periods, although the amount of available relevant data varies by region. The physiographic and hydrological characteristics of the three southern regions and the intervening sierras have a striking effect on the clustering and distribution of pre-Hispanic settlements, as well as on modern populations. In the internally drained Babícora Basin with its large intermittent laguna, settlements clustered in side drainages where there was arable land and into the edges of the main basin along these arroyos. Early archaeologists defined three major clusters of Medio Period sites in the 1920s and 1930s. One of these sites, subsequently tested by the PAC, included a Viejo Period component. A few additional sites were located inside valleys and at the basin periphery before the PAC suspended work in this region.

In the Santa María, pre-Hispanic Chihuahua culture communities appear to be concentrated in an area in the big bend of the river stretching from roughly the Ejido El Pacifico to Ejido San Blas. Within this section, sites occur beside the main river and across the broad valley next to the arroyos coming from the adjacent sierras. In contrast, the majority of known residential sites along the Santa Clara are concentrated along the main river valley in a rather linear pattern. This pattern is constrained by the distribution of springs that feed the river from Santa Clara pueblo for some distance to the north. This includes two other Chihuahua culture sites upstream at the confluence of side drainages in the vicinity of Santa Catarina.

The PAC focused on the Medio Period for several field seasons, and recognition of Viejo Period sites came later in the project. Three complete arroyo surveys failed to locate any Viejo Period sites, although a number of lithic and brown ware pottery scatters could pertain to this period. The fullest information about Viejo site distribution comes from the Santa María valley where five Viejo Period sites are known, and distances between them vary from 5 to 11 km; additionally, radiocarbon dates within the Viejo period have been obtained from three Medio Period sites. Two of the known Viejo Period sites are along the main river; two are on side arroyos in the central part of the valley; and one is on an arroyo at the extreme western edge of the valley.

Most information comes from the Calderon site (Ch-254) in the Santa María valley. At this site, six structures have been excavated. The house numbering system is misleading because one of these, Structure 5, actually consists of three or four superimposed structures making eight or nine excavated structures. Ground Penetrating Radar (GPR) located another 29 probable houses within a 100 × 150 m GPR survey area *if* all the probable houses are real houses. Previous testing and recent deep plowing outside of the GPR survey area suggests additional houses. In total, this site contained appreciably more individual structures than the Convento site. While Ch-254 is the largest known Viejo site in the southern zone, Ch-218, just 3 km away from Ch-254, contained 21 probable structures revealed by the GPR survey (100 × 100 m grid). Four of these have been excavated. At Ch-315 in the Santa Clara valley, some 28 structures were identified.[2] Other GPR surveys of limited grid areas have indicated settlements with four to six or more probable houses. A southern zone site hierarchy seems likely based on apparent site size, number of structures, and the presence of possible specialized structures at three of the southern sites that are similar to the "community houses" at the Convento and Reyes sites.[3]

Although the three complete valley surveys (the Zurdo arroyo in the Bábícora Basin, the Raspadura drainage in the Santa María valley, and the Picacho drainage, also in the Santa María) produced no new information about the Viejo Period usage of those drainages, the patterns indicated are worth noting. We hypothesize that Viejo and Medio Period settlements will tend to mirror each other. The Zurdo survey found extensive evidence attributed to the Medio Period among its short length of field houses, satellite sites on either side of the main site (Ch-159), and lithic procurement and workshop localities. In contrast, the Raspadura survey showed only surface scatters of lithics and a few ceramics from the upper valley well within the sierra, to the west, and all the way to the modern Pueblo of Oscar Soto Maynez on the main river. The lack of evidence of other sites for the entire length of that drainage (which supports the largest Medio Period site known for the southern zone) was unexpected.[4] Similarly, the Picacho survey (from the protected valley where Pancho Villa prepared for the Columbus raid to the drainage entry into the main Santa María valley) failed to locate more than artifact scatters in addition to the three previously known sites.

In summary, the southern zone has clusters of sites in three upland basins separated by sierras offering access to upper biotic zones. The northern zone has a number of rivers that drain into the Rio Casas Grandes and have patchy environments fostering site clustering, which may prove to be similar to the clustering seen in the southern zone. The Rio Casas Grandes itself provides more continuous arable land and more evenly distributed resources for pre-Hispanic agriculturalists throughout the grasslands (see Minnis and Whalen, this volume). Special-function sites are located from the uplands to the desert. Further survey of this major water source is needed in order to identify settlement patterns.

Subsistence and Acquisition of Perishable Resources

In the absence of evidence for the beginning of irrigation in the northern zone, we postulate that the northern and southern zones practiced *de temporal* agriculture (dry-land farming plus pot watering, spreader dams, and the like) during the Viejo Period to raise the traditional triad of maize, beans, and squash, all of which have been found in the southern zone. Only maize is reported from Viejo contexts in the north, but at the time of the JCGE, field techniques did not include flotation. Isotopic analysis of human skeletal remains from the Calderon site indicate a major dietary dependence on C_4 plants. Maize, or animals fed on maize, made up as much as 80% of the diet (Webster 2001; Webster and Katzenberg 2008).

Di Peso wondered if the arrival of *maiz de ocho* was an impetus for moving into heavy duty farming at the beginning of the Viejo Period (in the revised chronology, ca. AD 800). Today's archaeobotanists, such as Paul E. Minnis and Karen R. Adams, place less weight on Manglesdorf's (1952) races of corn and more on other variables in terms of understanding pre-Hispanic agricultural strategies and results. While a new flour corn may have been introduced at the beginning of the Viejo Period, archaeobotanical remains do not allow such determination in most cases. Rather, the move to sedentism would have increased the time allotted to caring for the crop and to the intricacies of storage of larger amounts of the resulting products. Drawing on analogy to contemporary and ethnographic situations, it seems likely that the pre-Hispanic Viejo farmers would have tried to maintain different varieties of corn with different soil, temperature, and moisture requirements in order to spread the risk. As an example, farmers today in the Babícora Basin, where hybrid corn cannot be grown, rely on a mixture of what are called *criollo* races, which vary in terms of length of a number of critical variables such as required growing season, yield, and intended end usage.

We postulate that agricultural production in the two zones was similar prior to the introduction of irrigation and other more specialized farming methods in the north. The Casas Grandes valley provided a continuous and less patchy environment for pre-Hispanic agriculture, enjoyed a longer growing season, and supported a larger and more evenly spread population than was the case in the south. The northern tributaries of the Casas Grandes exhibited separate site clusters confined to relatively small areas that combined sufficient water and arable soil, rather more like the southern zone. The southern zone may have had a rainfall advantage, since the precipitation cline in Chihuahua increases from north to south, and the higher elevations of the upland basin floors would have enhanced this advantage. Clearly, the southern zone was sufficiently successful with temporal agriculture in that irrigation was never implemented there, or if so, we have yet to find evidence of it. It is likely both areas would have suffered from droughts and faced uncertainty. In our opinion, we lack evidence in any part of the Chihuahua culture area to determine whether short-term sedentism, as presented in the volume edited by Nelson and LeBlanc (1986), is applicable to Chihuahua. Chihuahua chronology is not sufficiently developed and will not be with only radiocarbon dating available to detect multiyear periods of abandonment of one locality as is now seen for the Mimbres area.

Whalen and Minnis (2001, 103) suggest seasonal occupation for Viejo Period sites, and they note that adjacent areas have "small, simple pithouses that are generally believed to represent short-term, seasonal residences," which we assume means that they think it is likely for Viejo Period sites. However, we wonder if this is true for larger sites such as the Convento site or the larger sites in the southern zone such as the Calderon site.

Viejo Period subsistence practices and crops seem to be quite similar over the entire area. Local variations were probably based on relations of soil and water. Moving into the Medio Period, it would seem that agricultural practices in at least some areas of the northern zone, and especially in the inner zone, became more intensive with variable amounts of irrigation (Doolittle 1993). At the present time, there is no evidence of a shift to any kind of an irrigation system in the southern zone, although such evidence may yet be found. If, however, the agriculture of the southern zone Medio Period continued with much the same technology as seen in the Viejo Period, while at least favored sections of the northern zone moved toward greater productivity with improved water control, then we might be looking at one of the variables involved in the apparent divergence of the northern and southern zones during the Medio Period.

Cunningham (2009) suggests that this divergence was related to people being tied more firmly to land in the northern zone because of Medio Period investments in irrigation technology. In the south, a smaller population may not have been as firmly tied to land. The latter groups' willingness "to vote with their feet," could have been part of the reason for the subsequent lack of Medio period socioeconomic differentiation in that area. Or perhaps, the more patchy nature of agricultural resources in the south was just as confining in terms of freedom to move to another jurisdiction as the labor investment in an irrigation system. It is something to think about.

We take as given that the Viejo peoples, northern and southern, knew their environment and its resources quite well. Di Peso notes that scant information—a "bare minimum"—about subsistence plant and animal species are available for the Viejo Period in the northern area (Di Peso 1974:1, 244; Di Peso, Rinaldo, and Fenner 1974:8, 242), but that minimum "indicated that the Viejo people relied heavily on the bison as well as the Pronghorn and dog in their diet" (Di Peso, Rinaldo, and Fenner 1974:8, 247). Jackrabbits, domestic dogs, antelope, and locally available American bison were in the latest Perros Bravos component. In addition, a Mexican duck, a common turkey, and an immature macaw were identified, indicating that use of turkeys and macaws predate the

Medio Period. Plant remains were similarly scanty. "Only 12 lots of corn, none of which could be identified to species" were present (Di Peso 1974:8, 242). Insofar as we can tell, no evidence for beans or squash was recovered from northern Viejo Period sites, but recovery techniques were different a half-century ago.

Evidence in southern Viejo sites shows that resources (including fish and mussels) were gathered from ecological systems ranging from the river valleys to the elevation at which pine and Douglas fir grew in the adjacent sierras. No bison bones have been found. Local artiodactyls constituted the largest game. Rabbits and other small animals were most numerous. In the Babícora Basin, waterfowl were unusually well represented at the El Zurdo site. This is consistent for a location so near to a major wintering locale for water fowl like the Laguna Babícora (Hodgetts 1996); waterfowl in lesser numbers are found in other Viejo sites as well. Hunting was not a major occupation in the south and can mostly be characterized as garden hunting with occasional procurement of more elusive animals such as bear and puma.

Although a single immature macaw is reported from the Convento site, indicating the presence of this species in the Viejo Period, no macaw remains have been found in either Viejo or Medio Period southern sites. However, the distribution of the so-called macaw stones in southern sites may indicate that macaws were also kept there during the Viejo Period (Minnis et al. 1993). One of these stones has been found immediately south of the Chihuahua culture area in the Laguna Bustillos region. This may suggest that, if these are macaw stones, the practice of keeping macaws extended southward, as well as northward into Mimbres sites. Turkey bones, identified in a DNA study as the local wild turkey and not the domesticated turkey of the NW/SW, occur at the Calderon site (Speller 2009). Medio and Viejo Period turkey burials (species not yet identified) also occur at the El Zurdo site (Kelley 2009b).

Domesticated crops in the southern zone are represented by the common occurrence of maize in excavation units; maize, of course, has the greatest chance of entering the archaeological record of the three major crops. Enough evidence of at least two kinds of beans (common and tepary) and squash have been found in southern Viejo Period contexts to confidently assert their presence. As an aside, at least two

Beginnings

kinds of beans, as well as maize, were found immediately to the south in sites in the Bustillos Basin that are contemporary with the Viejo Period (MacWilliams 2001). Cotton was recovered from a possible Viejo Period context at the El Zurdo site in the Babícora Basin. It must have been imported from lower climes with a longer growing season—presumably the northern zone. In addition, a number of wild plants are found in the archaeobotanical remains of the south: pine, juniper, oak, manzanita/madrona, walnut, Douglas fir, willow, amaranths, cheno-ams, physalis, and grasses, along with *carrizo* and monocots. The latter were used for weaving mats and various other purposes.

Isotopic studies indicate that as much as 80% of diet was based on C_4 plants like maize. It follows that significant facilities would have been needed for people to be able to store sufficient food stuffs, including maize, beans, squash and gathered plants. There is no clear evidence for storage at the Convento and Los Reyes sites, although there are a number of pits (usually trash filled) that could have served that purpose. Di Peso (1974:1, 185) discusses storage bins for the Perros Bravos Period.

Three kinds of storage have been identified for the southern zone. One is a floor feature interpreted as an oval, plastered storage device roughly 1.5 m in its longest direction that extended beyond the outer wall of the oddly shaped Structure 2 (Ch-240) in the Santa Clara valley. At the same site, pot storage is demonstrated by a remarkable floor assemblage of pots crushed with their contents of corn, beans, wild products, and other materials in a rectangular storage structure adjacent to a circular house. In addition, the fixed base of a basket or fiber structure embedded in a clay housing was present in the same store house. A similar fiber/clay fixed structure (with floor dimensions of 65 × 30 cm) was encountered on the floor of a large domestic structure in Ch-218 in the Santa María valley. This structure also had a small round structure immediately adjacent that is interpreted as an external storage room. Some understanding of Viejo Period storage strategies is emerging.

Community Organization Across the Landscape

The starting point for a discussion of Viejo Period architecture is the JCGE information about architecture in which three distinctive house types formed the basis for Di Peso's three Viejo Period phases:

houses-in-pits characterize the Convento phase, pithouses the Pilón phase, and adobe-surfaced, contiguous rooms the Perros Bravos phase. Nine of the 10 houses-in-pits had unplastered floors and walls; hearths were of the category called Crude Type 3; and floor area inside the wall posts (the "living area") of 9 of the 10 domestic structures varied from 4.91 to 12.88 m². One larger example had a floor area that measured 24.02 m² (Di Peso, Rinaldo, and Fenner 1974:4, 154). The latter was unusual in having internal posts interpreted as a possible remodeling intended as a bench or to make the house smaller. It could also have been an internal screen that facilitated dramatic performances. Artistic reconstructions of these houses show domed structures with covered entryways that look like igloos. The entryways showed no directional patterning. In addition, there was the Convento phase community house (reconstructed as a cone shape) with six interior support posts and a double row of wall posts.[5] The floor area of this community house is estimated at ca. 45.25 m². Only intrusive pits from later occupations are mentioned for Convento phase houses. No houses-in-pits, and therefore no Convento phase houses, are reported from Los Reyes sites 1 and 2.

Figure 1.2. Community House 1 after excavation at the Convento site (Courtesy of the Amerind Foundation).

Pilón phase pithouses are also depicted as dome shaped with short covered entries and with a conical-shaped community house. Wall posts moved from inside the pit wall to the exterior of the pit. The houses tended to have more irregular forms than the houses-in-pits, and several are described as "D" shaped or as having one flattened wall; 11 of the 12 houses had plastered floors; and all had plastered walls. Hearths included crude and plastered basin types, usually placed off-center toward the entrance. Usable floor areas ranged from 2.6 to 20.03 m^2. Some of the smaller structures lacked internal features and can be reconsidered as possible store rooms given recent findings in the southern zone. The Pilón phase community house, rebuilt directly over the earlier one, has 6 internal support posts like its predecessor, a single row of peripheral posts, and a fire hearth placed farther from the entryway than most Pilón phase hearths. A single Pilón phase pithouse at Reyes site 1 with a central post was thought to have had a conical shape, two off-center hearths, and a step entrance. Reyes site 2 also had a pithouse with a central post (dome shaped), a hearth, and an ash pit, as well as a community house with a central support and four others placed adjacent to the pit walls.

The Perros Bravos phase architecture, representing the pithouse to pueblo transition here, consists of rooms created with adobe wall bases into which posts were set to form the wattle and daub walls for room blocks. A community room similar in size and plan to the ones associated with the two previous phases is, like those, reconstructed as a round or conical structure. The sketch of community house "R" (Di Peso, Rinaldo, and Fenner 1974:4, 192) appears to have an adobe wall base. And it is an example of the kind of structures that are common in the southern zone, a fact that suggests that the use of adobe is later here than in the southern zone. Evidence of a village palisade encountered at the Convento site has no known parallel in the southern zone, but then PAC has not used the large-scale horizontal excavation strategies of the JCGE (i.e., mechanical stripping).

In contrast to the Convento and Reyes sites, the architecture of the southern zone is not so easily placed into neat categories. It shows considerably more variation and does not segregate chronologically by types. Many southern houses have adobe wall bases, making this the earliest documented use of adobe in Chihuahua and possibly in the

NW/SW. Entrances are not as easily identified in the southern Viejo Period structures. Possible step entrances and one possible ramp have been noted. Most structures are approximately round; one irregularly shaped house is known. Several wall types have been found: shallow pithouses with presumably domed or *jacal*-style superstructures; surface jacals; round houses with adobe wall bases set into trenches inside the excavated pits that supported wattle and daub walls; and round structures with sod wall bases. Internal primary support posts vary from none to one, two, and four with variable numbers of additional posts that could have served as supports for the superstructure. Some of the southern houses are larger than the northern houses-in-pits and pithouses (sizes of domestic structures range from 7 to 38 m^2); consequently, there is less of a size differential between some of the structures of a presumed domestic nature and possible community houses.[6] All excavated southern houses have plastered floors. Plastered basin hearths are the most common, although some houses only have burned areas on the floor, and some lack evidence of hearths. Groups of post holes in a few houses suggest internal furniture such as benches, shelves or tables.

When it comes to architecture, as well as site size and artifact density, the available data sets from the north and south are not commensurate. Perros Bravos adobe-wall-based room blocks are prominent in the north according to the Whalen and Minnis survey (2001), but we have no indications of these types of room blocks in the south except in one Medio Period site. That single example seems more substantially built than Perros Bravos examples. Rather, southern zone discussion of Viejo Period architecture is pretty much limited to scattered, individual, mostly round structures in settlements that, while being different from the Convento and Los Reyes sites, share more with those sites than with the information available from the surveyed sites.

Other forms of sites described by Whalen and Minnis (2001) include rock-shelters and structures with simple, single course rock foundations. The south has produced a number of undated brown ware pottery, lithic scatters without other visible features, and a few rock-shelters with modest artifact assemblages, but these were not assigned to periods. One southern site (Ch-223) with small huts made of stacked rocks associated with rock outlined "plaza" spaces could be Viejo in age but lacks radiocarbon dates.

Whalen and Minnis give a size estimate of 7,700 m² for one site with Perros Bravos architecture (94–448) that we infer is one of the larger Viejo Period sites noted in their surveys. They mention that this site indicates that "large settlements had begun to form by the end of the period" (Whalen and Minnis 2001, 101). In contrast, the Calderon site in the southern zone is estimated to cover an area roughly 150 × 100 m, or 15,000 m². Other sites in the range of at least 100 × 75 m in the area are known. None of the single-period sites in the south have Perros Bravos architecture on them. Far from having sparse and limited artifact inventories, the scale of artifact density for Ch-254 can perhaps be appreciated by noting that roughly 50,000 sherds have been tabulated from this one site.

Because of the apparent scarcity or lack of Perros Bravos architecture in the southern zone, workers there tended to think that Viejo-to-Medio transition occurred after the pithouse era, moving into the full-fledged adobe architecture of Medio Period room blocks. But in the northern zone, this transition is made on Viejo Period sites, is clearly differentiated from the Medio Period, and is presumably from the pithouse era. If the history of archaeology had been different and the transition defined in the southern zone, it would have been placed at the end of the "pithouse" era.

Within the limits of available information, and with due respect for the present lack of comparable information, small communities of individual houses, with specialized community houses, occurred in the northern and southern zones. But the house plans show more variability in the southern zone, and no evidence of fenced or palisaded perimeters have been found in the south. The first use of adobe occurs in the south. Southern houses were often larger, perhaps implying differences in social structure. The first move to above-ground adobe room blocks occurs in the north, while pithouses continue in the south with a more rapid shift to Medio style pueblo architecture.

Durable Symbols of Identity

The JCGE ceramic typology relied heavily on whole vessels, while the PAC assemblages were almost exclusively made up of sherds. The basic Viejo Period pottery suite in all regions includes plainware, textured wares, and red-on-brown pottery. The JCGE created multiple types for, especially, the red-on-brown and textured wares. Red slipped and black wares are not reported for the northern area but are present in the south from at least AD 900. Linear and branching design motifs were used on red-on-browns and textured wares and, late in the period, on the local polychromes. Various attempts by PAC analysts to use the red-on-brown categories of the JCGE ended up with identification of the more distinctive Anchondo Red-on-brown and Mata Red-on-brown, but we were not as likely to identify the other less distinctive types and more likely to end up with a "generic" group. Local polychromes emerge fairly late in the sequence and are later joined by Mimbres Black-on-white. Nevertheless, it is clear that the most distinctive types can be recognized in both areas as can more generic examples. It is also apparent that the entire culture area shared a pottery tradition with local and regional variations. Sizes of vessels may be another point of difference between north and south. Di Peso, Rinaldo, and Fenner (1974:6, Figures 1–6) show the maximum size for Viejo Period ollas as approximately 2 gal. (7.6 L), whereas southern vessels of 4–5 gal. (15–18 L) are known. Some of the larger southern storage vessels have holes in the vessel walls, presumably to allow air to move through the stored foodstuffs.

Various attempts to determine the extent of movement of Viejo Period pottery between regions have consistently indicated that ceramic production was rather firmly based in local production, but it is not clear whether this was at the level of the household or drainage area (Burd-Larkin 2006; de Grandpre 2011; Fralick and Stewart 1999; Fralick, Hollings, and Stewart. n.d.). Sherds departing from the local geochemical patterns are often plainware that would not have been separated on macroscopic examination. Weak evidence for more limited production of some of the late Viejo polychromes has emerged, and there are rare white wares (including corrugated and red-on-white sherds) that need more attention. More trade wares might emerge as analysts control ceramic typologies from the west and south.

Sherds from beyond the southern zone and from outside of the Chihuahua culture area are rare, and the only currently identified external type to reach the southern zone is Mimbres Black-on-white late in the period.[7] The three sherds of Mimbres from the Calderon site sourced at the University of Missouri and included in the Mimbres sourcing data base are believed to have come from Swartz ruin or its immediate environs. Red slipped vessels, plainware, and textured wares could have been exchanged with areas immediately to the south, but more sourcing studies are necessary to evaluate this possibility. In contrast, the northern zone appears to have had an expectable complement of trade sherds from north of the international border, and possibly from Mimbres sites in the extreme north of Chihuahua. Red-on-browns, the hallmark of the Viejo Period, are found in diminished numbers in southern Medio Period levels, suggesting that these continued to be made, in contrast to the north (Burd-Larkin, Kelley, and Hendrickson 2004).

Social Differentiation

No one has seen much evidence of complexity in terms of social hierarchy in the Viejo Period, a position with which we concur. Major debates about the role of foreigners in the development of complexity and with the development of complexity at the primary site of Paquimé and in Whalen and Minnis's inner zone, are left to Medio Period discussions. Using primarily analogies to other small-scale farming societies, we suggest that there was a modest site hierarchy with larger sites having more locality-wide, integrating functions as reflected in the larger community structures. Religious rites and developing ritual power were tied to water, growth, and renewal, probably with a visible leader who may have had personal leadership abilities that functioned in the face of a great many leveling devices that forestalled the accumulation of too much power. We postulate a reasonably common base for a basic shared ideology with local expressions, which, in Viejo, does not find as much expression in iconography as it does in the Medio Period. Families and lineages would not have had quite equal status, and lineage status might have been related to first arrivals and property rights.

Evidence for some of these inferences include site size, presence or absence of community houses, variation in house size and construction, and the social memory represented in the construction of four houses in exactly the same place in the southern Calderon site. In one of those four houses, house 5B II, the very richly endowed burial of a baby judged to be 6–18 months old suggests that this was the location of a multigenerational lineage with enough resources over and above

Figure 1.3. Medallion found with infant burial at the Calderon site (Jane Kelley).

those available to other households to provide the infant with a most amazing medallion, a large marine shell pendant, and 940 beads, mostly of marine shell. Since this expression of the control of scarce goods was with a baby, it cannot be that an individual's achieved status was being celebrated. Rather, it suggests that the combination of the multigenerational houses and the rich burial reflects lineage status. The medallion, incidentally, shows that the symbolism expressed in the Mound of the Cross was present by AD 1000 in the southern zone; the latter has in turn been interpreted as a Venus symbol and as having astronomical significance (Thompson 2006).

Trade and Exchange

Medio Period trade and exchange of goods within the northern inner zone is, of course, one of the preeminent factors in recognizing and interpreting the development of Medio Period complexity. Bradley (1993, 1996, 1999, 2000) postulated that Paquimé and other sites gained more control of the trade of exotic goods, such as marine shell from the west coast of Mexico, in the core during the Medio, replacing a procurement system in which all regions of the Chihuahua culture had fairly equal access to imported goods during the Viejo Period. She also points out that after the core area assumed some degree of control over trade of certain commodities, there are many small Medio Period sites in the northern zone, as well as the southern zone, that appear to have had limited access to shell in that more controlled network. Marine shell occurs in various parts of Chihuahua in Archaic Period sites, indicating that marine shell had long been procured by earlier residents of the state, and that in all likelihood earlier trade networks existed for this same commodity. For the Viejo Period, modest amounts of marine shell seems to have been widely distributed across the entire culture area, suggesting fairly open access to this resource, although whether it was obtained by journeys to the coast, as Douglas (2000) suggests, or any one of several trade patterns is not clear.

We hypothesize that each region in the southern zone will share more with immediately adjacent sectors of the lower-elevation grasslands (the northern zone) than other areas. Thus, we predict that the upper Santa María valley and the Babícora Basin (as well as its northern neighbor, the Zaragoza Basin, which contains some of the headwaters of the Rio Casas Grandes) will show closer ties to sites such as Galeana, while the Santa Clara valley will show more ties to the downriver sites around Villa Ahumada. While such patterns are visible during the Medio Period, they are not yet clear for the Viejo Period. However, a more definitive sorting out of the late Viejo Period local polychromes might move the discussions in a useful direction.

It is not clear when copper objects from the west coast of Mexico began to enter the Chihuahua area. Di Peso (1974:8, 353) reports a single copper sheet in a "questionable Perros Bravos phase burial," and it should be remembered that he felt local mining and processing of copper occurred at Paquimé. One copper bell was found recently at a Viejo Period site in the northern zone near Mata Ortiz, but particulars in regard to its place in Di Peso's phase sequence is unknown. No copper objects are known from Viejo Period contexts in the southern zone.

If more copper objects occur in Viejo Period contexts, and if those are shown to be from West Mexico, they may have arrived via the more southern shell routes. The coastal route around the northern end of the Sierra Madre seems most likely (Kelley 2009a). The major differences in imported pottery between northern and southern zones have been mentioned, and the northern zone is strongly oriented toward the U.S. Southwest during the Viejo Period. The upper Santa María valley, at least, fits well with a down-the-line model for the Medio Period. The southern zone is the end of the line—at least for imported pottery—and the same appears to be true for other trade goods during the Viejo Period, with the exception of marine shell. Clearly we need more information before making pronouncements about the role of trade in the development of complexity in the north and the apparent lack of it in the south. For now, it appears the north was always better connected to foreign goods throughout the sequence than the southern zone, although acquisition of shell may have been rather parallel in the Viejo Period.

Summary

We have lumped rather large geographical areas actually composed of several poorly defined regions into the two loosely conceived northern and southern zones as used in this chapter. At that level, there are overall similarities in house types, pottery assemblages, subsistence practices, settlement patterns, and in the timing of the pithouse-to-pueblo transition. What stands out is that there is much more variability in house types than Di Peso found, and there seems to be a substantial overlap in the sizes of domestic structures, with the southern zone having some larger structures. Both had "community houses." The transition from pithouse to pueblo seems, on the basis of present evidence, to have occurred differently with northern Perros Bravos architecture on the same Viejo Period sites as earlier pithouses, while that does not seem to be true in the south. Nonetheless, radiocarbon dates in both zones strongly suggest that the transition occurred at much the same time. With regard to extra-areal relationships, the northern zone was always better connected to other regions, although the Viejo Period distribution of shell seems to be quite similar throughout the area. Indeed, the largest single concentration of Viejo Period shell is the infant burial from the southern Calderon site.

We see much more pronounced continuity in the southern zone between the Viejo and Medio periods than is evident in the north. We postulate that farming without major irrigation continued to provide basic sustenance for the population and appears to have been at least as large as that found in the northern zone during the Viejo Period. The use of adobe in the southern zone is earlier than in the north, and certain pottery types seem to be earlier. Red slipped and black wares occurred throughout the southern Viejo Period from at least A D 900 or earlier.

With regard to the emergence of complexity, we would argue that the seedbed for that emergence was the widespread Viejo Period that offered centuries of agricultural adaptation, a substantial and widespread population, and some established external relationships such as that represented by the marine shell trade. New research is expected to increase our knowledge of variability by localities and regions. It also carries the potential to introduce new evidence that will disprove our current views and suggest new directions of inquiry.

Notes

1. It is necessary to lay out certain terminological practices that have become established in the PAC codirected by Jane Kelley. The PAC worked in three higher-elevation basins/valleys in what we call the southern zone of the Chihuahua culture: the Santa Clara valley, the upper Santa María valley, and the Babícora Basin. As a corollary, we think of the lower-elevation grasslands of the Santa María valley from Buenaventura north, the Casas Grandes drainage, and the Carmen valley (which is the lower reaches of the Santa Clara River) as the northern zone. This terminology bears no relationship to the inner and medium zones of Whalen and Minnis (2001). We suppose that in their scheme, our "southern zone" would be relegated to an extreme outer zone.

2. Site Ch-315, or the Cienega Apache site, contains an I-shaped ball court of approximately the same size and orientation as the northern ball court at Paquimé.

3. Di Peso recognized community houses for each of the three Viejo Period phases at the Convento site, as well as at Los Reyes I, on the basis of size differentials between the larger structures and the domestic ones, as well as the structural details of internal support posts.

4. This is Ch-011 (the Raspadura site), which is a locally well-known Medio Period site that runs for 650 m along the Raspadura arroyo, and which has radiocarbon dates within the Viejo Period.

5. We have found it difficult to estimate Convento phase pit depths; step entrances appear to have been quite shallow (ca. 22–25 cm); however, depth of floors from the surface at the time of excavation varies from 22 to 115 cm.

6. Chiykowski (2011) argues that the lack of a major size differential between a postulated community structure (Structure 1 at Ch-254) and other excavated structures at that site casts doubt on the proposed function of Structure 1. However, we argue that the presence of additional architectural features, such as a large pit in the floor that had previously been covered with floor plaster, and a row of small pole holes extending around much of the periphery (interpreted as evidence of an internal screen) suggest that this was a special-use structure.

7. A single Mimbres Black-on-white sherd was found outside of the Chihuahua culture area near General Trias, Chihuahua, indicating exchange with nonagriculturalists (MacWilliams and Kelley 2008).

2

Ecology and Food Economy

Paul E. Minnis and Michael E. Whalen

Introduction

Paquimé's goodies and glitter, such as the 1.5 t (1,360.5 kg) of shell, the hundreds of macaw remains, copper artifacts, and massive architecture, as components of its political and ritual economies merit attention. Although not as visually impressive as its goodies, we consider how the food economy—production, distribution, and consumption—were essential factors in the rise and nature of Paquimé. Here we explore four points. First, one of the major recent advances in our understanding of Paquimé has been in its food economy because of the previous lack of research on this topic. Second, the Casas Grandes area was an especially favorable place in northwest Mexico and the U.S. Southwest (NW/SW) for pre-Hispanic economies. Third, farming was an economic foundation of Paquimé. Fourth, food provisioning was an integral part of Paquime's political economy, not just its domestic economy.

Unfortunately, the Joint Casas Grandes Expedition (JCGE) occurred before adoption of modern techniques to recover a wide range of plant and animal remains such as consistent small screening and flotation. In general, JCGE's excavated deposits that were screened were passed through large mesh screen, which is much larger than is now common. Consequently, small and inconspicuous remains, such as small bones and plant fragments, were rarely collected. On occasion even conspicuous remains were not collected. The clearest example is the plant material from what is likely the largest earthen oven in the NW/SW. The Unit 9 oven is described as having been filled with agave/mescal and sotol based on field observations (Di Peso, Rinaldo, and Fenner 1974:4, 468). Presumably this was a field identification by nonspecialists. Although related, mescal/agave/century plant (*Agave*) is a different plant from sotol (*Dasylirion*), so we do not know which plant was being cooked in this unique and important oven, and none of these specimens seem to have been saved (Minnis and Whalen 2005). The general paucity of organic remains, for example, can be seen by contrasting the coverage of plants and animals with that for stone and ceramic artifacts in the final JCGE volumes. For the Viejo Period, only a half-page each is devoted to animal and plant remains. Discussion of Viejo stone artifacts is 21 pages, and Viejo ceramics coverage is 55 pages. While the description of Medio Period animal remains is 60 pages, 40 of these are devoted to turkeys and macaws, neither of which were eaten. Only 9 pages describe Medio Period plant remains, mostly of maize. The Medio Period stone section is 444 pages, and 222 pages are devoted to Medio Period ceramics.

Some indirect evidence of the food economy, such as agricultural features and processing tools, were studied by the JCGE. For example, Di Peso (1974:2, 336–43) discussed the many human-made terraces on the hills and mountains of the Casas Grandes region and the tool inventory associated with food production, processing, and storage of foods (Di Peso 1974:2, 604–11).

More recent research, particularly of organic remains from our excavations around the Casas Grandes region, study of pre-Hispanic agricultural facilities (Minnis, Whalen, and Howell 2006; Whalen and Minnis 2009a), and the archaeobotanical data from the Proyecto Arqueológico Chihuahua (e.g., Adams 2013) to the south provide a more complete view of the ecology and food economy. This has greatly extended our understanding of the food economy of the Casas Grandes tradition.

Local Environments: Natural and Otherwise

The food economy of the Casas Grandes region is based largely on the local environment. To the west of Paquimé is the Sierra Madre Occidental, a continent spine of massive mountains running north-south in Mexico. According to Brown's (1994) classification, there are two major biotic communities in the mountains near Casas Grandes. The Rocky Mountain Madrean Montane Conifer Forest occurs in the higher elevations and is dominated by conifers, particularly pines but also spruce and fir. Lower mountainous elevations are covered by Madrean Evergreen Woodlands dominated by oaks, junipers, piñon pine, and other small trees and shrubs. Important natural resources in the mountains include acorns, pine nuts, juniper berries, various fleshy fruits, cacti, agavacous plants, and large and small mammals.

To the east are the foothills grading into desert and semi-desert plains interrupted by river valleys and isolated mountain ranges. Brown's Plains and Great Basin Grasslands, Semidesert Grassland, and Chihuahua Desertscrub are the three major biotic communities in foothills and plains. Within each of these major biotic communities are smaller communities such as the extensive dunes and playas of northeastern Chihuahua. The seemingly sparse vegetation of the plains can hide important food resources, such as mesquite and grasses, as well as animals such as rabbits, antelope, bison, and migrating fowl, among others.

Of special importance are the major rivers of the region, Rio Casas Grandes, Rio Santa Maria, and Rio del Carmen, were especially important locations for pre-Hispanic farmers. This was noted in the first description by European explorers to the region. In the 1560s, Baltasar de Obregón, Ibarra's expedition chronicler, marveled at the Rio Casas Grandes valley: "this is the most useful and beneficial of all the rivers we found in these provinces. Its shores are covered with beautiful and tall poplars, willows, and savins. It can readily, at little cost, be utilized for irrigating the fertile shores" (Hammond and Rey 1928, 205). We believe that Obregón was essentially right, the Rio Casas Grandes area was "a most useful" valley, for irrigation but also for access to a diversity of resources from the local sustaining area.

In sum, the mountains, valleys, desert plains, and dune fields are not only diverse but large. However, neither qualitative nor quantitative studies of this abundance as it relates to ancient communities have been conducted—research waiting to be done.

Environments are dynamic, but we have very little data about how Medio Period environments differed from current ones. Major changes documented in adjacent areas probably also occurred in northwest Chihuahua. Two are likely. First, the pre-Hispanic water table was higher with different river flow patterns than at present as is the case in adjacent areas of the NW/SW (e.g., Hubbs 1990; Webb, Leake, and Turner 2007; Webster and Bahre 2001). Second, low-elevation pine-juniper-oak woodlands and various shrub communities were sparser and more restricted in the ancient past; the pattern of increasing of woodlands is

Figure 2.1. The wide Rio Casas Grandes floodplain and modern fields. Paquimé is in the background (Courtesy of the Amerind Foundation).

widespread throughout the NW/SW and beyond such as the Southern Plains of the United States (e.g., Humphreys 1987; Turner et al. 2003). While smaller-scale changes are certain, gross general environmental patterning seems to have remained similar from Medio to modern times. We will discuss later another form of environmental change, anthropogenic ecology, that is, changes caused by humans.

The Food Economy Before the Medio Period

Farming was present in the NW/SW by 2000 BC, but its intensity seems to have varied widely. If research at the Archaic Period site of Cerro Juanaqueña, to the north of Paquimé near Janos along the Rio Casas Grandes, is a guide, then farming probably was the important economic mainstay for thousands of years before the apex of Paquimé's power and influence (e.g., Hard and Roney 1998, 2007). Archaeologists have recovered evidence from this impressive village, such as charred corn, beans, and possibly domesticated amaranth seeds, indicative of farming's importance at a time when most people in the NW/SW were hunter-gatherers or casual cultivators. This site, along with the recent research in the Sonoran Desert (*Archaeology Southwest* vol. 23 no. 1, 2009), is one of the most important projects on the role of farming during the Late Archaic Period in the entire NW/SW.

The nature of the domestic economy during the time between the Archaic and Medio Period is poorly documented. The quality and quantity of these data limit our interpretations of the food economy of Paquimé and other communities in northwest Chihuahua, as well as related areas. The only crop remains found by JCGE's Viejo excavations were corn (*Zea mays*) (Di Peso, Rinaldo, and Fenner 1974:8, 286). Recent pre-Hispanic ethnobotanical research at Viejo Period sites, central Chihuahua, has recovered the remains of a number of taxa (Adams 2013; see Searcy and Kelley, this volume). Maize is the most common macroplant taxon, but the remains of other cultigens, beans and squash, are also present. As well, cotton (*Gossypium hirsutum*) twine was recovered from a Viejo Period context at the El Zurdo site. In addition to crops, the remains of native types recovered include: piñon, grasses, juniper (*Juniperus*), bulrush (*Scirpus*), and chia (*Salvia*). Much more research is needed on the Viejo Period. For now, we suggest that it is best to assume that farming continued to be an economic mainstay during the Viejo Period.

Medio Period

More research on the food economy during the Medio Period has been conducted, but it still pales in comparison to some other regions of the NW/SW. While plant and animal remains have been reported from cave sites in the Sierra Madre Occidental west of Paquimé (e.g., Guevara 1984; Lister 1953;), the only systematic samples, from fine screening or flotation, are from sites excavated by only two projects: those directed by the authors and Kelley's project in central Chihuahua. Additional data, such as farming features, are available.

Farming

We suspect that the region around Paquimé was one of the better locations for farming in the NW/SW. Here we discuss two major farming locations: lowland river valleys and upland settings. Unfortunately, we know more about the latter, even though it was most likely less central to farming and the role of food production in the political economy of the Paquimé polity.

LOWLAND RIVER VALLEY FARMING. Scholars have long believed that farming of lowland river valleys was the foundation of ancient Chihuahuan agriculture, and most assume that irrigation was the most productive strategy (e.g., Di Peso 1974, vols. 1–3; Doolittle 1993; Minnis, Whalen, and Howell 2006). Unfortunately, there has been little research on these locations because scholars have assumed that pre-Hispanic irrigation features have been destroyed or modified over many centuries of very intensive post-contact valley farming. There have been massive modifications of flood plains for industrial-scale agriculture during the past century. For example, a substantial portion of the Rio Casas Grandes flow near Buena Fe is diverted away from the valley to large lakes southeast of Nuevo Casas Grandes, and portions of the channel edges have been severely modified within the past few years (P. Minnis, personal observation, 2011).

The geographer William Doolittle (1993) describes what he thought might be the remnant of a pre-Hispanic canal just south of Paquimé and suggests that Casas Grandes stands out as a center of sophisticated irrigation compared with other areas of the NW/SW. We estimated that there were around 2,000 arable hectares on the Rio Casas Grandes flood plain within 5 km of Paquimé (Whalen and Minnis 2001). Paquimé is located where the Rio Casas Grandes widens from its narrow upstream flood plain which limited ability to expand fields. We would be surprised if this correlation is a coincidence. Rather, we believe agricultural surpluses from such especially abundant and rich fields were an essential source of wealth for Paquimé and close-by communities. The larger size of the Rio Casas Grandes watershed, 16,600 km^2 (Schmidt 1973) or 1.4 times the size of the next largest river in the region, likely provided an abundant and reliable water supply. Other major rivers of northwest Chihuahua are smaller and presumably had correspondingly smaller amounts of arable land. Not only is there substantial arable land in the major river valleys of northwest Chihuahua, but their watersheds in the Sierra Madre can be quite large and provide a very desirable water supply for irrigation and domestic uses. The region today remains an important agricultural area as we suspect it was in its ancient past.

With the use of recovery techniques, such as small-mesh screening and flotation, not usually used by archaeological research at the time of the JCGE, we have more data about what crops were being grown. Study of plant remains from sites along the Rio Casas Grandes within 2 km of Paquimé indicates that maize was the primary crop. Also grown were cucurbits (squashes [*Cucurbita*] and gourds [*Lagenaria siceraria*]), beans (*Phaseolus* cf. *vulgaris*), cotton (*Gossypium hirsutum*), and chiles (*Capsicum annuum*) (Minnis and Whalen 2010; Morgan 2010). Tepary bean (*Phaseolus acutifolius*) remains have been reported from a site with Viejo/Medio contexts in central Chihuahua (Adams 2013). The importance of the three-sister complex, corn-bean-squash, and especially of corn, is its pattern of commonality in the NW/SW.

There are three especially interesting patterns regarding agriculture. First, there appears to be differences in crop assemblages within different environmental settings. Along with maize, beans and cotton seem to have been more intensively grown along the lowland flood plains around Paquimé, whereas agave, along with maize, were more common crops in upland settings in the region near Paquimé (Morgan 2010; Whalen and Minnis 2009a). Interestingly, agave remains have not been reported from central Chihuahuan sites (Adams 2013) in stark contrast to the situation around Paquimé. Second, we reported the discovery of the first pre-Hispanic cultivated chile seed (*Capsicum annuum*) from the NW/SW (Minnis and Whalen 2010). It was recovered from Site 315, which is within 2 km of Paquimé. Subsequently, analysis of flotation samples have revealed up to 20 more chile seeds from Site 315 along with another site (565) that is also within 2 km of Paquimé. Contrary to the popular image of highly spiced southwestern food, the widespread use of chiles in the NW/SW arrived with the Spanish, except in part of the core Casas Grandes region it seems. Was chile a common domestic ingredient, or was it used only for special meals by special people? That is, was chile part of the domestic or political economy? The answer is not yet clear. Third, charred little barley (*Hordeum pusillum*) seeds were recovered from Site 315. This plant is an indigenous domesticate found in Eastern North America and the Hohokam region of Arizona (Adams 2014). We believe that this is the first example of cultivated little barley in Mexico.

UPLAND FARMING. While the flood plains in northwest Chihuahua were the most productive farming locations, other settings were farmed. Uplands cultivation, both in the Sierra Madre and on the slopes of small hills, was ubiquitous. In fact, some of the best early research on terraced fields in the NW/SW was conducted in the 1960s by University of Denver geographers in the Rio Gavilán drainage southwest of Casas Grandes (Herold 1965; Howard and Griffiths 1966; Luebben, Andelson, and Herold 1986). These scholars mapped, recorded, and studied four types of sophisticated terraced systems. Terraces covered about 10% of their study area, but the geographers did note that the distribution of terraced agriculture in the Sierra Madre is patchy.

While terraced fields are common in many areas of the NW/SW, we suspect that northwest Chihuahua had some of the densest concentrations of terraced fields. The density of these features lead Di Peso to interpret them as parts of a coordinated system to control water flow in order to protect river valley fields. While an interesting argument, it has been rejected by others who have studied terraces in the northern Chihuahua (e.g., Minnis, Whalen and Howell 2006; Schmidt and Gerald 1988). We have recorded a sample of nearly 400 such terraced fields within 20 km of Paquimé (Minnis, Whalen, and Howell 2006). Most are quite small, less than 0.8 ha with an average of 11 terraces, a size likely

Ecology and Food Economy   49

Figure 2.2. An example of upland agricultural terraces just west of Paquimé (Paul Minnis).

controlled by individual families (Figure 2.2). However, 6 exceptionally large fields, up to 10 ha with hundreds of terraces each, are uniquely situated. This leads us to suggest that they were the chief's field, also known as *cacique* fields. All but one of these large fields were near special sites that we believe were centers of Paquime's power in outlying areas and not near population concentrations. If they were like chief's fields known to have been used among Puebloan communities in the northern Rio Grande region near Santa Fe, New Mexico, then they were controlled by leaders, and labor was provided by the local population (Parsons 1996). If our interpretation is correct, then these fields are the first archaeologically known example of cacique fields in the SW/NW.

Terracing is not the only form of upland farming. Earlier scholars have noted small canals. We have recorded a few small irrigation canals off of seasonal drainages, and we believe that we have located two small dams on these drainages. In addition, some rock mulching features have been found on the foothills of the Sierra Madre. These are similar to rock mulch features recorded from the Sonoran Desert of Arizona (e.g., Fish and Fish 2014). They are not common; only about one in 10 agricultural systems had rock mulch features. An early Mormon colonist mentions the presence of a number of reservoirs in the area north of Paquimé along the Rio Casas Grandes (Romney 2005).

Preliminary technical study of terraced field soils in several foothill locations west of Paquimé lead soil scientists to conclude that these soils can be very productive given sufficient water (Homburg et al. 2010; John Sandor, personal communication, 2006). As expected, more study is needed to understand the productivity potential of other field locations, especially those used for dry farming.

Fields systems do not tell us what crops were grown on these hill slopes. Analysis of lithic tools and debris found on fields in the Arroyo la Tinaja valley, just west of Paquimé, yielded a substantial number of artifacts associated with mescal or century plant (*Agave*) processing (Minnis, Whalen, and Howell 2006). The remains of agave are more common in flotation samples from upland sites than lowland sites in the Casas Grandes area. However, preliminary palynological research of soils from terraced fields near Paquimé yielded a single corn pollen grain, hinting that agave was not the only crop grown on upland terraces (Fish 2009).

Native Use of Plants and Animals

No human populations have lived solely on crops. Both native plants and animals offered resources to the intensive agriculturalists of the Paquimé tradition. If organic remains recovered from sites in the more intensively studied area of the northern NW/SW are guides, then we would expect a maize-centric diet supplemented by native plant use that varied widely depending on the local site setting and its resources (e.g., Fish 2004; Minnis 1989b).

PLANTS. While crops, and especially maize, seem to have been the mainstay of the diet for communities of the Chihuahuan tradition, there is little doubt that naturally available plants were consumed as much welcomed daily additions to the staple, especially when crops were in short supply and for ritual use. Additionally, communities not as well situated for farming may have relied on nature's bounty more than villages with access to better fields.

Initial documentation of how native plants were used had to wait until specialized techniques, such as flotation, became standard parts of

Ecology and Food Economy

archaeological protocol that occurred after the JCGE. Archaeobotanists working on projects in northwest and central Chihuahua have identified the remains of dozens of plants types found in Paquimé-related sites, but such data do not easily tell us how important these plants were in the diet, and some plants food are very unlikely to be recovered during excavation. For example, *quelites* (greens) and root/tuberous resources are more difficult to detect in the archaeological record compared with hard seeds and fruits.

Despite analytic and interpretive problems, we can suggest that several types of plant foods were valuable to the ancient peoples of the area. Cacti, such as prickly pear fruits and pads and cholla buds (*Opuntia*), likely were dependable foods as were agavacous plants that include agave, yucca (*Yucca*), and sotol. Although uncommon in the archaeological record, acorns (*Quercus*), piñon pine nuts (*Pinus cembroides*), and juniper berries would have been eaten. There are too many plants producing small edible seeds available in riparian, hillside, mountain, and desert plains to enumerate. Weeds, such as goosefoot (*Chenopodium*), pigweed (*Amaranthus*), and purslane (*Portulaca*) in particular, likely increased with more extensive land clearance and longer-term village occupations and are the most common "seed" remains from sites around Paquimé (Whalen and Minnis 2009a) and central Chihuahua (Adams 2013). Note that Morgan's (2010) observation that weed seeds were not as common from a site near Paquimé was based on the examination of a flotation sample from only the first field season. More data from these sites are consistent with the general pattern for ancient Puebloan sites in the NW/SW where weed seeds are very common.

ANIMALS. The JCGE recovered animal bones for many types of animals, from large mammals to various birds and reptiles. Some appear to have been the remains of nonfood use. For example, the large number of macaws and turkeys seem not to have been consumed for food (Di Peso 1974, vols. 1–3). Other animals, such as bear and water birds, probably were also the remains of ceremonial use rather than food use.

While there was a substantial diversity of faunal remains recovered by the JCGE, some meat sources were more commonly eaten than others. Typically, archaofaunal assemblages from the deserts of the southern

NW/SW are dominated by the remains of rabbits, both cottontails and jackrabbits, with medium-sized mammals, such as deer and antelope, also present but far less frequent. Faunal remains from more recent research at Chihuahuan sites conform to the typical pattern of rabbits and medium-sized mammals. This pattern seems to have a long history, as the bones of rabbits and some medium-sized mammals dominate the faunal remains from Cerro Juanaqueña. Medio Period sites also follow this pattern. Nearly all faunal remains from Villa Ahumada, for example, are from rabbits (Rafael Cruz, personal communication 2009). A similar situation is present from sites in the Babícora Plains and around Paquimé itself. The general pattern does not mean that there was no variation in the use of animals for food. For example, a turkey bone was recovered from El Zurdo, a Medio Period site, in the Babícora Plains (Kelley 2009b). Turkeys at Paquimé were not eaten but rather were used ceremonially. Were turkeys used in a similar way at El Zurdo or were they eaten?

Di Peso suggested that bison was a major meat source at Paquimé, which would have been quite different from most communities in the southern NW/SW. One could argue that the large number of bison bones was an artifact of JCGE's large-size screening that skewed the percentage of large animal bones retrieved, because smaller bones passed through the large mesh and were lost to the archaeological record. However, evidence from special sites west of Casas Grandes might suggest that Di Peso's interpretation that bison was especially common at Paquimé might be correct. We excavated an unusual site (Site 242) a few kilometers west of Mata Ortiz (Whalen and Minnis 2009b). We interpreted this site as a secondary center where administrative and ceremonial activities were concentrated; this site had Paquimé-like architecture, a very large ball court, and the only platform mound known from a site in the region other than Paquimé. An unusually large percentage of faunal remains from this site were from large mammals. Similarly, Pitezel (2011) excavated the special site El Pueblito located on a flat ridge on Cerro Moctezuma west of Paquimé. Large animal remains were concentrated in an adobe room block that might have been the abode of leaders or ritual specialists. It may have been that elites or some special segments of the Paquimé-dominated group, both at Paquimé and other special sites, had access to and control of better meats such as those from large mammals. If so, the "overabundance" of bison at Paquimé may reflect the ancient pattern of bison consumption and that it was more common among special people.

The Domestic and Political Economy of Consumption

Consumption is normally a communal activity. Since Paquimé was a domestic community, as well as a regional center, it is not surprising that food was consumed both in smaller familial settings and at larger events. The most obvious evidence of feasting is the large earthen ovens that produced substantial quantities of food for feasts. We believe one oven, next to the Unit 9 platform mound, was the largest earthen oven in the NW/SW and could have prepared over 3,000 kg of agave per cooking episode, special events that could have fed large numbers of people assembled for important ceremonies and other events (Minnis and Whalen 2005). There are four other exceptionally large ovens clustered at the north edge of Paquimé, but none are as large as the Unit 9 oven.

There is evidence of the consumption of food at ceremonial feasts outside of Paquimé. Large earthen ovens are found within 30 km of Paquimé (Whalen and Minnis 2001). Excavations at the special site west of Mata Ortiz suggest that another form of large-scale food preparation occurred there (Whalen and Minnis 2009a). This site had an unusually high percentage of pottery fragments from large vessels. The sherds have interior pitting that might have been the result of erosion due to the fermentation of a beer or from the alkaline treatment of large amounts of corn. Either way, this is most likely evidence of feasting activity at this special site.

Our eyes, quite naturally, are drawn to the large and exotic, and we too often do not see the seemingly mundane. As such, we do not discuss daily domestic food consumption by the many families that called Paquimé home. The JCGE's excavations recovered abundant evidence of items used for daily food preparation and consumption, including: nearly 500 heating/cooking hearths, vast quantities of utilitarian plainware, and a large assemblage of grinding stones. Some proveniences had cooking vessels still resting on hearths (Di Peso 1974, vols. 1–3). In addition, JCGE recovered hundreds of stone items associated with processing and cooking; manos and metates are but two examples. While not all manos and metates were used only to grind food, it is likely that the majority were. The JCGE retrieved over 1,200 manos and nearly 250 metates, a clear indicator of the frequency of food preparation. We do not know exactly what food was being ground, and likely sophisticated residue and chemical analyses of bone in the future will document how various food plants and animals were combined to form a cuisine that provided daily sustenance. We suspect that such analyses would identify meals based on corn with "relishes" of various native plants, other crops, and small amounts of meat. Such studies likely will shed more light on the use of food in the political economy of Paquimé.

Anthropogenic Ecology

It is now widely understood that people affect environments, often substantially so. This is not just, as is often thought, the unintended consequences of human activities, such as farming, wood harvesting, and water manipulation, among others. Rather, indigenous people typically consciously and actively manage plants, animals, and entire biological communities. Given the size of the Medio Period human population and the intensity of its economic activities, we might expect the archaeological record to show the ecological effects of humans, the area's anthropogenic ecology.

Interestingly, this issue was raised many decades ago by one of the founders of the modern environmental movement. Aldo Leopold's (1949) influential book, *A Sand County Almanac*, has a chapter on Chihuahua. After visiting the remote Rio Gavilán canyon in the Sierra Madre Occidental during two hunting expeditions in the 1930s, he wrote, "there once were men capable of inhabiting a river without disrupting the harmony of life. They must have lived in the thousands on the Gavilán, for their works are everywhere. Ascend any draw debouching on any canyon and you find yourself climbing little rock terraces or check dams, the crest of one level to the base of the other" (Leopold 1949, 162). The apparent irony is that Leopold used pre-Hispanic terraces—by their very nature modified the local landscape—as evidence of a balance between people and "nature." Leopold's statement should be considered a hypothesis rather than a conclusion, one that requires archaeological research. There are examples of human alterations of environments on the ancient NW/SW. For example, Jon Sandor

(1990), a soil scientist, found that soils on ancient terraced fields to the north in the Mimbres region of southwestern New Mexico were degraded, and the effects are detectable even centuries after they were no longer farmed.

Given the apparent intensity of economic activity and relatively high population density in the Casas Grandes region at least during the Medio Period and perhaps before, we could expect substantial human alterations of their environment. The ubiquity of weed seeds, from plants such as pigweed, goosefoot, and purslane, from recent projects likely is indicative of substantial soil disturbance. Their presence is not unique to the Casas Grandes tradition; weed seeds are often the most common plant remains from archaeological sites in the NW/SW. There is some evidence that can be interpreted that wood harvesting on upland slopes west of Paquimé might have reduced the density of woodlands. One might expect deforestation of flood plains with a dense human population requiring substantial field clearance and use of wood for fuel, a situation noted on other areas of the NW/SW including the Mimbres River Valley to the north in southwest New Mexico (Minnis 1985). This does not seem to be the case for the Casas Grandes region, as wood charcoal from streamside trees, such as cottonwoods, willow, and walnut, is commonly recovered from the excavation at sites along the Rio Casas Grandes.

There is some evidence of alteration of animal populations. There was change from earlier cottontail remains to jackrabbits later in a stratigraphic trash column from a large site west of Paquimé (Whalen and Minnis 2009a). This pattern has been noted elsewhere in the NW/SW and is often interpreted as evidence of land clearance. Jackrabbits tend to prefer open areas whereas cottontails tend to prefer more densely vegetated locations. Finally, chemical and physical analyses of terraced soils around Paquimé do not show evidence of soil deterioration that one might expect with intensive cultivation. Perhaps the current archaeological evidence suggests that Leopold was partially right after all.

Concluding Thoughts

Perhaps, more than any other aspect of the peoples' daily lives in ancient Chihuahua, recent research has expanded our understanding of their food economy. The JCGE simply occurred before adequate techniques for the recovery of a wide range of plant and animal remains. Also, the project focused on the Herculean task of excavating one of the premier archeological sites in the NW/SW, as well as several other smaller sites, so it had to forego large-scale regional reconnaissance or survey. Fortunately, Di Peso and his staff at the Amerind were dedicated enough to persevere for a decade and a half to produce one of the most extraordinary classic site reports in the NW/SW. These volumes allow subsequent researchers to evaluate Di Peso's interpretations and address questions that the JCGE did not have the time or resources to investigate fully.

The post-JCGE research discussed here helps put the JCGE's results in context and to view Paquimé in new and interesting ways. Paquimé was more than a site with "cool" stuff, such as a maze of massive architecture, hundreds of macaws, a spectacular collection of copper, nearly obscene concentrations of shell, and surprisingly diverse public architecture. Rather, it reminds us that Paquimé and outlying sites, both near and far, were living communities where the vast majority of the population were involved in farming far more than they attended ostentatious communal events. It also reminds us that all aspects of culture are interrelated. Some farming and food consumption, for example, were a part of the ritual life of Paquimé and other communities in Chihuahua. Food was a part of the political economy of Paquimé. It also reminds us that one cannot dismiss farming, hunting, and gathering as mundane and uninteresting; this premier regional center was unlikely to have arisen in the absence of surpluses provided by its setting.

The potential value of understanding Paquimé and its allied communities also transcends regional or even national borders. Are there useful lessons that Paquimé may provide the modern world? More and more, archaeologists and others are looking at how archaeology might address modern problems. The detailed archaeological record of the Ancestral Pueblo and Hohokam has been used as lessons about the fragility of the human experience. The most recent example, Jared Diamond's *Collapse: How Societies Choose to Fail or Succeed,* (and its detractors) includes an example that focuses on Chaco Canyon in the northern NW/SW. Others, especially those using Resilience Theory, contrast areas of the NW/SW to model the complexities of environment/human relationships.

Paquimé and sites of the Chihuahuan traditions should be a part of that conversation, as it may well have been one of the better areas for ancient communities, unlike some other locations in the NW/SW. How did the documented environmental and social dynamics in such an area differ from more "marginal" locations?

Organization of Production at Paquimé

Gordon F. M. Rakita and Rafael Cruz

Introduction

It is an often-repeated observation that Paquimé is one of the most—if not the most—complex communities in the pre-Hispanic, North American desert west. The great size of the ruins speaks volumes. It is an extremely large site and was certainly a population center. The diversity of the architecture also bespeaks of the complexity of the community. Few sites in the region contain ball courts, roasting pits, a canal, a reservoir system, platform and effigy mounds, colonnades and wooden pillars with stone foundations and bed-platforms, and T-shaped doors and stairways. This list is all the more impressive when one considers that much of the architecture was made of coursed adobe mud, wooden beams, stones, and plaster. But beyond the size and architectural variety, when the complexity of Paquimé is spoken of, it is usually the material goods that are most impressive. Richly decorated polychrome ceramics, turquoise beads, warehouses full of vast quantities of shell, copper bells, turkeys, and macaws—these are the material evidence that make prehistorians gape in astonishment. Understanding how these various crafts and commodities were produced and consumed is an important part of understanding the lifeways of the ancient Paquiméans.

Archaeological Approaches to the Organization of Production

Examining the production of critical commodities can provide a great deal of information about a community. To begin with, organization of production can be an indicator of general sociopolitical organization and complexity of a society. Communities in which each household produces and consumes all of the commodities required to maintain themselves are different from communities where different households produce different commodities and thus are dependent upon each other through exchange. Likewise, societies that produce more of a craft item or commodity than they need and exchange that resource with other societies are linked into regional trade networks as compared to more isolated societies. As Costin (1991, 2) noted, "our studies must never lose sight of the fact that production is embedded in political, social, and/ or economic systems." Additionally, the organization of production can have significant impact on gender roles and relations, kinship organization, and the nature of domestic life (Hendon 1996).

Organization of production can thus be a useful way to dissect the inner workings of a community. However, more than simply being a passive reflection of those arrangements, the organization of production can be an active force in the evolution of sociopolitical arrangements. This aspect of craft production has not gone unrecognized by previous archaeologists; however, it is receiving greater attention in recent years. For example, Schortman and Urban (2004, 186) note that "artisans are increasingly envisioned as having actively participated in fashioning the social and cultural worlds they inhabited." Thus an examination of commodity and craft production within a community can provide a window into not only how a society is organized and how it functions, but also how it got that way, and why it may have ceased to function.

We contend that a more thorough examination of the organization of production at Paquimé will help elucidate some of the enigmatic aspects of this community. For example, most researchers accept that Paquimé was a complex pre-Hispanic community. But in what way was it complex? Was there a political social hierarchy that organized the ancient Paquiméans into groups of elites and commoners? Did a few individuals control the lives and material conditions of the vast majority? Paquimé's relations with its surrounding region are likewise being debated. Was Paquimé a regional economic powerhouse? Did it produce commodities for export into its periphery or was it a consumer of items produced in outlying regions and traded in to the community. Did Paquimé control the flow of all goods or just a select few? Still other scholars are exploring the nature of ritualized activities at Paquimé. Did Paquimé produce goods only of secular value or did it have its hands in the production of both secular and religious items? A detailed examination of the organization of production can help answer these questions and others.

How Do Archaeologists Examine Organization of Production?

Costin (1991, 18) divides the evidence that archaeologists use to assess production of crafts and commodities into two categories: direct and indirect evidence. We follow this division here. Direct evidence for craft production typically includes production debris and tools used in production. For example, sherd wasters and a kiln feature would be direct evidence of ceramic firing. The clustering of raw materials, debris, and tools in a location is also a form of direct evidence for craft production. Finally, the presence of large amounts of a commodity may be evidence of production. Certainly, large quantities of a material goods might be due to trade and stockpiling. However, large quantities of crafts or commodities that could only be produced locally or are unlikely to have been traded long distances would be direct evidence of production.

We further consider evidence relating to a variety of other factors of production (what some might call the *modes of production*). In the case of some crafts and commodities found at Paquimé, there is robust evidence that allows for an assessment of the organization of production. In other cases, teasing out the nature of production is more difficult. Additionally, some commodities have been the focus of sustained interest since the Joint Casas Grandes Expedition (JCGE) completed their work. In these cases, the literature relating to production is rich. In other cases, scant or limited work has been done. Finally, we must be mindful of the different implications and archaeological evidence for various types of production, be it by individual specialists or groups of households. Below we review the types of direct and indirect evidence of production we have attempted to synthesize. We also discuss the various modes of production factors we considered. At the end of this chapter, we make some observations regarding the meaning of the commodities discussed.

The Meaning of Commodities and Crafts

We are sensitive to the fact that social meaning of crafts, and indeed even craft production, can have a profound impact on both the organization of production and the use of products. Much like Douglas's

(1992, 8) observation that the "social importance of interaction cannot be determined by ceramic counts," so too, the social importance of production and consumption of crafts should not be determined by counts. Small quantities of a given commodity may indicate a low scale of production. However, the social, political, or ideological meaning and value of that commodity might be considerable. Additionally, the unique production process or the production of that item by particular individuals within a society can greatly impact the social meaning of a commodity. Moreover, the lack of large-scale production and consumption of an object may reinforce the high value of such a commodity. "One must hope to achieve some grasp of the social meaning attached to categories of goods produced by specialized labor" (Cobb 2000, 36).

Commodities and Crafts at Paquimé

In his 1988 article, Paul Minnis was the first to examine the organization of production at Paquimé since the publications of the JCGE. He reviewed evidence for production of four commodities associated with Paquimé: shell, agave, turkeys, and macaws. Many researchers have followed and delved deeper into several of these commodities (for agave, see Minnis and Whalen 2005; for shell, see Bradley 1999; McGuire et al. 1999; for macaws, see Minnis et al. 1993; Somerville, Nelson, and Knudson 2010). Other researchers have investigated polychrome ceramics (Bishop et al. 1998; Carriker 2009; Sprehn 2003; Woosley and Olinger 1993), metates (VanPool and Leonard 2002), turquoise (Maxwell 2006; Maxwell and Cruz 2008), and copper (Vargas 1995, 2001). Here we focus on the products. However, we are cognizant that other "products" within a society exist.

"Most often, archaeologists use the term *crafts* to refer uncritically to a category of tangible, portable things such as pottery; metal tools, weapons, and jewelry; stone tools and ornaments; shell tools and decorative objects; basketry; and textiles" (Costin 2007, 146–47). Costin, however, notes that crafts also can include nontangible items (like poetry, dance, or music), food, and large immovable objects (like monuments and wall decorations). Here we focus on some key tangible craft items, including shell, turquoise, copper, polychrome ceramics, metates, macaws, turkeys, and agave that have attracted the attention of Casas Grandes scholars. However, we do mention some less tangible "commodities" at the end of our discussion.

We group our examination of the various crafts and commodities at Paquimé into two broad meta-categories: those of principally local origin and/or production and those with extra-regional connections or sources. The division allows us to examine differences in production and consumption of commodities at the two different regional scales.

Commodities of Local Origin

POLYCHROME CERAMICS. No material object associated with Paquimé attracts as much attention from both the public and scholars as the delightful polychrome pottery vessels. "The ceramic craft among the Casas Grandes people of the Medio Period was a highly developed art form." So begins Di Peso and colleagues' (1974:6, 77) discussion of pottery from Paquimé. While they extol the "unusual degree of control and precision" of the decoration and the quality of the paste and surface treatments, they do acknowledge that the pottery from the site "exhibited the wide range of proficiency expected in any mass-produced item."

Ramos Polychrome is 12% of total ceramics found in all contexts. Large quantities of whole and broken vessels were found throughout the site (Woosley and Olinger 1993, 108–10). Woosley and Olinger (1993, 105) also state that Ramos Polychrome "represented the greatest quantity of decorated whole vessels and sherds recovered during the excavations" at Paquimé. Over 129,000 Chihuahuan polychrome potsherds were recovered from Paquimé, of which 68.7% were Ramos Polychrome (Di Peso, Rinaldo, and Fenner 1974: 6, Figure 653–6). The JCGE also recovered a total of 276 whole or reconstructible Ramos Polychrome vessels. However, Ramos Polychrome is a ubiquitous decorated ceramic type across a large portion of northwest Chihuahua and the International Four Corners region.

Di Peso (1974:2, 533) describes raw lumps of clay, clay coils and a "firing wad" found in Unit 16 which he argues suggests that some of the pottery was made within the city. Di Peso (1974:2, 533–34, notes 126–27) also notes that Paquiméan ceramists probably used multipurpose tools (which were found at the site), including tools for mining clay and grinding stones for clays and pigments. Also found were polishing stones and sherd scrapers. Many (39%) of the polishing stones were found in Unit 16, and 22% of the sherd scrapers were found in Unit 8. However, Douglas (1992, 7) notes that no ceramic production loci was found at Paquimé. No specific kiln areas or locations of pottery firing were identified, though one might surmise that such a fuel dependent activity might occur closer to wood sources in the Sierra or that firing might take place off-site to manage debris.

On the basis of chemical analysis of sherds of Chihuahuan Polychrome, Bishop et al. (1998) and Woosley and Olinger (1993) conclude that there were production loci throughout the Casas Grandes region. Woosley and Olinger examined 382 sherds of Ramos Polychrome (146 from Paquimé) using X-Ray Fluorescent chemical analysis. They conclude (Woosely and Olinger 1993, 119) that "certain, perhaps most, of the Ramos Polychrome pottery from southern Arizona and New Mexico sites originated at a source or sources other than the Casas Grandes Valley." Using Instrument Neutron Activation Analysis, Bishop et al. (1998) confirm that various groups around Paquimé were manufacturing Ramos, Babícora, and Villa Ahumada Polychrome vessels. Thus, the available chemical analysis studies indicate that Paquimé was not the sole producer of Ramos Polychrome and there was probably production both at and around Paquimé.

Sprehn (2003), on the basis of an analysis of vessel morphology and production skill, argues that polychrome production is part-time. Polychrome types display a range of production skill, and Ramos Polychrome is perhaps the most skillfully executed. "Based on a high level of skill, high degree of labor investment, and CVs [coefficients of variation] still falling under the .10 mark for specialization, I suggest that the potters who made the Ramos ovoid jars produced at a higher degree of intensity than other potters. However, the Babícora and Villa Ahumada ovoid jars also have low CVs for morphological attributes, suggesting that the potters who made these vessels also worked at a level of intensity characteristic of specialists." (Sprehn 2003, 239–40). She also notes that the large mortuary urns that held the secondary remains of individuals buried in Unit 4 were more than likely specially commissioned (Sprehn 2003, 240). Interestingly, Carriker (2009) shows that Gila polychrome bowls are much more standardized (and larger) than other types at Paquimé, including Ramos and Escondido Polychrome, Ramos Black, Madera Black-on-red, and Casas Grandes Plainware.

Woosely and Olinger (1993, 122) conclude that "it does appear that Casas Grandes, as a central place, to some extent did control ceramic distribution throughout the region. Its potters, together with others from adjacent villages in the valley, may well be responsible for the bulk of Ramos Polychrome pottery found elsewhere in northern Mexico." However, polychrome ceramics are found in all contexts at Paquimé, including public, private, and domestic and ritual spaces. Moreover, given the wide regional distribution of the Chihuahuan Polychromes, and the fact that they are found in all sorts of contexts, it seems difficult to conclude that consumption or production of these ceramics was restricted to any one group. Raw materials, technology, and knowledge to produce polychromes likely were available widely. Bishop et al. (1998, 6) argue that "in some cases the same raw materials were used to make the ... different polychrome types." Woosley and Olinger (1993, 122) conclude that the "vast quantity of Ramos Polychrome pottery from Casas Grandes, with its characteristic signature, suggest the general location for clays used to manufacture vessels together with the ceramists who created them—namely, Casas Grandes and its immediate environs."

While little direct evidence of pottery production exists at Paquimé, what there is of it does not suggest a level of production technology above that of other pre-Hispanic communities in the region. Nothing at Paquimé suggests a level of production above the household specialist, a pattern that is common throughout the Southwest (see Hagstrum 2001, 50). However, if contemporary ceramists in the nearby village of Mata Ortiz are any indication of skill level—the Mata Ortiz pottery and finely crafted Ramos Polychromes show a similar level of production ability—then certainly some of the ancient ceramists were able to produce pottery of the same quality as modern-day, full-time specialists. This meshes with Sprehn's (2003, 241) observation that during the Medio Period "people throughout the area [30 km around Paquimé] had access to vessels made by specialist potters." She (2003, 244) further suggests that the "evidence for specialized production of the several Chihuahuan Polychrome classes shows that the development of specialized production was not a temporary variant of production organization, but a process associated with increasing complexity."

Numerous studies (e.g., VanPool and VanPool 2007) have suggested that the Chihuahuan Polychromes are ideologically rich in their symbolism. In this way, they are very similar to the Salado Polychromes (Crown 1994). That Ramos Polychrome is so suffused with macaw imagery suggests a symbolic connection between this type and those important birds. Woosley and Olinger (1993, 124–25) suggest that the standardization of the design elements on Ramos Polychrome may indicate a similar standardization of beliefs.

Crown's (1994) work on Salado Polychrome makes a convincing argument that Gila Polychrome was produced throughout the Salado area. However, the cache of 49 vessels of this type within Room 18-8 at Paquimé suggests a degree of control over access to this commodity. Given the high standardization of this type relative to other polychromes at the site (Carriker 2009), it seems reasonable to suggest that the cache was probably produced by specialist ceramists, though it is unclear if these specialists worked at Paquimé.

METATES. Di Peso (1974:2, 606) claims that "the metate stood out as particularly elegant Paquimian design. These neat-edged, closed trough rectangles were manufactured in the city in legless, tripod, and double forms." He claims that the metates were manufactured at Paquimé. However, he provides no evidence for this conclusion.

There were 102 type 1A and 27 type 1B metates, as well as 106 metate fragments found at Paquimé. There were 1,249 whole or fragmentary manos found at Paquimé (Di Peso, Rinaldo, and Fenner 1974:7, 171–72). By contrast, Neitzel (2003, 108) reports that 787 manos and metates were recovered from Pueblo Bonito. Shelley (2006, 1031) reports 51 metates and 123 manos were found at Salmon ruin. Only 9 metates (or fragments) were found in the Convento site excavations (Di Peso, Rinaldo, and Fenner 1974:7, 24–25). Thus, the scale of metate production at Paquimé does not seem out of place for a site of its size and duration of occupation.

Minnis (1988, 185) notes that "Unit 14, Room 24B contained 10 metates that were reported as evidence of a metate workshop (Di Peso 1974:2, 396). However, other rooms also contain as many metates, and Room 24B does not seem to have a tool assemblage which might have been used for metate production." The assumed production tool kit—hammer and grinding or pecking stones—would have been available to most or all Paquiméans. Moreover, these tools more than likely would have been multipurpose tools, and thus their use in metate production would be difficult to discern. Metate production debris would include basalt fragments and stone dust, hardly the sorts of items to stand out in an archaeological excavation. Di Peso, Rinado, and Fenner (1974:7, 163, 169) report one metate blank was recovered at Paquimé in a test trench in Unit 23.

VanPool and Leonard (2002) conducted a statistical analysis of morphological metrics of the metates from Paquimé and compared them with a sample of Mimbres metates. They found that type 1A metates were significantly more standardized than type 1B and Mimbres metates. "Ultimately, we argue that individuals specializing in ground stone production produced most of the metates from Paquimé. The fact that specialized ground stone metate production was present illustrates that specialized production was present at Paquimé and that it was not limited to 'elite' items." (VanPool and Leonard 2002, 712). Presumably, the type 1B metates (which are similar to metates found throughout the Southwest and northern Mexico) were reproducible by most individuals. The more standardized type 1As may not have required more skill than type 1Bs, but they did probably take more time and care to manufacture. There is no reported evidence for advanced production technology for groundstone objects at Paquimé.

VanPool and Leonard (2002, 725) suggest two possible explanations for the patterns in standardization they identify. The first posits that the greater standardization of the type 1A versus 1B metates may be due to the fact that the type 1B versions are from an earlier (prespecialized metate production) period. The second explanation is that some Paquiméans may not have had access to the more standardized 1A metates and thus had to make their own (type 1B) grinding stones. However, access to both 1A and 1B metates does not seem to have been restricted. For example, 26% of the type 1A metates were found in Unit 8, 32% in Unit 14, and 23% in Unit 16. Further, up to four metates were found in many of the other units. There were clusters of these metates in certain rooms (e.g., four in Room 10A and five in 6B of Unit 8). However, most rooms had but a single metate. The distribution of 1B metates was similar. Whalen and Minnis (2009a, 208) report that they recovered four type 1A and 9 type 1B metates from sites 204, 231, and 242. They argue that the low frequency of the type 1A metates at these sites (type 1As are the second least common type) indicates that specialist-produced metates were more common at Paquimé than at other sites in the region. Thus, the intraregional distribution may suggest that the benefits of finely crafted basalt tools may have been differentially accessible (Whalen and Minnis 2009a, 216).

The standardization of the type 1A metates suggests a level of specialization in ground stone production above that found throughout the region—indeed north of the Mesoamerican culture area. It is unclear if this standardization is the result of full-time or part-time specialists. It seems reasonable to imagine a few part-time specialists producing all of the type 1A metates over the course of the Medio Period. The raw materials are pretty widely available within the region, though special sources may have been preferred. Vesicular basalt is available in most of the mountain ranges around Paquimé, however, large enough blocks used to produce the type 1A metates may have been difficult to acquire. It is interesting to note that there is a drainage in the Sierra La Fortuna and Sierra America approximately 24 km south-southeast of Paquimé called *Los Metates*.

The intrasite distribution of metates at Paquimé suggests that most residents of the community were able to procure and use one for domestic grinding purposes. Additionally, the clusters of metates found in some rooms (like the 10 found in Room 24b in Unit 14) may represent special corn grinding locations. Evidence for such specialized milling rooms has been recovered in the U.S. Southwest (e.g., Mobley-Tanaka 1997; Reed 2008, 50–52). VanPool and Leonard (2002, 725) also suggest that the spatial clustering of metates at Paquimé might indicate that grinding (presumably corn) was a communal activity. Given the aggregation of population at Paquimé and evidence for significant consumption of corn (Rakita 2009, 31–32), efficient processing of this important foodstuff would have been vital.

TURKEYS. Di Peso saw a fairly large-scale turkey domestication and production system at Paquimé (1974:2, 602–3). He concluded that hundreds of turkeys were raised; they were "herded" during the day and allowed to roost in pens at night. He further argued that the Paquiméans kept three different breeds, one of which was a hybrid of their small and large turkeys (Di Peso et. al 1974:8, 275). Since limited cut marks were found on the few turkey remains recovered from trash deposits, he concluded that the turkeys were raised for feathers and as sacrificial animals, not for food (Di Peso 1974:2, 735).

Turkey remains were found throughout the site (Di Peso 1974:8, 274), though their distribution was concentrated in certain locations. Most (2,410 or 69.9%) were found in Unit 13. Unit 16 contained 6.7% of the turkeys; Unit 12 had 6.1%; Unit 8 had 5.8%; and Unit 11 had 4.9%. Units 1, 3, 14, 20, 21, and the central and southern plazas all had less than 4%. Two hundred and twenty of the turkeys were found intentionally buried, articulated, and headless, suggesting that they were used as sacrifices (Di Peso, Rinaldo, and Fenner 1974:8, 269). Of these, most (197 or 89.5%) were found in Unit 13; 9 were in Unit 12; 8 were in Unit 16; 5 were in Unit 11; and 1 was in the central plaza. It seems that the people living in Unit 13 had considerable access to turkeys, though by no means were turkeys unavailable to those living in other units.

Di Peso argues that the largest concentration of turkey raising occurred in Plaza 3 of Unit 13 where a number of roosting pens were located (Di Peso, Rinaldo, and Fenner 1974:5, 584–92). Given the large number of pens in Unit 13 and the fact that the majority (70%) of the turkey remains found at the site were in Unit 13, this room block seems to have been the key locus for turkey production. A total of 35 to 40 turkey pens were located in Plaza 3–13 and 7 or 8 pens in Plaza 5–8. Minnis (1988, 188) notes that given the lack of distinctive entrance stones like those used in macaw pens, and if turkey pens were constructed on upper stories at Paquimé, their discovery would be difficult. However, Minnis (1988) concluded on the basis of numbers of pens and recovered skeletons that turkey production was at the same scale as that of macaw production.

Neither Di Peso nor Minnis discuss tools or special technology that would have been associated with turkey breeding and raising. However, it is reasonable to assume limited technology would have been needed beyond the roosting pens and the plaza. Some food (possibly corn) would have been needed to supplement what the birds naturally foraged. Indeed, recent chemical analysis of turkey remains reported by Rawlings and Driver (2010) indicate that domesticated turkeys in the northern San Juan region subsisted on high levels of C_4 grasses, most likely corn. Watering dishes or troughs would be required. Bedding (corn husks?) would have probably been provided as well. Di Peso's evidence for turkey aviculture at Paquimé includes the roosting pens, some eggshells, and evidence of hybridized birds (Di Peso 1974:2, 734).

The localization of much of the turkey production in one area at the site, suggests that a subset of the population was involved in the work. Minnis (1988, 188) posits that turkey production "may have transcended the household organization" level. If Di Peso's conclusion about a distinct "Paquimé" hybridized breed of turkeys is accepted, it would seem that some level of specialized turkey aviculture knowledge was to be found at Paquimé. However, it is unclear if that knowledge was restricted to a few people.

Unfortunately, it is unclear whether turkey husbandry at Paquimé was a short-lived, high intensity production event or was an effort that occurred on a low but sustained production level. Both possibilities might produce the same material evidence. If Di Peso is correct that turkeys were used for ceremonial sacrifice, and some scholars agree (cf. Rakita 2009), then a sustained, low-intensity production may have supplied turkeys for ceremonials over the span of the community's existence.

While herding and care for the birds would have required some time, stocking food and water and cleaning of waste would have taken more time. Presumably, everyone would have had the necessary raw materials to raise turkeys, yet they are concentrated in certain portions of the site. This centralization may have been made for sanitary reasons. More likely, it limited control of these ritually important birds and their feathers.

Turkey remains are found in pre-Hispanic sites across the U.S. Southwest and northern Mexico. Thus there is no reason to believe (in contrast to macaws) that Paquimé was the production center for distribution of turkeys to a wide region. Di Peso contended, and Minnis agreed, that turkeys were raised at Paquimé for ritual purposes. Certainly the fact that 300 of the 344 turkeys found at the site were recovered in intentional burials and not trash middens suggest they were not consumed as food. Most turkey remains look to be the results of intentional sacrifice, though some are included in human burials. If turkeys were raised at Paquimé for ceremonial purposes, then this represents a difference from the use of turkeys in the northern San Juan region. As reported by Muir and Driver (2002), the use of turkeys shifted over time. Their data suggest that turkeys were used for ritual purposes in the Basketmaker II and Pueblo I periods, but that by Pueblo II, turkeys were increasingly used as food. Thus the ancient Paquiméans were using turkeys for ritual while those groups in the northern U.S. Southwest were increasingly consuming turkeys.

AGAVE. Di Peso contended (1974:2, 405) that Unit 1 was a center of alcoholic beverage production. The unit consists of a small house cluster, a large, low mound (26 m in diameter but only 2 m high), and four large roasting pits. One other very large pit oven was located near Unit 9. Di Peso argues that agave hearts were roasted in these pits and liquor made from the caramelized results.

Minnis (1988, 189) notes that the large size of both the debris mound and the ovens at Paquimé suggests a scale of agave roasting rarely seen in the region. Minnis and Whalen (2005, 118–19) suggest that the oven near Unit 9 at Paquimé may be the largest earth oven in northwest Mexico and the U.S. Southwest (NW/SW). They estimate that this one oven could have produced over 7,000 lb. (3,200 kg) of cooked food in one use. They also point out that the four Unit 1 ovens had features typical of economic specialization, including "large-scale production, formalized production facilities, stockpiles of raw materials, production standardization, and large trash deposits from production." Di Peso, Rinaldo, and Fenner (1974:4, 268) indicate that all of the ovens "were found full of baking material, i.e., lenses of fire-fractured stone; firewood . . . as well as layers of agave (sotol) hearts." They further state that the mound at Unit 1 was "not constructed as a single operation, but was an accretion mound composed of the accumulated fill from the pit ovens located around it."

The fact that four of the five Paquimé pit ovens were located at Unit 1 suggests that this was indeed a centralized location for roasting agave (or sotol; see Whalen and Minnis 2009a, 218 for a discussion of the difference between sotol and agave). Four of the Paquimé ovens are located slightly apart from the main room blocks at the site and have their own small household block. It may be reasonable to assume that the inhabitants of the household were responsible for maintaining and preparing the ovens for use.

Minnis and Whalen (2005, 121) feel that agave production was likely for both "ritual and 'secular' purposes." It is possible that the Unit 9 oven was ritually significant, located as it was near a platform mound. On the other hand, the unit 1 ovens may have had a more economic orientation. Regardless, feasting on a large scale probably occurred at Paquimé and at some neighboring sites.

The question remains, however, how often these agave roasting ovens were utilized. Given their large size (especially the Unit 9 oven) and the amount of labor, agave, and wood that would have been needed for one roasting event, it seems unlikely that such events occurred frequently. The centralized location and large size of the roasting ovens at Paquimé are indicative of a production system requiring organization, planning, and control. It is likely that this activity was highly regulated. As such, decisions regarding the distribution of the results of roasting events probably were similarly regulated. However, with the potential to produce thousands of pounds of roasted agave, it seems hard to imagine that consumption would be substantially restricted.

Similar, though smaller, roasting pits are found at other Medio Period sites in the region. Whalen and Minnis (2009a, 17–21; see also Minnis and Whalen 2005) report that they have located similar pit ovens at 25 Medio Period sites and 18 isolated others. However, they cluster in Whalen and Minnis's (2009a, 266) core zone around Paquimé and may be associated with sites that exhibit what they refer to as "architecture of power." While the five they have excavated are smaller than those found at Paquimé, their morphology and features suggest a similar food roasting purpose. Perhaps these ovens at nearby, smaller Medio Period sites were used for roasting events that mirrored or mimicked larger but rare feasting events that took place at Paquimé

Commodities with Nonlocal Connections

SHELL. In total, 3.1 million pieces of marine, land, and freshwater (worked and unworked) shell were recovered from Paquimé (Di Peso, Rinaldo, and Fenner 1974:6, 401–3), most of which originated along the west Mexican coast. Di Peso and colleagues argued, on the basis of the location of large quantities of shell in two rooms (15-8 and 26-14) and the access and morphology of one of these rooms, that shell production was the activity of a group of slaves or forced-labor workers. "The implication was that one segment of the Casas Grandes population that was involved in the production of shell commodities worked under duress and probably had a very low status" (Di Peso, Rinaldo, and Fenner

1974:6, 402). However, they also argued that some of these low status, corvée shell workers were able to acquire a rank as "artisans," and they operated workshops throughout the city as evidenced by caches of shells, manufacturing debris, and tools.

Certainly, Minnis (1988, 187) is correct when he observes that the "1.5 tons of shell, most of which were cached in two rooms, are indicative of the importance of shell and the centralization of its distribution." By contrast with the volumes of shell found at Paquimé, only 8,309 pieces of shell were recovered from Pueblo Bonito (Neitzel 2003, 108). McGuire et al. (1999, 144) estimate comparative numbers of shells for the Cerro de Trincheras site in Sonora and conclude that "the difference remains on the order of three times more shell at Paquimé than at Cerro de Trincheras." The sheer amount of this item at Paquimé indicates that it was important to the inhabitants. Of the over 3.7 million shell artifacts, 99.3% were beads, and most of these (99.4%) were found in rooms (Di Peso, Rinaldo, and Fenner 1974:6, 405). As McGuire et al. (1999) and Whalen (2013) observe, the vast majority of the shell objects at Paquimé were beads and specifically beads made from *Nassarius* species (a total of 3.7 million or 98.2% of the beads and 95.3% of all shell). Using this species for shell beads is fairly unique or atypical within the NW/SW.

Di Peso (1974:2, 501–4; Di Peso, Rinaldo, and Fenner 1974:6, 402) claims that shell was worked in two "slave" workshops (Rooms 15-8 and 26-14) and also by specialized shell artisans in locations "scattered throughout the city." However, only 20 unfinished shell objects and 22 pieces of "worked shell" were found at the site (Di Peso, Rinaldo, and Fenner 1974:6, 405). Tools similar to those used for turquoise working would have been required. These are found throughout the site. Minnis (1988, 186) points out that there is a paucity of shell-working tools in one of the hypothesized shell warehouses/slave working quarters (26-14), though Room 15-8 has a collection of shell working tools. Di Peso (1974:2, 694) offers an example of a pit with shell, a quartz pestle, and flaked stone gravers found in Room 9-14 as an example of a shell artisan's tool kit. Minnis (1988, 186) takes exception to this feature as a shell-working tool kit. As McGuire et al. (1999, 145) observe, "overall, there is negligible manufacturing debris recorded for Paquimé, suggesting that many artifacts must have been imported as finished products. Bradley

(1995) indicates that the lack of manufacturing debris most likely results from the emphasis on only slightly modified gastropod beads at the site and the resulting minimal manufacturing debris that the methods of production would produce."

They further conclude that the great majority of finished shell objects at the site were imported from elsewhere, including at least some from the Trincheras region. Over 3.7 million perforated *Nassarius* sp. shell beads were found at Paquimé, and Whalen (2013) has recently explored this hoard of shell. Perforation would seem to be a fairly simple task, requiring little if any standardization of effort. Similarly, the skill level necessary for perforating these shells would have been negligible even though the enormity of the task (viewed in its totality) would have been daunting. The lack of evidence for perforation at Paquimé and the possibility that these items were brought from their origin on the west Mexican coast as strings of beads suggests that (at least for these items) shell working was not a major effort at Paquimé. Whalen (2013, 636) has suggested that rather than part of a prestige good economy, the hoarded *Nassarius* beads were "a powerful object that was a critical part of the community's ritual system."

The distribution of shell and the tools for working shell at Paquimé do not suggest a significant control of the means of production. While there are concentrations of vast quantities of shell (especially in Unit 8), access was not exclusive to a few loci. Certainly, the fact is that much of the shell comes from outside the local Casas Grandes region, and the sheer quantity of shell at Paquimé suggests that there was some coordinated acquisition of this nonlocal raw material.

Paquimé was undoubtedly acquiring vast quantities of shell from the south-southwest. The source of most of the shell at Paquimé is the Pacific and Gulf of California coast of Mexico. It is also fairly reasonable to assume that the site was acquiring finished shell objects from the Cerro de Trincheras site (McGuire et al. 1999). Bradley's (1999, 224) analysis of shell object diversity across the NW/SW region supports the conclusion that Paquimé was not simply a consumer, but also "an active supplier and participant in the exchange of the material."

Minnis (1988, 187) argues for "small-scale" specialized shell production in the two shell warehouses (Rooms 15-8 and 18-8). However, shell is not the only commodity being worked or stored in these rooms, as the cache of Gila Polychrome bowls and some mined mineral materials were also found there. Despite the quantity of shell recovered from Paquimé, there is no indication that shell-working technology is any more specialized than in the Viejo Period or at other Medio Period sites.

It is unclear if shell objects were important for economic or ideological reasons, though Whalen's (2013) interpretation favors the latter. The scale of shell at Paquimé certainly bespeaks of an important commodity. The fact that a majority of the objects found in burials were shell ornaments likewise indicates an economic or ritual function or role. At least some of the people who were buried with shell ornaments presumably benefited from the abundance of shell at Paquimé. The meaning or role of shell in Casas Grandes society may have changed from the Viejo to Medio Period. Almost all of the shell from the Viejo Period Convento site was found in human burials. During the Medio Period, the frequency of shell ornaments in burials decreases, but of the over 11,000 objects found in Medio Period burials, 72% were shell ornaments (Rakita 2012). The fact that many of the objects have motifs also found on polychrome ceramics, however, suggests that they did communicate some ideological information (Bradley 1999, 227). Bradley (1999, 227) does note that the distribution of shell in the NW/SW mirrors the distribution of macaws.

The importation and caching of 3.7 million *Nassarius* shell beads, probably preperforated at their location of origin on the west Mexican coast, is enigmatic. Certainly these objects inflate the quantity of shell found at the site to unimaginable levels. While some of these beads made it into human and bird burials, ceremonial troves, and offerings, over 99% was stored in architectural spaces. These items may represent not ornaments but animate objects, material agents of a supernatural sort (Whalen 2013).

TURQUOISE. According to Di Peso, turquoise "may have been the inspirational quest that drew the original *puchteca* to Casas Grandes.... The Paquimians used turquoise primarily as offerings to their gods, while the Bonitians of Chaco Canyon permitted their ranked personages to wear this precious gem, as did the Zuñi of Hawikuh" (Di Peso 1974:2, 629–30). Despite this pronouncement, the amount of turquoise recovered from the site, the context of its recovery, and the lack of significant production debris suggest that Paquimé was principally a consumer of turquoise objects.

Di Peso (1974:2, 745) indicates that 5,895 pieces (worked and unworked) or 1225.8 g of turquoise were found at Paquimé. By contrast, Neitzel (2003, 108) reports that 61,650 turquoise objects were found at Pueblo Bonito. Maxwell and Cruz (2008) report that at the sites of Villa Ahumada and Los Patos west of Paquimé over 3,600 pieces of turquoise were found. This is despite only very limited excavations at both sites in comparison with the massive excavations at Paquimé. Thus it would seem that the volume of turquoise at Paquimé is not very great.

Of the 5,895 pieces of turquoise from Paquimé, 4,190 (or 71%) were recovered from Units 8, 13, 14, and 16 (Di Peso, Rinaldo, and Fenner 1974:8, 187). These units are also the only places where raw materials and waste are reported. Those pieces of turquoise found in the site are finished pieces. It is possible that these units represent areas where turquoise was worked. However, there is better evidence for production of objects from turquoise from the sites of Villa Ahumada and Los Patos in the Rio Carmen valley to the east of Paquimé (Maxwell and Cruz 2008).

In contrast, explorations at the site of Villa Ahumada have recovered a total of 1,075 pieces representing 18% of that recovered by Di Peso at Paquimé. Of these, 3% was raw material, 83% was production waste, and 13% was finished artifacts. At the Los Patos site, 2,528 pieces of turquoise were recovered, which represents 43% of the total found at Paquimé. Of these, 4% was raw material, 95% was production waste, and no finished pieces were found. At Paquimé, 6% of the turquoise was raw material, 11% was production waste, and 81% were finished pieces. The Villa Ahumada and Los Patos sites are much smaller than Paquimé. In fact, Villa Ahumada is only 1.5% of the size of Paquimé. Additionally, Di Peso excavated close to 50% of Paquimé, while the excavations at Villa Ahumada covered 5% of the site. Thus, proportionally speaking, Villa Ahumada and Los Patos have more turquoise than Paquimé.

At Paquimé the "evidence for onsite manufacture of turquoise objects in organized workshops is slight" (Maxwell and Cruz 2008, 3). Presumably stone drills, polishers, and abraders would be used to work turquoise. These are found in abundance and are widespread at Paquimé. A total of 99 abraders in a variety of forms and 15 drills were found throughout the ruin (Di Peso, Rinaldo, and Fenner 1974:7,

49–56, 356–59). However, the lack of production debris in the form of waste pieces suggests that these objects were used for other purposes.

There is no apparent standardization of turquoise products at Paquimé nor any indication of the development of specialized skills or knowledge in working this material. Turquoise mosaic work (Di Peso 1974:2, 615–16) would have required a degree of knowledge and skill. However, these objects are rare, so if mosaic specialists existed, they did not produce a significant amount of these objects. Maxwell and Cruz (2008) conclude:

> Turquoise pieces from Paquimé have not been analyzed in this fashion so no comparisons in production methods can be made. However, interregional differences across the Southwest may have occurred. A visual photographic comparison of turquoise beads and tesserae from the Casas Grandes region with similar pieces recovered in Chaco Canyon suggest that different manufacturing techniques were used. The Casas Grandes forms tend to have greater thickness, but it is undetermined whether this is due to dissimilar production techniques, raw material variations, or desired end product.

Most of the turquoise at Paquimé was found in the ceremonial cache placed at the bottom of Reservoir 2. Thus, turquoise was not used by many "consumers" for personal adornment. Di Peso (1974:2, 630) recognized this point and stated, "very little turquoise—less than 6% by weight and a little more than 1% by numerical count—was used as personal ornaments in graves. The actual figures were 338 (5.7%) objects that weighed 15.5 g (1.3%)" (Di Peso 1974:2, 749). Maxwell and Cruz (2008) make a convincing argument that Paquimé was principally a consumer of finished turquoise objects. With the exception of the Los Patos and Villa Ahumada site, turquoise objects are rare, but ubiquitous across the region. Thus, the level of turquoise production, organization, and technology at Paquimé is probably no greater than any other site in the region. Any production occurring at Paquimé probably would have been part-time and at the domestic or household level.

COPPER. Di Peso (1974:2, 511–12) not only argues that copper objects were produced at Paquimé, but that copper smiths were organized into a craft guild that had kinship ties to populations on the west Mexican coast. Moreover, while he claims that copper production was third in quantity (behind shell and turquoise), he asserts that it was preeminent in terms of technical quality. In Di Peso's reconstruction, those working copper were adept at smelting, cold-hammering, and mold techniques. They worked with nearly pure copper and produced a diversity of objects including, crotal bells, tinklers, wire, a ceremonial axe head, plaques, beads, and pendants.

The JCGE excavated many (664) copper artifacts at Paquimé (Vargas 2001, 198). As Vargas notes, this is "more than the combined total of copper items recovered from all other Southwest/Northwest region sites." For example, only 11 copper objects came from Pueblo Bonito (Neitzel 2003, 108). In total, 57 pieces of copper ore weighing roughly 14.6 kg were recovered from Paquimé (Di Peso, Rinaldo, and Fenner 1974:7, 500–503). The vast majority (94.3%) of this ore was found in Unit 8. Eighteen pieces of sheet copper were also found at Paquimé. Seven pieces (38.9%) were found in Unit 8; 5 (27.8%) were recovered from Unit 13; 4 (22.2%) were in Unit 16; and 1 piece (5.6%) each was present in Unit 14 and the central plaza. If copper was being smelted and/or worked at Paquimé, Unit 8 would have been a likely location. Di Peso (1974:2, 515) claims that no special tools were found that indicate hammering of copper, and no molds from casting were found.

Vargas (1995, 2001) convincingly critiques Di Peso's evidence for pre-Hispanic copper smelting and production of copper objects at Paquimé. To begin with, the chemical analysis used by Di Peso and colleagues was too imprecise to definitely match raw materials with finished products. Second, the "workshop" materials found at the site include four worked nuggets showing no signs of smelting, and the piece of sprue was an unprovenienced surface find that could have been historic. Third, the two pieces of "slag" available for analysis have not been tested for traces of copper and come from secondary contexts. Fourth, no positive identification of a smelting location showing significant thermal alteration has been found at the site. Finally, Vargas efficiently dispenses with Di Peso's argument that some of the copper objects at Paquimé were morphologically unique to the site and unlike objects found elsewhere. While not dismissing the idea that some copper may have been worked at Paquimé, Vargas (1995, 14) concludes that "copper production at Paquimé is not substantiated by the available evidence."

Significant knowledge, technology, and raw material resources would have been required to make the copper objects found at Paquimé (a point Di Peso acknowledges). However, Vargas (1995) has argued on the basis of technological and morphological style that West Mexico is probably the production loci of most of the copper objects at Paquimé. It is possible that copper artisans originally from West Mexico produced the copper objects found at Paquimé. However, the lack of evidence for production at Paquimé suggests otherwise.

Access to copper objects at Paquimé was not equally distributed across the population. Vargas (2001, 206) makes three observations: 1) few copper objects were found in mortuary contexts; 2) many copper objects were found in nonmortuary and ritual contexts; and 3) some copper objects were found in domestic contexts. Moreover, "access to copper artifacts, even among households possessing them, was not equal" (Vargas 2001, 206). Most households with copper objects had less than 6. However some households had up to 10 pieces, and 1 household had almost 100 pieces. Vargas concludes that there is strong evidence that copper objects were used for ceremonial purposes, and that those domestic areas where copper was found may represent the households of ritual specialists. If Vargas's conclusions are correct, ritual specialists and their families benefited from the acquisition of copper objects from West Mexico.

Since production most likely occurred in West Mexico, no one at Paquimé had control over production; however, control over intrasite distribution may have been exercised by a subset of the population. It is unclear what relationship existed between the West Mexican producers of the copper objects and the people of Paquimé. Were objects acquired directly or through down-the-line trade? What commodity was exchanged for copper?

Vargas (2001, 200) points out that the majority of copper bells distributed throughout the NW/SW date prior to Paquimé's fluorescence, suggesting that its role in the distribution of copper may have been less robust than once thought. She concludes (1995, 70) that "Paquimé appears to have been primarily a large-end consumer of bells and only involved in small-scale trade of a few bells northward to several sites in the southern portion of New Mexico and perhaps to northern Sonora."

MACAWS. Macaw production at Paquimé was so unique and extraordinary to Di Peso that he referred to Unit 12 as the House of the

Organization of Production at Paquimé   79

Macaws (1974:2, 599–600). Di Peso interpreted the various evidence for macaw husbandry at Paquimé as indicative of full-time, specialized aviculture. He even goes so far as to suggest that the craft was passed down from generation to generation. He sees these specialists as attending to daily chores of feeding and watering the birds and tending to their nesting boxes.

An astonishing 322 scarlet macaws were recovered at Paquimé (Di Peso, Rinaldo, and Fenner 1974: 8, 275), which is considerably more than the 37 at Pueblo Bonito, 5 at Pueblo del Arroyo, 1 at Kin Kletso (Mathien 2003, 129), the 27 from Point of Pines, and the 12 from Turkey Creek (Hargrave 1970). An additional 81 military macaws and 100 macaws of undesignated species were also discovered at Paquimé (Di Peso, Rinaldo, and Fenner 1974:8, 274). There is little doubt that Paquimé represents a pre-Hispanic concentration of these valuable birds.

Minnis et al. (1993) identify six areas at Paquimé with variable numbers of nesting boxes and suggest that cage stones scattered throughout the site represent other possible production loci. The total number of nesting pens that existed at Paquimé is unknown due to preservation issues, though Di Peso, Rinaldo, and Fenner (1974:4, 267) report at least 69. Fifty-six pens were discovered with macaw remains and feces (Somerville, Nelson, and Knudson 2010, 126). However—and luckily for archaeologists and unluckily for macaw breeders—macaws are notoriously destructive of cages. Thus the Paquiméans built cages with stone ring doorways and stone plugs that the birds could not destroy with their powerful beaks. Moreover, 125 of these fairly indestructible remains attest to nesting boxes at Paquimé, and 95 nesting door plugs were also recovered (Di Peso, Rinaldo, and Fenner 1974:7, 42–45). The lack of macaw eggshells—only one sample was recovered—is explained by Minnis et al. (1993) as related to poor preservation and the lack of fine screening by excavators. As with turkey aviculture, tools associated with raising macaws would have included food and water containers for them.

Somerville and colleagues (2010) examined 30 samples of macaw bones from Paquimé using stable light and heavy isotopes (delta 13 C and delta 18 O) to examine the diets and source of the birds. The results of their carbon analysis suggest that the birds were raised on diets heavily enriched with C_4 plants, presumably corn. Their oxygen isotope results indicate that many of the sampled birds were born and raised at Paquimé (though several samples indicate possible importation). Thus, it seems that the ancient Paquiméans had not only imported these tropical birds from farther west and south in Mexico, but they had established and maintained a breeding population.

The scale and wide distribution of evidence for and debris from macaw aviculture at Paquimé suggests that many individuals were involved in the practice. As with turkey husbandry, the number of nesting boxes may represent either a short-lived, high intensity production period or a low, sustained production level. A fair degree of knowledge and skill would have been required for successful macaw breeding and raising. This is especially true of the scarlet macaws, which are not indigenous to the Casas Grandes region. Indeed, Somerville, Nelson, and Knudson (2010, 125) indicate that "the Paquimeños had in fact developed the breeding technology and cultural knowledge to sustain a reproducing population of scarlet macaws in the highlands of northern Chihuahua." They further argue that their evidence "suggests a tradition of macaw keeping at Paquimé where specialists were familiar with the needs of the parrots and put them on a pure maize diet only after the delicate nestling phase of development." (Somerville, Nelson, and Knudson 2010, 133)

At Paquimé (Di Peso, Rinaldo, and Fenner 1974:8, 274–75), 54% of the 322 scarlet macaws were recovered from Unit 12, 28.3% from Unit 11, and 11.8% from Unit 8. Trace counts (less than 6 birds) were recovered from Units 6, 15, 16, 18, 21, and the central plaza. Sacrificed macaws were found only in Units 8, 11, and 12. Thus, those individuals living in, or with access to, Units 8, 11, and 12 seemed to have relatively good access to macaws. The wide but variable (in quantity) distribution of pens at the site suggest that the practice of raising macaws was not strictly controlled or centralized. Minnis (1988, 188) states, "it appears that many groups of Paquiméans raised macaws, although some areas seem to have produced larger numbers of these birds than others." The wide distribution and lack of centralized production at Paquimé lends itself to envisioning a range of production intensities at the site. Those areas with only a few nesting boxes may be evidence of sporadic or very part-time macaw keeping while those areas with larger-scale production areas (i.e., more nests) as evidence of more intensive production.

Within the region, however, it does appear that there was a fairly tight control over macaw production centralizing it around Paquimé and its immediate sphere of influence (Minnis et al. 1993). The use of macaws for sacrifice and feathers is almost undoubtedly of a ceremonial nature. For example, VanPool (2001, 81–5) provides convincing evidence that sacrifice of macaws is symbolically represented on at least one Ramos Polychrome vessel.

Conclusions

Di Peso's reconstruction of production at Paquimé as a series of craft guilds was clearly inspired by the pochteca explanatory framework he developed for the rise of the community. However, a more critical review of the evidence suggests that commodity production at the site was not so centralized nor access so controlled. In many ways, craft production at Paquimé was much like that seen in other areas of the U.S. Southwest and northern Mexico. In terms of the locally produced commodities (e.g., ceramics, type 1B metates, and turkeys), household or extended family production probably accounts for much of the materials recovered. There is limited evidence for a restricted distribution of these objects. Certainly most Paquiméans were able to acquire polychrome ceramics, metates, and turkeys for sacrifice and probably participated in large feasting events represented by the roasting pits. In terms of the nonlocal commodities, it appears that Paquimé was principally an end consumer of items like shell, turquoise, and copper objects. Turquoise was probably acquired in finished form from areas to the north and east, while shell and copper almost assuredly came from the west Mexican coast. Macaws were also probably originally acquired from West Mexico, though subsequently the Paquiméans may have managed a breeding population to supply their needs. Each of these nonlocal commodities was probably ritually or ceremonially important.

However, there are examples where craft production was more standardized, larger in overall amount, or otherwise different than that seen in the southwest or northern Mexico. For example, type 1A metates show standardization unparalleled in the region. Domesticated turkey husbandry, while perhaps no more than observed at other late ceramic period sites, was unusual in that these animals seem to have been used for ritual not subsistence purposes. Paquimé stands out as having significant agave roasting capacity, and production of this commodity was probably at the community (certainly above the household) level. Finally, the ancient Paquiméans maintained a breeding population of macaws far north of their native habitat and most assuredly served as a distribution point for birds or their feathers moving into the Southwest.

There are, of course, a number of products that have not been examined by scholars coming after the efforts of the JCGE. Di Peso (1974, 2) offered specific interpretations regarding various types of specialized producers, including builders of architecture, woodworking, weavers, and those making bone tools. These reconstructions have not been examined in detail. Further work should also be directed at the nature of production of plainware ceramics, other ground stone tools, and flaked stone objects.

4

Religion and Cosmology in the Casas Grandes World

Christine S. VanPool and Todd L. VanPool

We have been asked to provide an overview of the various thoughts on Casas Grandes religion. Religion is central to human culture in general but is particularly important to the current discussions, because: 1) whatever else the Casas Grandes phenomenon is, it reflects the spread and adoption of a distinct ritual and cosmological system; and 2) perhaps because of its very placement on the landscape, Casas Grandes religion is part of a larger debate concerning Mesoamerican influence moving into northwest Mexico and the U.S. Southwest (NW/SW). Our discussion is organized into three sections. First, we outline the views of Charles Di Peso (1974, vols. 1–3), which have framed the consideration of Medio Period Casas Grandes religion. We then consider more recent discussions using a thematic framework. We conclude by identifying broad areas of agreement that can serve as the basis for further synthesis.

The Point of Departure: Charles Di Peso and Mesoamerican Cults

Di Peso and his colleagues (1974, vols. 4–8) continue to structure discussions of Casas Grandes religion, just as they continue to structure discussion of most aspects of Medio Period archaeology. They suggested that Mesoamerican *puckteca* (named after the Aztec trading class of merchants, warriors, and priests) built and administered Paquimé and the surrounding area to gain resources such as turquoise. According to Di Peso (1974, vols. 1–3), puchteca traders introduced Mesoamerican cults (where "cult" is narrowly defined as a religious institution stipulating a specific deity and that deity's associated ritual system) to organize and facilitate their relations with the local inhabitants. There were four such cults: 1) the *Quetzalcóatl* cult, which was preeminent; 2) the *Xiuhtecutli* complex; 3) the *Xipe Tótec* complex; and 4) the *Tláloc* cult (Di Peso 1974:2, 548–69). The Quetzalcóatl cult focused on the Mesoamerican feathered rattlesnake (Quetzalcóatl) that was the "old creator god" and "the giver of all things" (Di Peso 1974:2, 548–49, 556). His domain was over water, and the ballgame and his cult was reflected during the Medio Period by murals of horned serpents, I-shaped ball courts at Paquimé and elsewhere, the thousands (perhaps tens of thousands) of serpent images on pottery and rock art throughout the region, and a serpent-shaped mound adorned with an eye containing the carved image of a Quetzalcóatl. Further, the acquisition of "scarlet macaws for use in various Quetzalcóatl religious ceremonies" consumed a considerable portion of the Medio Period economy as evidenced by macaw aviculture and the sacrifice of hundreds of macaws at Paquimé (Di Peso 1974:2, 552). Quetzalcóatl could also take the humanoid form of *Ehécatl*, the wind god, who is associated with wind spirals and *Strombus* shells, which are naturally spiral shaped. Di Peso (1974:2, 548–49) suggested Ehécatl is reflected by *Strombus* shell jewelry at Paquimé, spirals in Medio Period ceramic iconography, and a spiral-shaped "temple" built on top of Cerro de Moctezuma, a substantial hill that overlooks Paquimé and the surrounding area.

Di Peso believed that the other cults at Paquimé were generally supplementary to the Quetzalcóatl cult. The Xiuhtecutli complex commemorated the Mesoamerican Lord of the Fire, who was often depicted by the Maya as a squatting old man (or woman in other areas) carrying a heavy backpack. Di Peso (1974:2, 557) proposed Xiuhtecutli was reflected by male and female humpbacked Casas Grandes effigies. Another manifestation of Xiuhtecutli was Turquoise Blue Snake (*Xiucóatl*), which has a "spiked and sectioned body wearing a helmet or a crest" (Di Peso 1874:2, 557). A copper back shield (CG/3844) with a sectioned serpent similar to Xiucóatl serpents on warrior shields at Tula and Chíchén Itzá was found in Room 13-13 at Paquimé. The Xipe Tótec complex focused on "nature's regeneration" and springtime, and was associated in Mesoamerica with offerings of the Flayed One (a skinned man), trophy heads, and effigy vessels that depicted Xipe with closed eyes and an open mouth. Related evidence from Paquimé include Xipe effigies, trophy heads, vestiges of cannibalism, and ceremonial drinking of the maguey plant (Di Peso 1974:2, 556–59). Finally, Di Peso (1974:2, 565) proposed that terraced headdresses found on human effigy vessels and human stone figures represented Tláloc, the water deity that controlled rain. He suggested that this deity was part of a larger rain making cosmology that was shared by Mesoamerican and Puebloan peoples. While Di Peso proposed that the hundreds of turkeys sacrificed at Paquimé were offerings to Tláloc based on his reading of historical accounts, Schaafsma and Taube (2005) note that child sacrifices were more common in Mesoamerica.

The Practical Importance of Mesoamerican Cults at Paquimé

As previously mentioned, Di Peso (1974:2, 574, 586) argued the Mesoamerican cults structured Medio Period economic and social relations and organized Medio Period life. According to Di Peso (1974:2, 574), the puchteca formalized priesthoods headed by male and female ministers from "noble families." The priests implemented the general Mesoamerican educational system and "state schools in which the children of the ruling class were educated." As part of his discussion, Di Peso (1974:2, 586) carefully distinguished between ministers/priests (who were dominant as part of the state religion) and shamans (a catchall term into which he lumped sorcerers, magicians, medicine men, witch doctors, and shamans as individuals that practiced magic and curing in private rituals). Following standard anthropological definitions, Di Peso (1974:2, 574) defined priests as religious practitioners who conducted "state controlled ceremonies" as part of "state religious organizations," whereas shamans were "self-employed" practitioners (i.e., outside of the dominant cult organization) who conduct "private rituals" for their clients (Di Peso 1974:2, 574). Given their state sanctioned ceremonial role, Di Peso contended the priesthoods of the four cults dominated the religion and by extension the political, economic, and educational systems. However, he followed Bernardino de Sahagún in proposing that shamans were necessary to work with the unseen world, and he suggests shamans and priests "overlapped in certain of their professional dedicatory duties" (Di Peso 1974:2, 589). For example, Di Peso (1974:2, 588–89) suggested that:

> The shamans were also responsible for the inducement of fertility, which was a primary concern of the people who wanted not only an abundance of children but also a plentiful harvest of both cultivated and natural goods. In this cause, the priests prayed to the earth goddess, to Xipe, and to a host of other fecundity deities on behalf of the community, while the shaman conjured his spirits on behalf of the individual, using such age-old paraphernalia as stone phalli and vulva rings or an occasional clay human fertility effigy.

Presaging many recent arguments, Di Peso (1974:2, 586–87) also discussed shamanism's deep roots in the Olmec and the Mesoamerican belief that shamans transformed into spirit animals to interact with supernatural entities. He further suggested this practice was present in the Medio Period world:

> Paquimian illusionists, who, according to the local effigy record, may have regarded the bear or the mountain lion as their principal animal metamorphosis. Some may even have chosen the bighorn sheep, coyote, wolf, or macaw as their appropriate totemic disguise. (Di Peso 1974:2, 587)

Ultimately, Di Peso's conclusions rested on the placement of ritual paraphernalia and ceremonial architecture at Paquimé and ethnohistorical records written by Sahagún in the Florentine Codex, which documented priests and shamans in several Mesoamerican groups in the sixteenth century. Di Peso's argument is quite simple. He argues that because priests' ceremonies are state sanctioned, they will be associated with public architecture, such as ball courts and the large mounds, which are inappropriate for any type of "private" ritual. Given that most artifacts apparently related to religious ritual were associated with architectural features indicative of public ceremonies, the priesthoods were the focus of ritual behavior. Not all architectural features were public, though, and Di Peso (1974:2, 589) states that shamans used turquoise ornaments to "pacify house spirits who cracked walls of private residences."

The Path to Here: Recent Discussions of Casas Grandes Religion

Di Peso's (1974, vols. 1–3) ideas continue to influence more recent discussion, and in the case of Riley (2005), are generally accepted. However, many subsequent discussions have a more limited focus on specific deities (e.g., Quetzalcóatl) or architecture (e.g., ball courts). Further, some of these discussions simply ignore Di Peso's proposed cults partly because of efforts to incorporate more recent anthropological perspectives regarding priesthoods, shamanism, and other aspects of religious organization into the discussion (e.g., Rakita 2009; VanPool and VanPool 2007), as well as more recent understandings of Mesoamerican religion and deities (e.g., Mathiowetz 2011). What is probably more significant, though, is the historical circumstance of the general evaluation of Di Peso's (1974, vols. 1–3) ideas outside of his consideration of religion. Problems with Di Peso's proposed chronology and Paquimé's subsequent redating demonstrated that it is too late to have been founded by Toltec traders as Di Peso (1974, vols. 1–3) originally suggested, and archaeologists have generally rejected the idea that Mesoamerican puchteca directly created a trading outpost (Bradley 2000). As a result, Di Peso's ideas regarding Medio Period leadership and interregional interaction with Mesoamerica have been rejected en masse by some archaeologists. This included his views of religion, despite the fact that there is no necessary inconsistency between the four cult institutions he identifies and the revised Paquimé dates or many of the subsequent models of Mesoamerican/Casas Grandes interaction. The cults Di Peso identifies had broad spatial and chronological distributions throughout Mesoamerica, and could have been adopted through various mechanisms ranging from direct introduction via contact with the (West Mexican) Aztatlán traders to indirect adoption from down-the-line diffusion of religious ideas and institutions (Mathiowetz 2011; VanPool et al. 2008). Furthermore, these ideas could have arrived in pulses at various times starting perhaps as early as the Archaic (Phillips 1989; Phillips, VanPool, and VanPool 2006). For example, Phillips, VanPool, and VanPool (2006) suggest that multiple feathered/horned serpent "cults" were introduced in the NW/SW starting around AD 1000 and again in the 1300s (see also VanPool and VanPool 2006).

The number of researchers interested in Medio Period religion continues to grow. Tables 4.1 through 4.5 help organize the differences and similarities in their perspectives, and will form the foundation of our discussion. These tables are not exhaustive and are meant to be heuristic aids for subsequent discussion. Even when multiple authors are lumped together, say, in regard to the I-shaped ball courts reflecting Mesoamerican ball games and rituals, they may have significant disagreements about other aspects of Medio Period religion and even about the specific topic (e.g., compare Harmon [2005] with Whalen and Minnis [1996] and Rakita [2009]). The remainder of our discussion will focus on a few central themes reflected in the five tables that we believe are the areas of greatest interest in current discussions and will be the basis of future growth regarding our knowledge of Medio Period religion.

The Nature and Dominance of the Casas Grandes Plumed Serpent

The plumed serpent (Di Peso's Quetzalcóatl) is typically viewed as the central Medio Period deity. Plumed serpent images are ubiquitous throughout Medio Period imagery as illustrated by thousands of depictions on pottery and in rock art, as well as the Mound of the Serpent and the wall murals at Paquimé (Schaafsma 2001; VanPool and VanPool 2007). Serpent icons on ceramics reflect substantial consistency, suggesting that the artists (and probably the rest of the Casas Grandes population), uniformly understood the knowledge, myths, rituals, and beliefs associated with these creatures. This in turn supports Di Peso's idea of a cult institution with a formal ritual structure. Newer models for religious organization include everything from priests to shamans to caciques (Table 4.1), but researchers uniformly acknowledge the plumed serpent's importance. However, there is considerable disagreement about its relationship with Quetzalcóatl (Table 4.2).

Researchers, such as Schaafsma (2001) and Riley (2005), see a relatively unambiguous relationship between the Medio Period plumed serpent and Quetzalcóatl. However, the Casas Grandes horned/plumed serpent is not a feathered rattlesnake as is the Aztec's Quetzalcóatl. Rather, it is a serpent with a two-fin tail and a horned/plume appendage coming out of its head or snout. As a result, other authors are more

Table 4.1. Medio Period Socio-Religious Organization

Puchteca priesthoods associated with four Mesoamerican deities (Quetzalcóatl, Xiuhtecutli, Xipe Tótec, and Tláloc)	Di Peso (1974); Riley (2005)
Cult of the Dead—similar to kachina societies with their focus on fertility, water, and regeneration	Ravesloot (1994)
Caciques "or sacred leaders" that have political power as well. These leaders also had knowledge of complex irrigation systems.	Schaafsma and Riley (1999:248)
Mesoamerican shamanic leaders concerned with fertility, water, and regeneration	VanPool and VanPool (2007)
Two distinct priesthoods that worked together: Cult of the Dead and an Earth and Fertility Cult. Cult of the Dead was for ancestor worship for negotiation of power. Earth and Fertility Cult was for regeneration and cosmology.	Rakita (2009)
Chaco elites (Paquimé's polity "was a canal economy and so was its hinterland's.")	Lekson (1999:137)

circumspect about drawing a direct historical analogy between the serpent traditions. Braniff (1999, 82) suggests that the Casas Grandes horned/plumed serpent represents a different deity, perhaps the Turquoise Serpent or the Fire Serpent. Taube (2006) and Mathiowetz (2011) posit a connection between the "flowered serpents" found in Late Preclassic Maya murals of San Bartolo (Guatemala), Techinantila murals at Teotihuacán, and Puebloan plumed serpents (which are somewhat later and distinct from the Medio Period serpents). Based on the prevalence of flowered serpents across these regions, Mathiowetz (2011) suggests that running bands of circles commonly depicted on Medio Period serpent icons are flowers reflecting the plumed serpent that embodies the flowery road and the path of the sun across the heavens in the Casas Grandes world. VanPool et al. (2008) have suggested that the Casas Grandes horned/plumed serpent is morphologically most similar to the Mimbres horned/plumed serpent and Zuni's Water Serpent *Ko'loowisi* from the Historic Period, both of which clearly fit into the pan-American water serpent tradition, but share an ambiguous relationship to Quetzalcóatl at best. Phillips, VanPool, and VanPool (2006) build on this theme. They observe that the Casas

Table 4.2. Proposed Mesoamerican Deities in the Casas Grandes Region During the Medio Period

Quetzalcoatl has "dominion over the rivers and irrigation systems of this arid land." Ehécatl was a kindly fertility spirit.	Di Peso (1974:2:548, 549); Kokrda (2005); Riley (2005;) Schaafsma (1998)
Xiuhtecutli: God of Fire	Di Peso (1974); Riley (2005)
Xipe Tótec: vegetation and rebirth	Di Peso (1974); Riley (2005)
Tláloc (rain and fertility)	Di Peso (1974); Riley (2005); Schaafsma (1999); Schaafsma and Taube (2006)
Young Sun God is reflected by macaw-headed anthropomorphs	Mathiowetz (2011)
Flowery Serpent as the path of the sun	Mathiowetz (2011)
Generic feather serpent associated with fertility, floods, and earthquakes	Phillips et al. (2006)
Tláloc associated with sacred water	Schaafsma (1998)
Generalized Ancestral Pueblo and Mesoamerican deities	Moulard (2005); Schaafsma (1999, 2000)

Grandes serpent shares as many or more similarities with the serpent tradition of eastern North America as it does with the Mesoamerican Quetzalcóatl tradition. One's view of the relationship among the various serpent traditions is quite significant. If one accepts a direct analogy between the Mesoamerican Quetzalcóatl and Medio Period serpent traditions, then the ball courts, macaws, and other aspects of the archaeological record fit within a more general, unified cult structure as Di Peso (1974, vols. 1–3) and Riley (2005) suggest. If one rejects this analogy, then the relationships among these aspects of the archaeological record must be reconfigured using other lines of argumentation. This is not to say that the ultimate connections must be different. There could be a connection between the ball game and the plumed serpent even if the Casas Grandes serpent is not a direct manifestation of Quetzalcóatl, for example. The point is that the lines of argument will necessarily be different, in that one cannot rely on direct analogy to the Mesoamerican Quetzalcóatl cult to explain the association (see Harmon 2008).

Priesthoods, Shamans, and Religious Leadership

One of the most extensively debated aspects of Medio Period religion is its leadership. Di Peso (1974, vols. 1–3) held that the priests of the four cults controlled religious power and worked with shamans who conducted ceremonies in private contexts. VanPool (2009) builds on more recent discussions of the integration of shamanism and leadership among New World peoples to challenge the old shaman/priest typology, which was central to Di Peso's (1974, vols. 1–3) leadership framework. Given that "priests" often perform "shamanic" activities, VanPool (2003, 2009) and VanPool and VanPool (2007) suggest that Mesoamerican-style "shaman-priests" (individuals who are part of a formal priestly system but perform shamanic activities as part of their official duties) were the focus of Casas Grandes iconography and the center of Medio Period leadership. In accordance with Di Peso's ideas, VanPool (2003) and VanPool et al. (2008) propose the Medio Period religious system was introduced from Mesoamerican sources (in this case the Aztatlán system) through direct contact and was used by elite shaman-priests to establish and maintain their authority. These shaman-priests performed both public and private ceremonies. During the ceremonies, they undertook "soul flights," during which the shaman-priests initiated a trance (using psychoactive drugs and other means) and had visions of transforming into a spirit creature that interacted with other spirits/deities. VanPool uses several lines of evidence to support this position. She argues that in Medio Period ceramic iconography soul flights are indicated by a rare design, the "pound sign," that with only two known exceptions[1] is limited to male smoker effigies, painted figures with horned/plumed serpent headdresses depicted in poses suggesting dancing or other movement, and macaw-headed anthropomorphs (VanPool 2003). Following cross-cultural patterns of shamanic behavior, she contends the pound signs reflect the same individuals who have undergone the transformation from humans, by consuming psychoactive agents, into macaw-headed anthropomorphs (Figure 4.1). Further, the anthropomorphs are associated with "odd" vessels decorated in ways that explicitly flaunt the rigid rules of Medio Period pottery decoration and design field composition (VanPool and VanPool 2007). VanPool (2003) and VanPool and VanPool (2009) further note that seven of

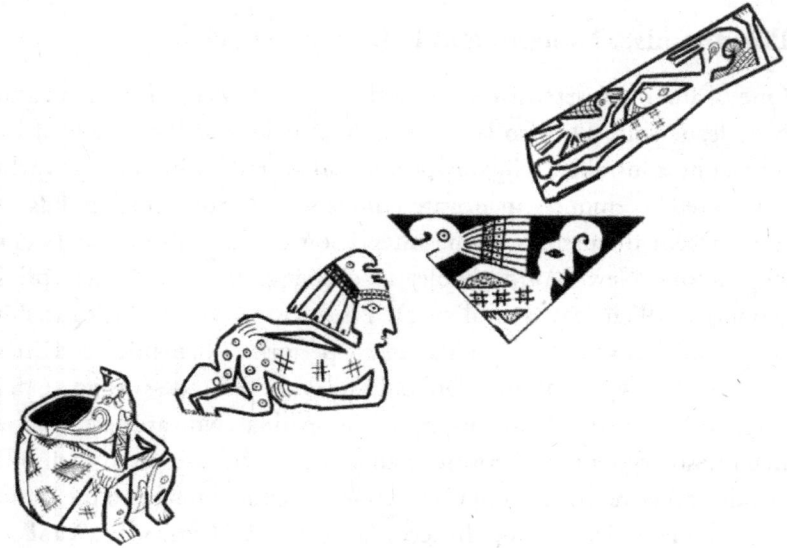

Figure 4.1. The transformation of shamans as indicated by the pound sign from a male smoking and dancing while wearing a headdress (the smoking male effigy and painted figure of a dancer wearing a horned-serpent headdress on the bottom left) to spiritual creatures who commune with supernatural entities (the painted images of the horned man beside the discarded headdress and the macaw anthromorph on the right) (Christine and Todd VanPool).

the nine stone pipes found at Paquimé were found in side rooms of a hidden Walk-In Well (Di Peso, Rinaldo, and Fenner 1974:7, 305–306), which also contained "shamanic caches" (jars with mineral concretions, quarts, and small fetishes) and a large jar depicting two shamans (VanPool and VanPool 2007). The pipes, which are identical to those held by the smoker effigies, indicate that smoking was an important part of water ritual, not just an activity portrayed on pots. Their association with shamanic caches and images of the shamanic anthropomorphs indicate that smoking rituals and other shamanic activity were associated with the House of the Walk-In Well (see the section on religious architecture below).

Smoking, pipes, and shamanic caches and iconography at the House of the Walk-In Well constitute an "iconic family" that, according to Knight (1986, 676), forms a "set of *sacra* particularly associated with a corresponding cult institution." Riley's (2005, 143) observation that our idea of shaman-priests is not incompatible with Di Peso's (1974, vols. 1–3) framework is correct, especially given Di Peso's arguments for cooperation between shamans and priests and his suggestion that shamans underwent spiritual animal transformations. Other authors have directly challenged the proposal of Casas Grandes shaman-priests. Moulard (2005) presents the most direct challenge and points out that smoking tobacco does not necessarily lead to shamanic trances and that it is a common component of ethnographically documented Southwestern ritual in which it is associated with clouds and rain, and therefore water. She further contends that shamanism is limited to simpler societies than those focused on irrigation agriculture. There is no inherent incompatibility with the use of tobacco in both nonshamanic and shamanic rituals or with an association between tobacco smoke and clouds and its use in shamanic ritual. Further, Moulard's (2005) citations regarding the limitation of shamanism to simpler societies are dated and ignore research demonstrating shamanic-based religious systems in more complex societies, including state-level societies in the Old World and the New World (Aldhouse-Green and Aldhouse-Green 2005; Chang 1983; Freidel, Schele, and Parker 1993). Moulard's interpretation also does not account for the macaw anthropomorphs that both VanPool (2003) and Di Peso (1974:2, 587) suggest were the "shaman's totemic disguise."

Rakita (2009) uses Victor Turner's conceptualization of ritual practitioners to develop one of the most thorough examinations of religious organization using Paquimé's mortuary data. He proposes a shift from shamans during the Viejo Period to priests during the Medio Period that is associated with the presence of two cult systems, one based on ancestor worship and the other on fertility. The cults formed as aspiring elites at the beginning of the Medio Period created a division emphasizing the ancestor cult, which helped establish and maintain elite authority through exclusionary ritual (e.g., playing the ballgame). They also manipulated human remains, allowing them to directly interact with ancestors through the periodic revisiting of specific burials. In contrast, the fertility cult emphasized inclusion and community bonds to help encourage community cohesion. The elites were also involved in this ritual, possibly using public spaces, such as the Mound of the Cross, but it was expressed through pottery and other means that were generally accessible and readily transmitted throughout the Casas Grandes world. Both of the cult institutions were dominated by priests, although Rakita (2009) allows for continued shamanic practice as part of the Earth Fertility cult. Again, Rakita's (2009) ideas are not inherently incompatible with either Di Peso's (1974, vols. 1–3) and Riley's (2005) proposed cult structures or VanPool's (2003) shamanic leadership model, but it does not adopt these perspectives either. In fact, Rakita (2009) does not mention possible Mesoamerican cults but instead employs a more broadly defined framework that is independent of arguments for particular deities.

Not all researchers adopt the priest/shaman framework implicit in the previously mentioned studies, in part because of a concern that the general terms do not accurately reflect the culturally specific variation in religious practitioners (Mathiowetz 2011; Moulard 2005). Schaafsma and Riley (1999) use a concept of caciques or "sacred leaders" that have political power (see Table 4.1). Although consistent with classically defined religious categories, such as shamans and priests, the cacique concept they employ emphasizes political leadership more than religious practice. They argue, for example, that Medio Period caciques' knowledge of complex irrigation systems was perhaps more important to their leadership and daily activities than were religious rituals associated with a given deity. This is not to deny that such rituals took place and were important, but it instead shifts focus away from debates about particular deities and toward the daily leadership activities of religious leaders.

Religious Architecture

Casas Grandes architecture reflects religious ritual, just as Puebloan and Mesoamerican architecture does. VanPool and VanPool (2012) discuss the significance of dedication ceremonies of various features at Paquimé, for example, and Di Peso (1974, vols. 1–3; see also Lekson 1999) proposes that the Mound of the Cross at Paquimé was a solstice (or Venus) observatory. We wish to focus attention here on several studies that we believe are particularly important. First, there is general agreement that the ball courts at Paquimé and scattered throughout the Casas Grandes region were religiously important and served as a location for elite competition (Rakita 2009; Whalen and Minnis 1996). Harmon (2005, 2006, 2008) conducted a phylogenetic analysis that indicates the Casas Grandes ball courts were a "blend of religious and ideological concepts tied primarily to Mesoamerican ballgame cults of the La Quemada-Chalchihuites complex of Durango and Zacatecas, the Toltec and Aztec cultures of central Mexico, and to a lesser extent Mimbres/Mogollon cults represented by communal structures (great kivas), square kivas, and large surface rooms" (Harmon 2006, 192). He further builds on previous arguments (e.g., Gillespie 1991) that the ball court represents a decapitated body (with the four corners of the I-shaped court representing the arms and legs and the ball reflecting the head) and proposes that the Casas Grandes ball courts reflect both human sacrifice and the "shamanic universe" tripartite division of an Upper, Lower, and Middle world (see VanPool and VanPool 2007). Human sacrifice is associated with the T-shaped court in Paquimé, which has been considered the most ritually significant court in the Casas Grandes region (Di Peso 1974, vols. 1–3; Harmon 2005). Sacrifices include a human female who had severed feet (which Harmon [2008, 41] considered analogous to the T-shaped ball court that is an I-shaped court with its lower limbs removed), a pregnant female, and a female with her severed right arm draped around her neck (both of which might be metaphors for the Mesoamerican hero twin stories [Harmon 2008, 41]). Harmon (2005) does not however attempt to tie the ball court to any specific Mesoamerican cult as Di Peso (1974, vols. 1–3) does. Rakita (2009) suggests these sacrifices, and the ballgame in general, were associated with ancestor worship.

Second, Pitezel (2011) presents detailed analysis of Cerro de Moctezuma (the previously mentioned hilltop that Di Peso [1974:2, 548] proposed contained a "temple" focused on Ehécatl) and more generally a framework for understanding the ritual landscape of the Casas Grandes region. He found that Cerro de Moctezuma was a ritual location constructed with a unique (in the Casas Grandes region) rubble core masonry, to create a ceremonial center that was the focus of pilgrimages from the densely settled valleys surrounding the hill. Its prominent placement on a tall hill overlooking Paquimé caused it to reflect a pan-regional emphasis on elevated positions. It fits within a larger ritual landscape composed of other hilltop shrines (called *atalayas*), ball courts, and massive agave roasting ovens. The atalayas formed local shrines, according to Pitezel (2011, 187–92), that were less elaborate than and subsidiary to those associated with Cerro de Moctezuma but that served a similar purpose (see Swanson [2003] for a more extensive discussion of atalayas). Likewise, the agave roasting ovens and ball courts at Paquimé are more extensive and impressively constructed than elsewhere in the Casas Grandes region. Based on this, Pitezel (2011) concludes that Paquimé (and the associated settlement atop Cerro de Moctezuma) served as the ultimate expression of Medio Period ritual authority, although he does not seek to tie this authority to any cult institutions.

Water Symbolism

Another area of nearly universal agreement is that water ritual and symbolism was central to Medio Period religion. Di Peso (1974, vols. 1–3) argued that it was part of the Quetzalcóatl cult's dominance. Schaafsma and Taube (2006) suggest that rituals for Tláloc, as a mountain God, were conducted at Paquimé. VanPool and VanPool (2007, 2012) argue it is a unifying theme in Medio Period ideology as well, especially at Paquimé where the ubiquity of water symbolism and ritual caused it to metaphorically be a "water city." Ravesloot (1994, 17) suggests that the skeletons of past leaders were sacred objects used, "in a critical role in the community's successful cycle of agricultural production and plentiful supply of water." [2] As noted above, Schaafsma and Riley (1999) observe leadership was needed to build the large Medio Period irrigation systems, so some of the authority caciques wielded was used for and derived from building and maintaining the extensive hydraulic system. As part of this effort, elites integrate religious activities and dedicational offerings to water features throughout Paquimé that reflect Mesoamerican and Southwestern water symbolism. For example, the Walk-In Well was a hidden subterranean water source with extremely limited access built in the heart of the village (Di Peso 1974:8, 356; Di Peso, Rinaldo, and Fenner 1974:4, 377). To enter it, one had to step over a human skullcap embedded in the floor of the room at the hidden entrance and descend 19 stairs (Di Peso, Rinaldo, and Fenner 1974:4, 372–81; Walker and McGahee 2001). Valuable artifacts and "ceremonial paraphernalia," such as copper tinklers, animal bones, small stone and ceramic effigies, and beads of turquoise and shell were strewn down the stairs (Di Peso 1974:4, 356; Di Peso, Rinaldo, and Fenner 1974:4, 377–81). The bones included bison, red-tailed hawk, pronghorn, bobcat, various other animals, and isolated fragments of human bone. Animals such as bear and badger were reflected as ceramic effigies, several of which were "decapitated" at the neck and were found without the associated pottery body (Di Peso, Rinaldo, and Fenner 1974:4, 379). Copper, shell, and green stone like turquoise are associated with water in Mesoamerica and the Southwest (Miller and Taube 1993, 174), suggesting that the artifacts and bones on the stairway were ritual offerings similar to those given to springs and caves throughout both regions (Di Peso 1974, vols. 1–3; McNatt 1996, 85–86; Miller and Taube 1993, 43). Such entrances into the underworld in turn represented the "axis mundi," the center place of creation at which the upper world, the lower world, and the four corners of this world were united (Garber and Mathews 2004).

The connection between Paquimé and water is also reflected directly throughout the city. Paquimé's farmers diverted water from a warm spring 3.6 km northwest of the site and from the Rio Casas Grandes into their village using a system of canals and drainages (Di Peso 1974:5, 830). As was the case at the Walk-In Well, significant animals may have also been placed in Paquimé's canals. Di Peso, Rinaldo, and Fenner (1974:8, 250) argued that 17 mud turtles (*Kinosternon sonoriense* and *Kinosternon* sp.) found in the canals were intentionally introduced from the mountains in Arizona given that they are ordinarily found in woodlands at an elevation above 1,550 m and are primarily aquatic animals that only occasionally take to dry land (generally after heavy rain). Although most of the turtles were found in the water system, four were found inside the room block, indicating their use by humans perhaps for food and for their carapaces (Room 7–8; Di Peso, Rinaldo, and Fenner 1974:8, 250). Turtles symbolized water throughout the Americas, and Southwestern Pueblo groups continue to this day to use turtle rattles, especially on the legs of some kachinas who stomp while dancing to make the rattles and their feet sound like rain and thunder (Miller and Taube 1993, 174; Parsons 1996; Wright 1973). The city also had two reservoirs, one of which had a Playas Red jar wrapped in a necklace of turquoise, shell, and slate that held several additional necklaces of the same materials and a horn, possibly from a bison or a mountain sheep, buried in a small shaft covered by a rock slab at the center of its basin (Di Peso, Rinaldo, and Fenner 1974:5, 836). Schaafsma and Taube (2006) believe that this offering reflects a shared rainmaking ideology that is found in the Pueblo Southwest and Mesoamerica. They and VanPool and Van-Pool (2012) agree with Di Peso, Rinaldo, and Fenner (1974:5, 83, Figure 215–5), who first suggested that this jar was a water offering that is "consistent with past and/or present beliefs in the Southwestern United States and Mesoamerica concerning the relationships between turquoise and water" (quoted in Schaafsma and Taube 2006, 247 [Tables 4.3, 4.4, and 4.5]).

The presence of spiritual/mythic creatures, especially the horned serpent, in rock art near water sources also emphasizes the cosmological importance of water (Schaafsma 1998). The association between horned

Table 4.3. Cosmological Principles

Multitier cosmos with a watery underworld	Schaafsma (1999); Harmon (2005); VanPool and VanPool (2007)
The flower world	Mathiowetz 2011
Cyclical rituals for cosmological continuity	VanPool and VanPool (2007)
Cosmological landscape with north pointing toward the ancestors	Lekson (1999)
Cosmological landscape	VanPool and VanPool (2007)

Table 4.4. Religious Metaphors

Clouds are ancestors	Schaafsma (1999); Schaafsma and Taube (2006)
Cruciforms are associated with Venus and warfare	Schaafmsa (2001); Thompson (2006)
Cruciforms are associated with the cardinal directions	VanPool and VanPool (2007)
Red and green symbolism	Di Peso (1974); VanPool (2001)
Animism	VanPool and Newsome (2012)
Double-headed macaw diamond represents cyclical time	VanPool and VanPool (2007)
Duality and twins	VanPool and VanPool (2007)

Religion and Cosmology in the Casas Grandes World   99

Table 4.5. Sacred Architecture

I-shaped ball courts reflect Mesoamerican ball games and rituals	Di Peso (1974); Harmon (2005); McGuire (1980); Rakita (2009); Riley (2005); Whalen and Minnis (1996)
T-shaped ball court, high ritual	Di Peso (1974)
Mound of the cross used for astronomical reasons	Di Peso, Rinaldo, and Fenner (1974); Pasahow (1993); Rakita (2009)
Mound of the Offerings had the original founders of Paquimé	Di Peso (1974)
Mound of the Offerings was revisited during ancestor worship	Rakita (2009)
Walk in well for water rituals	Di Peso (1974); Walker (2002); VanPool and VanPool (2007)
Mogollon-style kiva associated with Mound of the Serpent.	Lekson (1999); Walker (2002)

serpents and water is further reflected by the "Mound of the Serpent," a platform mound at Paquimé, 113.3 m long and shaped like a horned serpent. The mound runs along one edge of the site and helped divert water around the main ceremonial complex (Di Peso, Rinaldo, and Fenner 1974, vols. 4–8). VanPool and Newsome (2012) use an animistic framework, the pan-Native American belief that spirits reside in objects and places (man-made and natural) to explore the religious significance of aspects of Paquimé. They suggest that the Mound of the Serpent as a water control feature was the direct personification of a water-controlling, terrestrial serpent similar to Quetzalcóatl and Ko'loowisi. In this personification, he is an active agent impacting the daily life of humans at Paquimé. The placement of the eyes as part of the construction of the serpent provides further insight into its interaction with humans. The western eye was etched with a Mesoamerican-style plumed serpent, indicating that the Serpent Mound was either seeing a reflection of itself in the sky or was viewing another serpent to the west. The eastern eye, which faces the city, was blank—perhaps to keep a watchful eye on the inhabitants, as the literal personification of the serpent emphasizes its active role in controlling water, and thereby promoting and maintaining life at the settlement. Furthermore, its tail turns to point directly at

Arroyo de Los Monos, a spring with a dense concentration of rock art 15 km away, further integrating Paquimé to water across the landscape (Schaafsma 1998).

The Kachina and Other Mesoamerican Religious Influence Throughout the Rest of the Southwest

Archaeologists have determined that Mesoamerican influence filtered through and fundamentally transformed the late pre-Hispanic cultures of the NW/SW in ways ranging from the introduction of new weaving techniques (Teague 1998) to new religious ideas (Riley 2005). Given the evidence of Mesoamerican influence during the Medio Period, it seems likely that it was the conduit for this influence. Mathiowetz (2011) uses comparisons of Mesoamerican, Casas Grandes, and Puebloan iconography/symbolism to propose the spread of specific religious concepts/practices such as the Sun Youth. These arguments do not focus on the specific cult institutions Di Peso (1974, vols. 1–3) identified, but are similar in the premise that specific Mesoamerican cults (in this case from West Mexico) were adopted. Mathiowetz (2011), as well as Schaafsma (1999, 2000) and Adams (2000), link the origin of the Southwestern kachina religion to Mesoamerican influence during the Medio Period. Schaafsma (1999, 2000) suggests the kachina are derived from the Tláloc cult. Tláloc, the rain god, is a mountain being for the Aztecs but who was commemorated with Tláloc statuary, Tláloc vessels, and other offerings atop many peaks (Broda 1991, 84–96; Townsend 1992). Puebloans likewise considered mountains to be the home of rain-providing supernaturals, commonly called kachinas in Southwestern ethnographies. Using this commonality, Schaafsma (1997, 2001) suggests that the adoption of the Tláloc cult at Paquimé influenced and perhaps led to the development of the kachina tradition to the north. Furthermore, she suggests that Tláloc figures are frequently found in the Casas Grandes and Jornada style rock art as figures with large "goggle" eyes and square bodies decorated with pecked cloud terraces, which she calls "*cartouches*." She believes that some of these cartouches are masks, which would be indicative of kachinas. To our knowledge, no masked dancers or clearly recognizable kachina dolls have been found in the Casas Grandes region, although a few terrace (cloud/cloud ladder) headdresses and horned/plumed serpent headdresses are represented in Medio Period ceramic and rock art iconography. Schaafsma (2001) suggests a ground stone effigy with a terrace headdress excavated by Di Peso represents a kachina, but Adams (2000) warns researchers to keep masks, which are indicative of kachinas, separate from headdresses, which have a broader distribution and are distinct from the kachina masks. Given the low number of terrace headdresses and the lack of masks, there does not seem to be a full-blown kachina tradition during the Medio Period, even if Medio Period religion contributed to it in some way.

Ceremonial Center

Regardless of the exact relationship between Mesoamerican and Medio Period cults, Paquimé clearly was unique in terms of its size and ceremonial architecture, and it has more "West Mexican prestige economy" goods than any other Medio Period (or for that matter southwestern) site (Bradley 2000; Lekson 1999). Given the emphasis on Aztatlan prestige goods and the city's "overbuilt" walls that reflect social and symbolic power (Whalen and Minnis 2001), Paquimé was clearly a center for political, social, and religious activity (Lekson 1999; VanPool, VanPool, and Leonard 2005; Whalen and Minnis 2009). Throughout much of North America and Mesoamerica, there was no separation between religious, political, and economic considerations. As a result, Paquimé's role as an economic and political center necessitates that is was also a religious center that was the focus of movement, perhaps even pilgrimages, from the surrounding settlements (Fish and Fish 1999; VanPool, VanPool, and Leonard 2005). People probably visited the city for a number of reasons, at least some of which included the cult institutions that formed the basis of Medio Period religion and elite power.

Conclusions

As is obvious from this and the other chapters in this volume, it is an exciting time to be a Casas Grandes archaeologist. Our increasing knowledge is allowing the creation and evaluation of a wide array of ideas. There is tremendous diversity of thought regarding Medio Period religion, but we do have a solid basis from which to grow. We wish to end our discussion by returning our focus to these. To begin with, there is general agreement that Mesoamerican interaction led to the adoption of Mesoamerican religious principles both in the Casas Grandes region and in many Pueblo groups in the U.S. Southwest. However, McGuire (2011) makes a salient point that the social contexts of these groups are vastly different, such that even though Mesoamerican and Southwestern priests could talk with each other about theological issues, these concepts were applied in very different ways. In McGuire's (2011, 49) terms, "we may come to better understand why Aztec priests wielded knives while Pueblo priests scattered corn pollen." Furthermore, there is an emerging consensus that Mesoamerican shamanic practice was a part of this system. David Freidel, at a workshop on Amerindian Cosmology and Society at the Santa Fe Institute, suggested to Michael Mathiowetz, Polly Schaafsma, and Christina VanPool that their interpretations on Casas Grandes iconography were compatible in that shamanism is a fundamental component of the Mesoamerican myths and rituals that Mathiowetz discusses (e.g., shamans can reenact the Sun Youth). Mesoamerican and NW/SW religion often employ complex metaphors that tie together multiple concepts into a meaningful mosaic. Sorting out the manner in which these metaphors were integrated into the Casas Grandes world will be one of the major themes that will continue to propel our studies forward. Second, there is also a general agreement that much of Casas Grandes religion focused on water and fertility, the sun symbol, and maize symbolism, although the specifics of this emphasis vary from researcher to researcher. There is also general agreement with Rakita's conclusion that elites used the symbolic and ritual system to parlay and negotiate their power at Paquimé to maintain the Casas Grandes cosmological and sociopolitical structures (Lekson 1999; Pitezel 2011; VanPool and VanPool 2007; Whalen and Minnis 2003).

Notes

1. The exceptions are on the vulva of a pregnant female effigy and on a snake's head.

2. Note that Rakita (2009, 157) suggests the manipulation of burials by elites was instead to "reinforce community cohesion and to affirm their authority roles," as previously mentioned.

5

Settlement Patterns of the Casas Grandes Area

Michael E. Whalen and Todd Pitezel

Archaeologists have long known the Casas Grandes area of northwest Chihuahua, Mexico, because it contains the large pueblo center of Paquimé. Most interpretations of the area's prehistory were made within the context of Paquimé and its immediate predecessors of pithouse times. Unfortunately, Paquimé always has been a large and obviously influential community without a firmly established regional context. The problem is that for most of the period of the community's notoriety, there have been few settlement studies, and the data have been imprecise to work with. A 1988 examination of the current literature on northwest Chihuahua found only a few hundred sites on record for an area about one-sixth the size of the state of New Mexico. Many of these sites were visited a half-century earlier, before topographic maps were available for northwest Mexico (e.g., Brand 1935; Carey 1931; Lister 1946; Noguera 1930; Robles 1929; Sayles 1936). Uniformly, locational information was vague, and site descriptions were very brief. There has been considerable improvement in this situation, but some aspects of past settlement pattern studies continue to cause confusion. The objective of this chapter is to summarize all known settlement pattern data for four time intervals: the preceramic; the pithouse adaptation (the latter part of which is known in Chihuahua as the Viejo Period); the pueblo apogee of Paquimé (known locally as the Medio Period and the region's peak of complexity); and post-Paquimé times. We will evaluate old interpretations and propose some new ones.

There are several major bodies of data to be considered. The first we term "the early reconnaissances." Most of this data set consists of sites recorded in the 1930s and 1940s by Donald Brand (1933) and Edwin Sayles (1936) through unsystematic reconnaissances that visited scores of sites in and around the Casas Grandes area. Some survey work was done by, or under the auspices of, the Joint Casas Grandes Expedition ([JCGE] Di Peso 1974, vols. 1–3). A large, intensive survey was carried out 20 years later from 1994 to 1995 (Whalen and Minnis 2001), and other small reconnaissance projects have taken place since.

The Preceramic Settlement System

Early reconnaissance provides no information on preceramic sites. Di Peso speculated on early life in the Casas Grandes area by drawing upon examples from what he called the Gran Chichimeca, a massive geographic space of which the Casas Grandes area is a small part, because there was little evidence for preceramic peoples in the immediate area. In fact, only a few reports of Clovis projectile points and other associated stone tools are known from the area (Di Peso 1974:1, 63). This time period also would include the Archaic and Early Agricultural periods. Di Peso says little of these times other than that the occupants of the area apparently did not adopt agriculture because of the abundant food that could be gathered from cacti (Di Peso 1974:1, 78).

Despite more recent attempts to locate valley settlements from the Archaic/Early Agricultural Period, evidence largely still eludes archaeologists. More stone tools have been recorded as isolated occurrences across the area, and only one Archaic site has been identified (Robert Hard, personal communication; Whalen and Minnis 2001). However, there is other evidence of life in this early time along the Rio Casas Grandes River and nearby. Between about 1500 BC and AD 300, or in the Late Archaic, people lived in settlements that were larger and more elaborate than anyone suspected.

Of the 14 hills that have been documented and termed *cerros de trincheras*, Cerro Juanaqueña is the most extensively modified (Hard and Roney 2007). It has almost 500 individual terraces along its upper and lower slopes that have a combined length of a little over 5 mi. Around 1250 BC and again around AD 300, perhaps 100 to 200 people lived on this hill. Macrobotanical analysis shows that the residents had a substantial dependence on maize agriculture. Possible domesticated amaranth also was identified. The documentation of these trincheras sites shows a complex local adaptation in Archaic/Early Agricultural times. This situation also has implications for the early part of the succeeding

Pithouse Period, and it is far from the perception of small, simple hunting and gathering bands moving widely about the landscape.

The Pithouse Settlement System

Brand, Sayles, and Di Peso focused their reconnaissance activities on "Casas Grandes" sites, and their results include practically no pithouse period loci. Given the nature of Late Archaic occupations in the Casas Grandes area, we expect that there is a substantial Early Pithouse Period occupation that presently is completely unknown. Di Peso's reconnaissance work focused on the Puebloan site of Paquimé and its contemporary neighbors. He undertook only limited excavation at three sites along the Rio Casas Grandes, and these were radiocarbon dated to about AD 700–1060, a time he called the Viejo Period (Di Peso 1974:1, 100–255). The Viejo Period is widely discussed as the pithouse period in the Casas Grandes area, but this is problematic. Di Peso's dates from the succeeding Medio Period are now rejected as too early, and his sequence has been extensively revised. Pueblo settlements are now dated from the late 1100s, thus setting the Viejo Period forward by a century. In fact, it seems highly likely that Di Peso recorded only the latest part of pithouse times and the pithouse-to-pueblo transition in what he termed the Viejo Period.

As noted above, the equation of pithouse settlement and the Viejo Period should be avoided because surely pithouse sites that are earlier exist in the area. We know from work in the Tucson Basin in Arizona, for example, that pithouse sites, or irrigation communities, date to at least 1200 BC, and pithouse sites on the Colorado Plateau date to about 1000 B.C, all well before the use of pottery (Mabry 2005). In the southern deserts of New Mexico and western Texas, Early Pithouse Period sites with plain brown ceramics date from ca. AD 300 to 700, and there is a Late Pithouse Period that dates from ca. AD 700 to 1000. There is a brief pithouse-to-pueblo transition period between about AD 1000 and 1150 (Whalen 1994). There is no reason to believe that adjacent northwest Chihuahua differed greatly from this pattern, especially given the large and elaborate Late Archaic occupations that characterize the area.

We think it probable, therefore, that Di Peso's Viejo Period includes only the last part of the Pithouse Period and the first appearance of mud-and-stick surface rooms. More recent work has identified a few other pithouse sites about 150 km south of the Rio Casas Grandes valley that immediately predate the Medio Period (see Kelley and Searcy, this volume). All of this means that there is a yet-undiscovered early Pithouse Period still awaiting definition in northwest Chihuahua. It may date to around the beginning of the Christian era, or even earlier, if the magnitude of the area's Late Archaic occupation is taken into account.

A little is known about the settlement pattern of the Viejo Period. Surveys along drainages in the Casas Grandes area in 1989, 1994, and 1995 recorded 15 Viejo Period sites (Whalen and Minnis 2001). This seems a small number considering that more than 7,000 km^2 were surveyed. However, 56 sites also were recorded with both Viejo and Medio ceramics. Of the 15 single-occupation Viejo Period sites recorded, 9 are on river terraces, a setting similar to the 3 sites excavated by Di Peso. In addition to these, 2 others on terraces have been more recently identified along the Rio Palanganas near its confluence with the Rio Casas Grandes. This type of site location is a contrast with Medio Period settlement that with few exceptions is in lower locations along watercourses. In addition, however, pithouses have been found in excavations underlying every medium or large Medio Period settlement that has been investigated to date. Most of these sites lie in the fertile river valley bottoms. At present, we have such poor chronological control of pithouse or Viejo times that we cannot say whether these two settlement locations are sequential or contemporary. Survey in the San Pedro area suggests contemporaneity, as late-dating Mimbres Classic Black-on-white sherds are found on pithouse sites in the river valleys and on terraces.

With the limited data, it appears that the Viejo Period settlement location more closely mirrors Medio Period locations given the 56 additional sites that have indications of both components. Most of these are located in or on the margins of river or drainage valleys, which is a characteristic location for Medio Period villages. Moreover, recent survey (Whalen and Minnis 2001) recorded upland field houses with Pithouse ceramics. These are small, very sparse occupations, which we presume to be temporary accommodations for upland agriculturalists as they were in the succeeding Medio Period.

Although these data indicate that Viejo Period site location was more diverse than in the Medio Period, the small data set prevents firm conclusions. We expect to see a good deal of variability in the locations of Pithouse Period sites, as we presently cannot separate early from late ones, and the early and late adaptations are likely to have involved substantially different types and intensities of agriculture. It may well be that the Viejo sites were more intensively agricultural, were more heavily occupied, and so are more conspicuous in the archaeological record than their early predecessors.

It is likely that Chihuahuan pithouse sites are difficult to recognize on the surface, a condition noted in adjacent areas of the Southwestern United States. Equally important is recognizing that many pithouse sites are deeply buried beneath later occupations. In short, we still have far to go toward an adequate understanding of Pithouse Period settlement in northwest Chihuahua.

The Paquimé Settlement System

The Early Surveys

Brand (1933) used the term "Casas Grandes" sites, for which we here use the more current term 'Medio Period.' These sites were briefly described, and Brand's reports sometimes gave estimates of room block mound area. It is evident, however, that he divided Medio sites into two classes: a) the larger and more conspicuous sites that he visited and briefly described; and b) smaller sites whose presence was noted but which were not individually described. He usually gave rough room block, mound size estimates (e.g., 50 × 60 yd) only when dealing with sites that he considered to be significant. In addition, Brand frequently describes a larger site and notes that there were several smaller ones in its vicinity. A picture thus emerges of a few larger sites surrounded by many smaller ones. Even his large sites were not enormous, however. These ranged from 900 to 2,850 m^2 of room block mound area, with an average size of 1,400 m^2 (standard deviation, 634 m). It also was clear that all of the significant drainages contained these sites near their watercourses. Brand did not examine upland areas. A similar impression comes from Sayles's reconnaissance (1936), and he examined areas outside of the lowland drainage channels. His descriptions of Medio Period sites are as brief as Brand's, and room block mound size information is lacking. Sayles notes, however, that almost none of the sites he visited seem to have had more than one story (Sayles 1936, 30). Like Brand, he described a pattern of large sites surrounded by more numerous small ones. All of this early reconnaissance thus showed a Medio Period settlement system headed by the very large center of Paquimé and consisting elsewhere of a few large communities and many small ones. The sparse room block mound size data suggested that the largest sites were not very large and that all of them were much smaller than Paquimé. They clearly were drawn strongly to the region's drainages, and their presence seemed to be in direct proportion to the available water and arable land.

The Joint Casas Grandes Expedition

Little more work was done in the Casas Grandes area for decades, until the beginning of large-scale excavation work at Paquimé in 1958 by Charles C. Di Peso and his colleagues of the JCGE. The focus of most activity was the center itself, but the report published in 1974 notes a survey of the Casas Grandes valley, plus reconnaissance trips elsewhere in the region. Mention also was made of a regional survey done in the summer of 1959. "These data," Di Peso wrote, "were added to the previous excellent work of Sayles and Brand" (Di Peso 1974:1, 38). This combination presumably produced the regional map published as an appended figure to a later Casas Grandes volume (Di Peso, Rinaldo, and Fenner 1974:5, Figure 284–5). This map is partially reproduced here as Figure 5.1. It shows more than 1,000 "Casas Grandes" sites that we assign to the Medio Period. The combined surveys of Brand and Sayles recorded some 200 sites in the same region, so that most of the localities (over 800 of them) must have come from the 1959 survey. Unfortunately, no records of any of these sites are known, and they exist only as dots on the Di Peso map.

Despite a lack of any site data beyond location, the Di Peso map echoes the findings of earlier work by showing river and drainage valleys full of sites. After evaluation of these data, Lekson, Bletzer, and MacWilliams (2004) argue that the site densities shown on the Di Peso map probably are accurate. We agree with this conclusion; the region's drainages contain many room block mound sites with Medio Period ceramics on their surfaces. The Di Peso map also shows many small sites and very few larger ones, again reflecting the findings of earlier work.

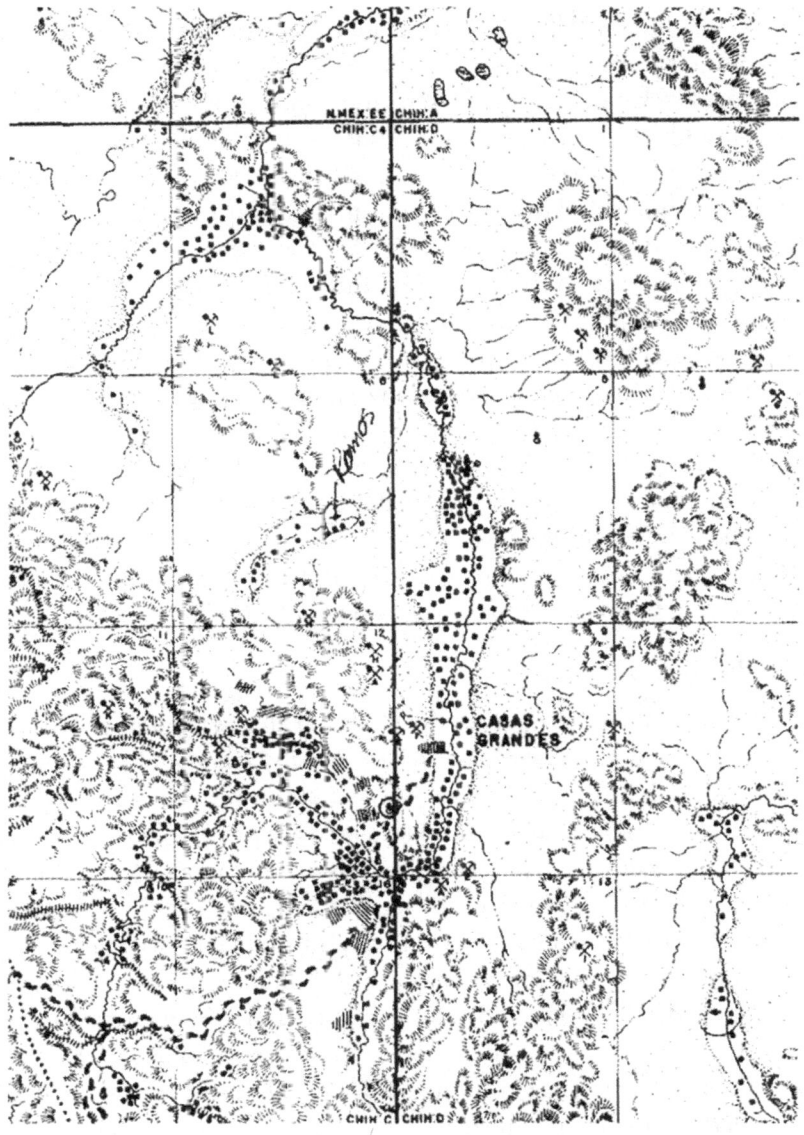

Figure 5.1. A portion of the Di Peso map. The small squares are sites with estimated populations of 100–500, and the squares bisected by horizontal lines are sites with estimated populations of 500–1,000 (Courtesy of the Amerind Foundation).

More questionable are the population estimates also present on the Di Peso map. Aside from Paquimé itself, the map shows two categories of room block mound sites: those with assumed populations of 100–500 people and a few with 500–1,000 residents. Lekson, Bletzer, and Mac-Williams (2004, 60) correctly term Di Peso's estimates "arbitrary," and there is no published discussion to justify the map's figures. Almost all of the more than 1,000 sites on the Di Peso map belong to the smaller of these two population size categories. This is more than 1,000 sites with 100 to 500 people each. The Di Peso map thus argues for a population of 100,000 to 500,000 people within about 60 km of Paquimé, assuming that all Medio Period occupations were contemporary. This is an incredible population density for anywhere in the arid U.S. Southwest and northern Mexico, but it is consistent with Di Peso's maximizing interpretation of everything about Paquimé. He argued, for example, that the center itself could have had as many as 5,000 residents (Di Peso, Rinaldo, and Fenner 1974:4, 207). Clearly, he saw an enormous center surrounded by an equally large regional population.

The 1994–1995 Survey

For more than two decades, the Di Peso map was the only published presentation of settlement pattern, site density, and population size in northwest Chihuahua. Comparative data ultimately were provided by an intensive regional survey in 1994–1995 (Whalen and Minnis 2001). This work recorded more than 300 Medio Period room block mound sites at a range of distances to the north and west of Paquimé. A number of these sites are identifiable on the Di Peso map, so the first point of comparison is site density in particular drainages. Figure 5.2 presents these data. The 1994–1995 survey units cannot be presumed to be exactly congruent with earlier ones. Even so, Figure 5.1 shows that site counts in major drainages do not differ greatly between the Di Peso map and the 1994–1995 survey.

The estimated size of these sites is another matter. The 1994–1995 survey recorded room block mound area as a measure of site size. Brand (1933) did the same to a limited extent, as noted in preceding pages. The 1994–1995 survey sites were divided into small, medium, large, and very large categories based on room block mound area (Whalen and Minnis 2001, 108–110). Small sites overwhelmingly dominated the

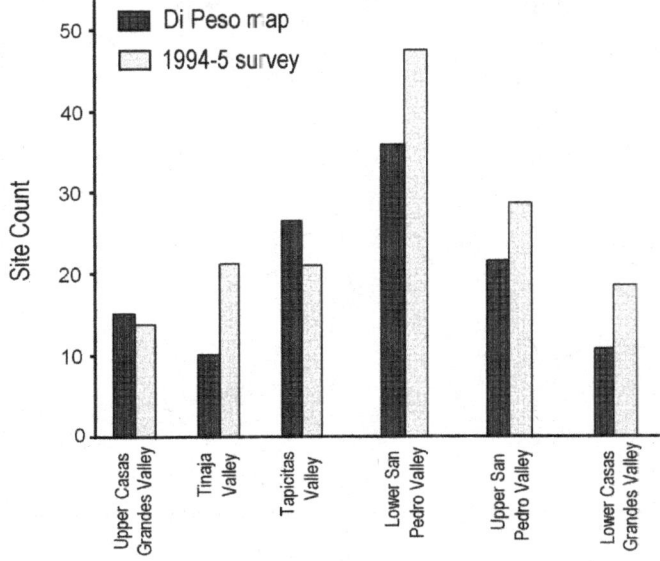

Figure 5.2. Comparison of site counts between the Di Peso map and the 1994–1995 survey (Michael Whalen).

settlement array in every part of the survey area, and the median size of all room block mounds was less than 500 m². To estimate the number of rooms that such sites are likely to contain, we simulated room block mound size by drawing boundaries around sets of rooms in excavated areas at sites 204 and 317 (excavation data from Whalen and Minnis 2009b). Drawings of each cluster of rooms were enclosed on paper by a round or oval outline of a room block mound. This outline centered on the room cluster and allowed about 15% of the room cluster's largest dimension for perimeter areas that contain no rooms. That is, the room block outline extended 7.5% of the largest dimension on all sides of the room cluster. Each excavated area thus became a room block mound of 300–600 m². The two sites used here are, respectively, large and small neighbors of Paquimé. We know that these outlying sites have much smaller rooms than the primate center, the rooms of which are not used in this calculation.

Figure 5.3 is a regression of simulated room block mound area on excavated room count. The latter is the dependent variable to be

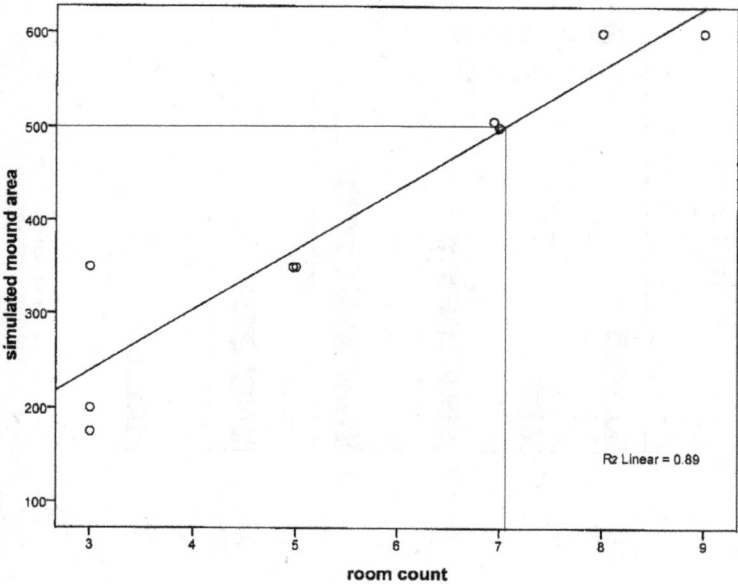

Figure 5.3. Prediction of room count from simulated mound area (Michael Whalen).

predicted from the former. The high value of the correlation coefficient (R^2 = 0.890) shows that estimated room block mound size is a good predictor of room count in this small sample. Estimated room count can either be read directly from the least-squares line, or it can be calculated using the values of constants provided by the regression analysis. In either case, these data show that a room block mound of 500 m^2 should have about 7 rooms, while one of 600 m^2 should contain on the order of 9. These estimates obviously are not very precise because of the small number of data points. Even if the estimated room count is doubled, however, we still have a situation in which half of all Medio Period room block mounds recorded by the 1994–1995 survey have fewer than 20 rooms.

There is no precise way to translate pueblo room count into a population estimate. The problems are well known, including abandoned rooms, changes in room function, cultural ideas of proper space allocation, and variable family sizes. A literature search shows that the number of people estimated per room by archaeologists varies from 0.5 to

2.0. If we take the highest of these figures, or an average of two residents per room, and multiply it by double our estimated room counts, we still have fewer than 30 people at half of the Medio Period sites recorded by the intensive survey. These are many of the same sites to which the Di Peso map assigned populations of 100 to 500 residents. We thus estimate a regional population only one-third to one-sixth of Di Peso's.

We cannot use the regression shown in Figure 5.3 for larger sites, as the analysis is only valid within the specified range of simulated room block mound areas (i.e., up to 600 m^2). To further complicate the matter, average room size also is larger on larger sites and smaller on smaller ones. We can, however, calculate the percentage of room block mound area excavated in the main mound at the large Site 204 and extrapolate the number of rooms dug to the whole room block mound. The area covered by the main mound at Site 204 is about 9,250 m^2. We dug about 800 m^2, or about 8.6% of the mound (Whalen and Minnis 2009a). The excavated areas that sum to 800 m^2 come from all parts of the main mound, and together they contain 31 rooms of a variety of shapes and sizes. If 800 m^2 contained 31 rooms, then 100% of the mound should contain about 360 rooms. We reduce this total by 15% to compensate for outward "smearing" of the room block perimeter, arriving at a total of about 290 rooms.

Applying the variable estimates of 0.5 to 2.0 people per room gives a population estimate at the site's peak of ca. 150–580 residents. Despite this range, we can say that the population of Site 204 seems to have been on the order of a few hundred people. We emphasize that Site 204 is one of the region's largest according to the 1994–1995 survey. It will be recalled that the Di Peso map's *smallest* sites were estimated to have had 100 to 500 people, while we estimate about that population to have been present at one of the 1994–1995 survey's *largest* communities. Our conclusion, then, is that the Di Peso map vastly overestimates the Medio Period population of northwest Chihuahua in general and of the Casas Grandes region in particular. We do not attribute this difference to change in site sizes (e.g., by erosion) between the times of Di Peso's work and the 1994–1995 survey some 35 years later. In the few cases where the 1994–1995 survey and Brand (1933) recorded what appears to be the same site, size estimates are comparable. This reconnaissance was done 61 years before the 1994–1995 survey. We recently have argued

(Whalen, MacWilliams, and Pitezel 2010) that the center of Paquimé itself was much smaller than Di Peso estimated, with a population on the order of 2,000 instead of the original estimate of up to 5,000 (Di Peso, Rinaldo, and Fenner 1974:4, 207). We now extend the same argument to the population of the center's hinterland.

More precise data came from an intensive survey of selected portions of the Casas Grandes region that was done in 1994–1995 (Whalen and Minnis 2001). The intensive survey areas were grouped into three large units, termed the Inner, Middle, and Outer Zones. The Inner Zone is around Casas Grandes, while the Outer Zone lies near the U.S.-Mexico border. This terminology has changed slightly over the years. The Inner Zone is now referred to as the Core Zone. The Core is the area within about 30 km of the primate center, while the Middle Zone lies between 60 and 80 km from Casas Grandes. Intensive survey in the Core and Middle Zones covered, respectively, 124 km^2 and 145 km^2. Intensive survey was not conducted in the Outer Zone. Core and Middle Zone coverage yielded, respectively, 141 and 168 Medio Period sites. In both zones, these occupations were found to cluster in areas with water and arable land. They fill the valleys of primary and secondary drainages, and many lie on the piedmont of the Sierra Madre. This is in agreement with the earlier reconnaissance discussed in preceding pages.

The basic residential units of the Medio Period are blocks of contiguous, adobe-walled rooms. These decompose into low adobe mounds. Most Medio Period settlements all over the study area had 1–3 room blocks; a few had 4–5 blocks; and there were a few settlements with 6 or more blocks. Since almost none of the recorded room block mounds appeared to have had more than one story, area was adopted as a simple measure of room block size. Settlement size was measured by the sum of the areas of component room blocks, and these values were divided into four size classes. Small settlements had up to 2,000 m^2 of room block mound area; medium ones had more than 2,000 but less than 6,400 m^2; large ones had 6,400–9,999 m^2; and very large settlements showed more than 10,000 m^2 of room block mound area. Room block mounds covered between 10,000 and 15,000 m^2 on the few observed examples of very large settlements. We note that Casas Grandes itself is completely off of this settlement size scale. It has some 40,000 m^2 of room block mound area in multiple stories, making it by far the largest settlement of the region. Settlement systems like this, where the largest site is many times the size of the next-largest one, are described by geographers as "primate" (e.g., Hagget, Cliff, and Frey 1977; Smith 1976).

The mere existence of a primate structure is meaningful to questions about the general level of organization of the Casas Grandes system's core. Primate centers characteristically are the foci of their areas' economic, ritual, and political structures. They are the residences of most of the elite of their societies, so that a large proportion of the decision makers and managers are concentrated in one spot. Primate centers are also the points of convergence and control of regional economies, and they dominate long-distance trade. To support the expenses of these activities, the areas immediately around primate centers often show substantial investment in facilities for the intensification of production. Finally, primate centers usually serve as paramount ritual loci, containing the most, largest, or most elaborate ritual architecture in their regions. Nevertheless, the centralization of regional control in primate systems is highly variable. Of what kind was the Casas Grandes polity? For an answer, we must examine the settlement system around Casas Grandes, proceeding from the core outward and employing such regional system descriptors as the extent of specialization and differentiation among settlement system components, as well as the kind and extent of regional control and integration strategies that were used.

The settlements of the Core and Middle Zones showed a grading from small to large or very large. Most recorded settlements were small ones, however, and settlement frequency in both zones diminishes rapidly with movement up the size scale. Both zones also contain about the same frequencies of settlements of each size category. There are, however, important differences between the two zones. Every Core Zone survey unit, for instance, contained settlements ranging in size from small to large or very large. Larger Medio settlements thus were accessible to their smaller neighbors all over the Core. The Middle Zone, in contrast, does not show this pattern. All of its largest settlements cluster on the easternmost edge of the survey areas and away from most of the area's small and medium-sized settlements. Average distance to a higher-order community in the Middle Zone was 15 km, or about 6 times the Core Zone average of 2.5 km, and many Middle Zone small and medium settlements lay 25–35 km from the nearest large settlement.

If we assume that the largest settlements discharge more functions, including administrative ones, than do their smaller neighbors, then we can conclude that there may have been a higher level of community organization in the Core Zone.

The range of features visible on the surfaces of Core and Middle Zone sites also is quite different. These features include large and small ovens, agricultural terraces, ball courts, and the stone doors of birdcages where macaws and other parrots (Minnis et al. 1993) were kept. Some of these facilities, namely ball courts, birdcages, and large ovens likely were used in such social-integrative activities as public feasting and other ritual activities. The center of Casas Grandes showed a level of elaboration of these integrative facilities that was far above any other Medio settlement, but the Core and Middle Zone settlements also differed notably. Utilitarian facilities such as small ovens were found in the Middle Zone, but ball courts, birdcages, extensive upland agricultural terrace systems, and large ovens were all rare or absent. All of these facilities, in contrast, were present at a number of Core Zone settlements.

However, these facilities were not uniformly distributed within the Core. The only ones recorded in the Core Zone are associated with the very unusual site of Cerro de Moctezuma, the only known hilltop settlement in the region. It has a very large oven and a series of agricultural terraces, and it may have been closely associated with the center of Casas Grandes. Apart from this site, no ovens, terraces, ball courts, or birdcages were recorded among Casas Grandes' near neighbors, or those within 10–15 km of the primate center. This is about the distance a person on foot can travel and return in one day, thus defining the limit for daily contact between communities (Wilcox 1996). It is now referred to as the Inner Core Zone. Casas Grandes thus appears to have absorbed from its nearest neighbors many of the social, political, and ritual functions that were linked to ball courts and the production of exotica. Beyond the limit of daily interaction, that is between 15 and 30 km from the primate center, in what we now call the Outer Core Zone, ball courts, bird cages, and large ovens are found at a range of small to very large Medio settlements. This is an area where an organizational structure involving the ball game ritual and exotic goods is clearly present, but without the pattern of monopoly seen in the immediate vicinity of Casas Grandes. These data make it evident that there are identifiable activities that are present on and around some Inner Zone core settlements, while they are absent at others. Even so, all of this adds up to no more than a moderate amount of functional differentiation among the core's settlements.

Another important observation is that two local settlement clusters exist in the Outer Core Zone. Each cluster contains the full range of Medio settlement sizes, from small through very large. The large and very large settlements of these clusters were located in their centers, and small and medium-sized settlements were scattered around them. Each cluster contains all of the features and facilities that have been identified in preceding pages as likely to have been organizational or integrative. There are ball courts and macaw cage door stones. On and around a number of settlements in each cluster are the vast ovens, which have been argued to be large-scale food processing facilities possibly associated with public feasting. Each cluster lies about 20 km from the primate center of Casas Grandes, and the two clusters are separated from each other by about the same distance. No such clusters were found in the Middle Zone.

We also might ask how the Core Zone was organized and integrated within its primate structure. Commonly recognized dimensions of control and integration in mid-level societies are economics, politics, ritual, and militarism, although we see little evidence for much of the latter in the Casas Grandes region. It was noted earlier that wealth, authority, and many of society's elite people would have been concentrated in the primate center of Casas Grandes. These elite are expected to have exerted a substantial degree of control over the regional economy and over long-distance trade. The presence of public architecture in a community is a widely recognized indication that local leaders were able to recruit labor and gather resources for communal activities. The fact that Paquimé has the greatest diversity and amount of public architecture of any pre-Hispanic community known from northern Mexico and the U.S. Southwest is a testimonial that a significant degree of centralization of authority and control over local productivity was to be found there. Other economic, political, and ritual structures by which the primate center supported itself and maintained authority over its neighbors have been discussed elsewhere (Whalen and Minnis 2001: 182–90; see also Douglas and MacWilliams, this volume).

Despite the settlement pattern differences discussed earlier, the Middle Zone strongly resembles the Core Zone in its ceramic assemblage and in the architectural elements observable in the many looted areas. The two zones likely were components of the same settlement system, although their attributes suggest that their roles were not the same. It seems that the Core Zone lies at the system's center, while the Middle Zone includes a part of its periphery. Furthermore, it has been argued (Whalen and Minnis 2001) that this core-periphery structure was of an elementary sort, where the core is small and where linkages with its periphery are relatively few.

Discussion elsewhere (Whalen and Minnis 2001) postulated a set of economic, political, and ideological structures upon which the organization and integration of the Casas Grandes core was based. In further pursuit of the question of regional system organization, we must now inquire into how far these structures extended out of the small Casas Grandes core and into its peripheries. This is a critical issue, as a major factor in evaluating different levels of regional system structure is the extent to which a core controls its periphery. The original interpretation of regional structure envisioned a high degree of control by Casas Grandes over a large periphery (Di Peso 1974:2, 314–15).

Preceding pages reviewed settlement pattern data to argue that the Middle Zone periphery was organized and integrated at a lower level than was the Core Zone. A settlement size hierarchy is present in the Middle Zone segment of the periphery, but it has been shown that the largest settlements of this zone were clustered in a short segment of the lower Casas Grandes River valley. Many of the small settlements of the periphery thus lay far from a higher-order settlement. This situation implies a generally lower level of settlement system structure and organization in the Middle Zone periphery than in the Core Zone.

A further indication of the disorganization of the Middle Zone periphery is the near-complete absence there of almost all of the integrative features and productive intensification facilities found in the Inner Zone core, from ball courts to birdcages to agricultural terrace systems. For instance, only one small, simple ball court was found among the 140 Medio settlements of the Middle Zone, and no macaw cage door stones were found in any of these communities. These data indicate that two of what seem to have been important organizational and integrative activities in the Core Zone were rare in the Middle Zone periphery.

Finally, the Middle Zone also lacks features and facilities for agricultural intensification and large-scale food production. These were common in the core, but intensive surveys in the Middle Zone periphery recorded few of the terraces and large ovens that were so conspicuous in the Inner Zone's core. This evident lack of productive intensification in the Middle Zone periphery is in keeping with literature on settlement system primacy, which reports that organization and productive intensification are characteristically seen near the primate center, while outlying areas display increasing self-sufficiency and production that is extensive as opposed to intensive. A measure of the primate center's level of greatest power, therefore, might be the distance from the center that its productive intensification is in evidence. In the Casas Grandes case, this distance appears to have been on the order of a modest 30 km.

There may have been an economic relationship between the primate center and its Middle Zone periphery. Literature on primacy and on core-periphery relations (for example, Paynter 1982; Santley and Alexander 1992) describe the movement of peripheral resources, especially food, into a primate center or a core zone in exchange for finished, exotic, or nonlocal things. Peripheral people require these things for social reproduction, of which they cannot secure a satisfactory supply by themselves, and which are concentrated at the primate center. This kind of economic interaction is likely to be visible in the archaeological record only as a distribution of finished or prestige goods in peripheral areas, as edibles have neither durability nor high visibility.

Nevertheless, our settlement pattern data provide one observation that hints at this kind of economic activity in the Casas Grandes periphery. Preceding discussion noted the concentration of large Medio settlements in a short stretch of the Middle Zone's lower Casas Grandes River valley. This pattern is consistent with a kind of settlement structure that has been identified in the peripheries of some primate systems (Paynter 1982, 141–42). Present in this case is a set of large, surplus-concentrating settlements (termed *entrepôts* in the literature) that are found in major ecological or transport corridors of peripheral zones, and that are linked to the primate center. These entrepôts are positioned for the convenience of the surplus-concentrating elites, not for that of the surplus-producing people. They are not found in the hinterlands among the smaller communities, which tend to be relatively poorly articulated, both to each other and to the larger regional system. This model provides a good description of the settlement pattern in the Middle Zone, and it tentatively has been interpreted to point toward the draining off of some of the periphery's produce by the Core Zone.

The Middle Zone could be considered a near periphery of the Casas Grandes core, as it has a settlement structure that not only suggests subordination but that also differs noticeably from its northern and southern neighbors. In this near periphery, some 60–75 km from the core zone, we may be seeing the farthest extent of a political economy centered on Casas Grandes. The data from more distant peripheries indicate return to settlement systems of intermingled large and small communities. This appears to be true of the Carretas Basin and Hidalgo County, New Mexico, to the northwest, of portions of the Sierra Madre to the west, the Santa María drainage to the southeast, and parts of southern Chihuahua. These more distant peripheries use Casas Grandes–style ceramics, including Ramos Polychrome, with its macaw and macaw-man motifs. We are also aware that ball courts exist in adjacent parts of the Sierra Madre and in the Carretas and Animas areas of northwest Chihuahua and southwestern New Mexico. No courts yet have been reported from the largely unstudied Santa María valley to the southeast, but their discovery there would not be surprising.

These data all indicate that the Casas Grandes regional system's periphery was far from a homogeneously organized entity. Instead, we see multiple levels and different kinds of interaction with the primate center and its small core. There is an inner core of settlements within the radius of daily interaction, or about 15 km, which appear to have been directly dominated by the primate center. An outer core of settlements within 15–30 km were closely tied to the primate center, but they show somewhat more autonomy than the settlements of the inner core. Near peripheries like the Middle Zone may be the outermost limits of a political economy focused on the primate center. More distant areas, including the middle Santa María valley to the southeast, the Animas area to the northwest, adjacent parts of the Sierra Madre to the west, and parts of southern Chihuahua contain extensive settlement hierarchies, plus Casas Grandes–style ceramic assemblages and architecture.

A few ball courts are known from the lower Animas, the parts of the Sierra Madre nearest to Casas Grandes, and adjacent southern Chihuahua. These intermediate peripheries appear to have been less closely tied into the core's political economy.

Far peripheries such as Villa Ahumada to the east, Babícora to the south, and northern Sonora to the northwest contain ceramic assemblages that show significant local differences while still implying some contact with Casas Grandes. Finally, there are neighboring areas, where Casas Grandes–style ceramics appear as minor components of assemblages that are overwhelmingly dominated by local wares. Much of the southern part of the Southwestern United States falls into this last category, for example, the Jornada Mogollon area around and above El Paso, the Postclassic Mimbres area, and the Animas area.

The rough limits of the Casas Grandes interaction sphere, then, seem to reach from the Babícora and upper Santa María valley in the south to Villa Ahumada and perhaps El Paso in the east, to somewhere in the southern Mogollon's Mimbres and Jornada areas in the north, to the Sierra Madres and northeastern Sonora to the west. Depending on where and by what criteria one draws boundaries, this region includes some 70,000 to 100,000 km^2, most of which is in the northwest part of Chihuahua. This Casas Grandes interaction sphere is about the same size as the Chaco and Hohokam regional systems of the Southwestern United States (Crown and Judge 1991, 2–3). By terming this an interaction sphere, we are implying the existence of some sorts of social and economic relations among the area's populations.

The import of this entire discussion is that there is little indication of the far-flung dominance originally assumed by Di Peso, who saw the center as exercising "sovereignty" over the entire 88,000 km^2 interaction sphere (Di Peso 1974:2, 328). Di Peso evidently assumed a uniformly high level of regional integration. He saw Casas Grandes as so large and elaborate, in other words, that a comparably large and elaborate regional structure was assumed to have surrounded it. This interpretation followed a common trend in the adjacent Southwestern United States, where perception of the complexity of the Southwestern regional systems has been "unequivocally tied to the elaboration of their centers" (Fish and Fish 1999, 47). We note that a recent study indicated that Casas Grandes was only about half the size originally assumed by Di Peso (Whalen,

MacWilliams, and Pitezel 2010). The complementary argument of this chapter is that the interaction sphere surrounding Casas Grandes was a less extensively organized entity than originally proposed.

The Post-Paquimé Settlement System

As with the preceding Medio Period discussion, Di Peso's idea of the post-Paquimé situation in the Casas Grandes area was the dominant one for a generation. In this view, violence destroyed the primate center; the surviving population dispersed north and west (Di Peso 1974:3, 321; see also, Phillips and Gamboa, this volume). For unexplained reasons, the Casas Grandes area, one of the best-watered in the entire region, was abandoned. The idea of a catastrophic collapse has been questioned, and doubt continues (e.g., Casserino 2009; Ravesloot 1988). Di Peso's notion of extensive abandonment of the area arose because of the absence of sites with recognizable post-Paquimé ceramic assemblages, and the 1994–1995 regional survey (Whalen and Minnis 2001) showed the same situation; only Medio Period ceramics were to be seen on site surfaces.

This may be a misinterpretation on all of our parts, however. The following discussion is abstracted from (Whalen and Minnis 2012). It is argued that the original Medio Period ceramic tradition mostly consisted of plain brown, textured brown, red-slipped, and black wares as its utilitarian component. It was supplemented by vessels painted in coarse, black and red geometric designs that are referred to as Design Horizon A, and it characterized the early part of the Medio Period. Design Horizon A recently has been shown to have continued into and through late Medio times. The late Medio, after about AD 1300, is marked by the *addition* of a new ceramic tradition (Design Horizon B) to the existing Design Horizon A. Figure 5.4 schematically represents this situation. Design Horizon B was produced from the older Design Horizon A by addition of a set of complex anthropomorphic and zoomorphic images that likely carried a variety of ritual and social meanings. These were done with increasingly fine brush work, as well. It is noteworthy that Design Horizon B images like horned serpents, macaws, macaw-men, Tlálocs, and a variety of fantastic creatures are religious images in the societies of Mesoamerica, as well as among the Puebloan peoples of the U.S. Southwest. Accordingly, we can assert

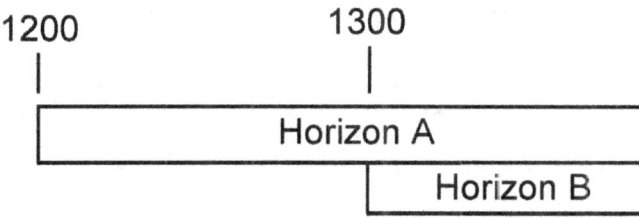

Figure 5.4. Supplementation of the old Design Horizon A tradition with the new Design Horizon B (Michael Whalen).

that at about AD 1300 (the opening of the late Medio Period), a new, complex set of religious and supernatural images was added to the older, simpler Chihuahuan Design Horizon A style of ceramic decoration, producing complex patterns like those seen on Classic Mimbres and Salado Polychrome vessels.

These elaborate Mimbres, Salado, and Casas Grandes ceramic designs most often are interpreted as religious in nature, representing to their informed beholders a spiritual world, a set of myths, and a perceived cosmological order. They communicate, in other words, what Rappaport (1999, 263) has termed a set of "ultimate sacred postulates." Religions, the same discussion asserts, have discursive aspects that are expressed in symbols. Moreover, these symbols establish and maintain the convictions and beliefs that are essential to all religions. Others have made similar points, terming such supernatural symbols "a visual language" (Townsend 2005, 62) that expresses "a corporate cognitive code" (Coon 2009, 61). This harks back to an earlier and highly influential interpretation of the Salado Polychrome ceramic designs as reflections of a shared ideology that was termed "the Southwestern Cult" (Crown 1994).

If this were so at Paquimé, then the frequencies of these information-bearing wares (especially Ramos Polychrome) should be highest during the center's growth and peak periods (Whalen and Minnis 2012). The following discussion is derived from the source just cited. Because these vessels were much more expensive than most in terms of labor involved in their production, they might be expected to have diminished with the center's decline due to their increasing irrelevance and high cost. It has been argued that the utilitarian part of the Medio ceramic assemblage—the plain, textured, red-slipped, and black wares that compose

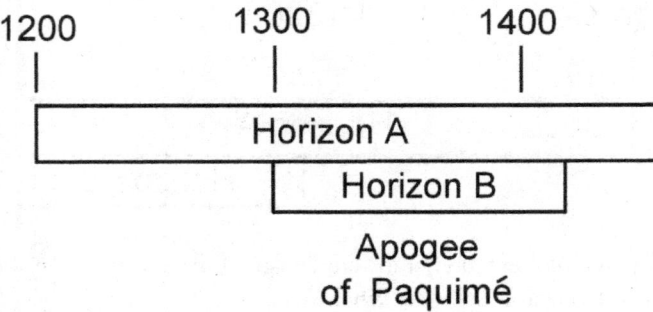

Figure 5.5. The postulated persistence of Design Horizon A after the decline of Paquimé (Michael Whalen).

80% or more of every site's ceramics—continued unchanged in form from early through late Medio times. The elaborate Ramos Polychrome tradition thus is seen as a Paquimé-inspired addition to a long-lived and stable utilitarian ceramic tradition, as shown in Figure 5.4. If Horizon B were to be removed from Figure 5.4 after the collapse of Paquimé in the early-to-mid 1400s, only the old, stable, largely utilitarian Design Horizon A would remain (Figure 5.5). As a result, surveyors would class as Medio Period those sites without polychromes but with the distinctive utilitarian wares on their surfaces.

Since we and all others always have understood the term "Medio Period" to mean "the time of Paquimé," then the region appears to have been uninhabited after the center's dissolution. It may be, however, that the long-believed fifteenth-century regional abandonment did not occur. Instead, the episode of population aggregation at the primate center could have been followed by dispersal of its inhabitants into small residential settlements located in the same prime agricultural zones as their predecessors, where they continued to use the utilitarian part of their old ceramic assemblage. Surveyors would classify these utilitarian wares as Medio Period, leading to the conclusion that there is nothing in the regional archaeological record after the Medio. There may also have been significant reduction of population. Situations of rapid population decline, dispersal, and even abandonment have been outlined in several parts of the Southwest, from the Mesa Verde area in the north (Varien 2010) and the Mimbres area in the south (Nelson

1999). A scenario of rapid population decline and dispersal is plausible for the Casas Grandes area, as we have no convincing evidence to show why one of the best-watered parts of the arid U.S. Southwest and northern Mexico should have been abandoned by farmers.

Earlier, we argued that the Medio Period settlement system was fairly well represented by the Di Peso map, while the population estimates associated with these sites were very much inflated. In contrast, we contend that the post-Paquimé settlement system has never been accurately described because it could not be recognized. It most likely consisted of small, scattered communities. We suggest this because the 1994–1995 survey recorded in every survey area a number of small sites with ceramic assemblages that contained the diagnostic Medio Period utilitarian wares, but elaborate polychrome ceramics were rare or absent. These sites had single room block mounds ranging from 100 to 1,000 m^2 in room block area, although most of them were 500 m^2 or less. They occur in the same river valley and piedmont locations as do larger residential sites, so that these small sites clearly are not restricted to poor, low-productivity segments of the environment. Some of them, for instance, lie within a few kilometers of Paquimé in the Rio Casas Grandes valley, the region's most productive agricultural setting. This would be the likely location of post-Paquimé occupations. In short, we raise the possibility that there is a post-Paquimé settlement system that has yet to be defined and investigated in the Casas Grandes area. Fragmentation and dispersal of the population of Paquimé in the mid- to-late 1400s may be the reason that every settlement pattern survey done in the region has found so large a proportion of small sites. This remains an untested hypothesis at present, and reading the palimpsest of Casas Grandes area settlement patterns continues to be a challenge to archaeologists.

Society and Polity in the Wider Casas Grandes Region

John E. Douglas and A. C. MacWilliams

Introduction

We take as our topic a single question: across the vast area marked by extensive use of Casas Grandes ceramics from the Viejo and Medio periods, how were communities organized socially and politically? Ultimately, we are interested in both "society," the organizing principles that established relationships between people within and between settlements across this large area, and "polity," the way these social relationships were expressed on the landscape to produce territorially defined units.

How this region was organized is among the most enduring questions facing archaeologists. Before the early 1930s, research was quite limited (see Minnis and Whalen, introduction, this volume), and to the extent scholars attempted to consider broader patterns, they drew rough comparisons with better-known regions of northwest Mexico and U.S. Southwest (NW/SW). It was Donald Brand's 1933 dissertation that reported an extensive survey across the entire Casas Grandes region and first provided a convincingly detailed understanding of the variability in Casas Grandes sites from watershed to watershed. Brand (1933, 64) knowingly spoke of the prevalence of *cimientos*, lines of stones left from adobe walls, in Sonoran Casas Grandes sites, the sheer density of sites in the Casas Grandes valley, and local perturbations in ceramic assemblages. Consistent with the thinking of his era, Brand (1933, 94) believed that all of Casas Grandes culture emanated outward from one "hearth area." Sayles (1936), who also surveyed vast areas of Chihuahua, likewise grasped the subregionalism of the Casas Grandes area. Although Sayles did not approach spatial variability with the same deliberateness as Brand, his ceramic analyses and descriptions, employing the framework developed at the Gila Pueblo, continue to provide the language to discuss regional ceramic variability.

A generation later, Charles Di Peso focused on the complexities of Paquimé. He did not delve systematically into the topic of regional variability in spite of his interest in regional interaction and its consequences—for example, the diverse rocks and minerals at Paquimé drawn from surrounding areas. He (Di Peso 1974:2, 335) was clearly aware of "districts" within the region, but understanding that variability was secondary to studying Paquimé, several highly informative excavations at outlying sites notwithstanding. Di Peso (1974:2, 328*ff*) generalized that the region was comprised of Paquimé and several thousand satellite villages. His belief that Medio Period events were triggered by an external source—*pochteca* who acted as professional traders, warriors, leaders, and/or social engineers from Mesoamerica—placed Paquimé as the indisputable locus of all innovation and the center of the most significant social interactions. Di Peso (1974:2, 331) explicitly rejected the idea of "endemic processual growth." This view led to Di Peso's dichotomized interpretation of the region, which can be highlighted with a few key oppositions:

Paquimé = Foundational, sophisticated, and affluent
The rest = Emulators, simple, and marginal

The idea that the Medio Period was sparked by interest-laden immigrants persists, although the proposed mechanisms of migration are altered considerably (Lekson 1999; Mathiowetz 2011; Schaafsma and Riley 1999, 248). Tellingly, these scholars, similar to Di Peso's approach, have focused on Paquimé without substantially considering the implications of regional variability.

In the half-century since Di Peso's herculean effort to comprehend the most complex site in the NW/SW, there have been several long-term projects within the Casas Grandes area. These projects have subregional foci, though each brings insights about the region as a whole. These projects inherently lean toward understanding the region in terms of endemic growth and change. They do not deny the unique qualities of Paquimé or its prominence; its size, architectural grandeur, amount of ritual space, and the seemingly endless collections of prestige goods greatly exceed its neighbors, near or far. But Paquimé did not develop in a vacuum, and its population was always dwarfed by the region as a whole. Not only did Paquimé develop within the region, but if Obregón's (see Di Peso, Rinaldo, and Fenner 1974:4, 114; Hammond and Rey 1928) account of warfare with people from west of the mountains forcing abandonment of Paquimé is accurate, then the immediate cause of dissolution of Paquimé must also be seen at this middle level of interaction.

The accumulation of information from subregions renders it possible to revisit the Casas Grandes region as a heterogeneous whole, an approach largely overlooked since the grand surveys of Brand (1933) and Sayles (1936). What follows is our effort to demonstrate that this approach can provide real insights into the region. These insights, naturally, are not complete. The local level is required for understanding any community, that is, the human landscape where most of the construction labor, craft activities, food, and core political alliances are drawn, as Whalen and Minnis (2000, 2001, 2009a) have demonstrated for Paquimé. Understanding Paquimé and the rest of the Casas Grandes region also requires the distant level. For both Mesoamerica and the NW/SW after ca. AD 1100, many large-scale processes played a role, including climate change, population dislocations, increased variability in settlement size and social organization, new political and religious systems, and expanding trade routes that generated novel, far-flung linkages—as Di Peso, and far more scholars than can be reasonably listed here, have argued.

The Casas Grandes region—defined by the ceramic and architectural characteristics employed in the farming villages and towns across the area—is undoubtedly large and varied, even though setting its outer boundaries and overall size is controversial (Di Peso 1974: 2, 328; Minnis 1989a; Schaafsma and Riley 1999). Figure 6.1, a conservative estimate, indicates that the Casas Grandes area slightly exceeds 75,000 km^2. Ecologically, this landscape ranges from Chihuahuan desert, to fertile riverine green belts, to grasslands, and into montane pine forests. Temporally, the late Viejo and Medio periods, spanning from roughly AD 1000 to 1500, are the focus of this chapter. As a simple, perhaps even simplistic, heuristic, this data review is organized by subregions beginning with the one defined by Paquimé and its proximate, closely linked neighbors, which we label as the "core." This subregion is surrounded by four additional subregions of varying sizes, labeled by the cardinal

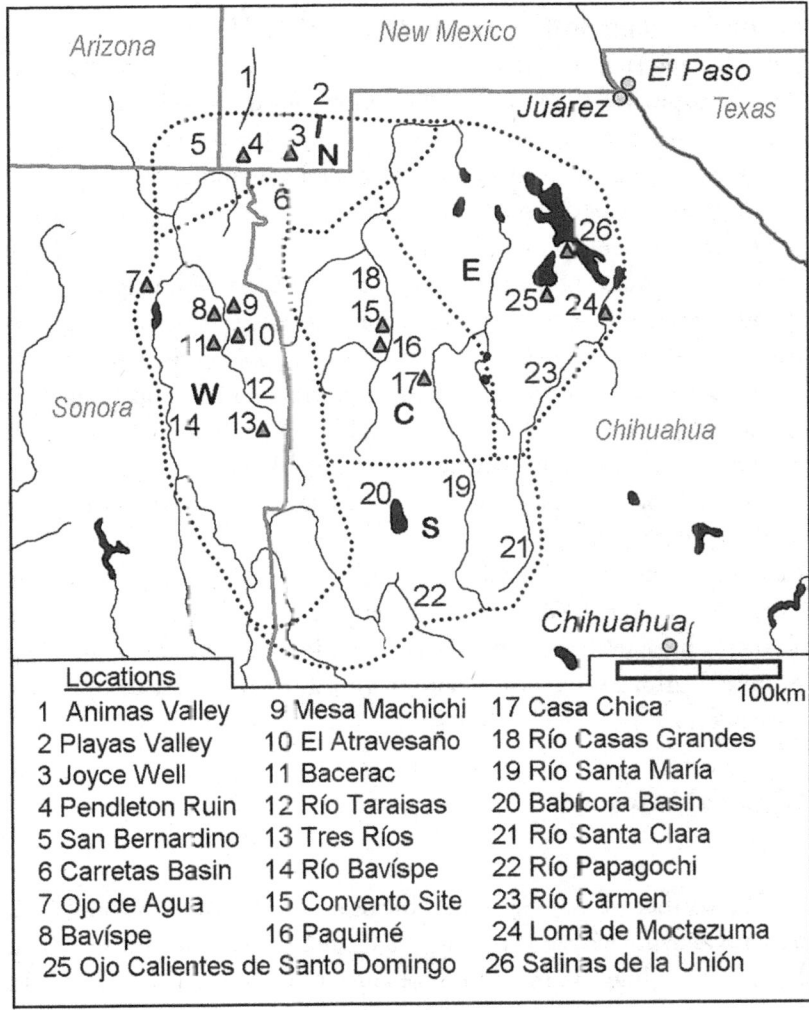

Figure 6.1. Map of the wider Casas Grandes region (A. C. MacWilliams).

directions, as shown in Figure 6.1. The Paquimé core approximates the "inner and intermediate zones" as defined and mapped by Whalen and Minnis (2001, 2009a). Note that the label "core" as employed here is not intended to indicate hegemonic control on the regional level or temporal precedence in all cultural practices. However, the core subregion likely includes the neighboring communities and hinterlands that Paquimé relied on for subsistence, labor, and other primary resources, presumably controlled by Paquimé's elite (Whalen and Minnis 2001, 2009a). This suggests that not only is the core subregion the most densely populated single area in the region, but it is also likely the location of the largest Medio Period polity within the region.

In examining the four provisionally defined subregions outside of this best-understood "core," we consider the archaeological evidence of society and polity in four overlapping areas: 1) the movement of goods that would indicate economic and/or prestige linkages; 2) settlement patterns, including evidence for social scale, social organization, and features linked to competition and possibly warfare, notably unoccupied zones between settlement clusters and hilltop refuges; 3) ritual and public architecture that might indicate regional systems of public activity, taken as evidence of ritual and belief that might indicate shared social frameworks and/or elite leadership and control; and 4) the general pattern of shared and unshared stylistic characteristics that might indicate social boundaries and organizational principles. There are not yet the data to quantitatively or systematically compare all these characteristics across the region. However, the accelerated rate of investigations since 1990 makes it possible to begin a comparative framework.

Regional Evidence

South

The southern Casas Grandes subregion includes the Babícora Basin, upper Rio Santa María, Rio Santa Clara, and the Rio Papagochi. Much of this area is high Basin and Range country with extensive grasslands. Precipitation in Chihuahua increases to the south and west, making this southern area better-watered and therefore the least likely to require elaborate water management strategies to support agriculture as compared with the rest of the Casas Grandes region.

Practically nothing can be said about the Archaic Period in this subregion, although sites from this interval are known. It is with the Viejo Period, which commenced sometime before AD 800, that the south can be meaningfully discussed, primarily thanks to the many years of work by Jane Kelley and colleagues. They have excavated several Viejo Period sites located approximately 160 km south-southeast of the Convento site (Kelley 2009; Kelley and Searcy, this volume). Within the scope of this chapter, the key points about the Viejo Period in the southern subregion are that it matches the timing of regional events and that there is a local distinctness within a broader scope of similarity to the rest of the region.

The southern Viejo Period is most readily likened to the Viejo Period in the Casas Grandes valley based on generally similar though not identical architecture, pottery, and chronology. This was a period of pithouse settlements at the scale of *rancherías* to small villages. There are considerably fewer than 100 recorded Viejo Period sites throughout the Casas Grandes region and none known that might indicate a large concentration of people. However, this situation does not necessarily mean that there were few people during the Viejo Period. Viejo Period site abundance remains an uncertainty, in part because these are not conspicuous sites. Kelley and colleagues have demonstrated that concerted efforts to locate Viejo Period sites can be effective. The southern subregion survey evidence indicates that Viejo Period sites are neither scarce nor as abundant as later Medio Period sites and tend to be grouped along well-established drainages. These southern Viejo people were agriculturalists with basically the same architecture, craft production, and imports as their counterparts elsewhere in the region.

This combination of apparent heterogeneous population density over a sizeable area and clear indications of shared cultural identity are intriguing points when considering how southern Viejo people organized and governed themselves. The basis for this shared development may partially reside in the dispersed population inferred to have existed—people would have had incentives to reach out to neighbors and develop cooperative relationships coincident with limited pressure to compete for resources. We do not know how residents of southern Viejo settlements were linguistically related to northern counterparts. Probably all were Uto-Aztecan speakers, though not necessarily speakers of the same or even mutually intelligible languages. There is no indication that a Viejo Period focal point, in the sense of Chaco Canyon or Medio Period Paquimé, had emerged anywhere in the Casas Grandes region. It is likely that people living in the southern Casas Grandes area during the Viejo Period were organized at a very local level without much institutional elaboration.

At the imprecise resolution of radiocarbon dating, the Medio Period, which lasted no more than three dynamic centuries, emerged from the Viejo Period at about the same time over the entire region, including the south. It was conspicuous Medio Period adobe pueblos that monopolized the attention of the first archaeologists in the southern subregion. Henry Carey (1931), who did fieldwork in the Babícora Basin during the 1920s, opined that the southern materials were "inferior" to those in the Casas Grandes valley. Today that stands as an ill-chosen term, but it does convey the reality that much of the conspicuous elaboration found in the Casas Grandes watershed was not matched in the south. There are some sizeable southern sites with multiple mounds left from adobe room blocks, but many of the more than 100 known southern Medio Period sites are small compared to those in the Casas Grandes watershed. The southern subregion, a sizeable area, likely included multiple polities. Pueblos in the Babícora Basin tend to occur in clusters while those along rivers are more dispersed (Kelley, Burd-Larkin, and Hendrickson 2004). We do not know if any larger southern Medio sites were regional centers. There are few hints to the affirmative and site scale may simply reflect the availability and productivity of nearby arable land. However, one ball court is known from the south (Kelley, Garvin, and Cunningham 2012; Kelley et al. 2012). Merely a few small check dams are known (Kelley et al. 1999), in stark contrast with the large roasting pits, dozen or more ball courts, and sprawling water management systems in the Casas Grandes watershed (Minnis, Whalen, and Howell 2006; Whalen and Minnis 2001). The complete repertoire of Medio Period pottery is not seen in the south. The pervasive iconography with ideological underpinnings conspicuous northwards in pottery, petroglyphs, carved stones, and other media is decidedly less common in southern Medio Period sites. Imported goods, such as marine shell, copper objects, and pottery from outside the Casas Grandes region likewise are rarities in the south during the Medio Period (Kelley et al. 1999).

Medio Period ascendency of the core subregion and specifically Paquimé is indisputable, but there is cause to believe that more distant areas, including the southern subregion, were full participants in the overall trajectory of Casas Grandes culture, though on local terms (Kelley et al. 1999). It is difficult to extract social organization and governance from archaeological remains, particularly for an under-researched area. However, the organization during the Medio Period for the south may plausibly be described as a segmented society that had a population never exceeding a few thousand people, communities integrated through kinship ties reinforced with at least several centuries of shared history, and rather weak, noninstitutional leadership. Of course coexisting in contiguous-room pueblos and an apparent upswing in population must have required some enhancement of leadership compared with the preceding Viejo Period. Yet, it is easy to believe that few people in the south fully escaped the responsibilities of farming through leadership roles or fulltime craft specialization. The Medio Period ideological transformation that swept the Casas Grandes region and which surely redefined leadership roles is not as conspicuous in the south. The near absence of water management features in the south and isotopic evidence from human skeletal remains (Webster 2001) provide evidence that southern Medio Period populations remained small-scale agriculturalists that were heavily reliant on maize.

West

Ceramically, the boundaries of the western subregion are delineated by relatively high frequencies of Carretas and Huérigos Polychrome. Geographically, it includes the Carretas Basin, just northwest of the core subregion; the high, but well-watered mountain valleys of the northern Sierra Madre Occidental on both sides of the continental divide; and the upper (and probably lower, as well) Bavíspe valley, the first drainage in a series of fairly narrow north-south trending valleys in eastern Sonora. The western edge of the Casas Grandes region in Sonora is distinct, delineated by an unmistakable boundary with the Sonoran culture of north-central Sonora (Amsden 1928; M. Pailes 2012; R. Pailes 1978).

Outside the Carretas Basin, this western zone consists of a fragmented agricultural landscape, with difficult transportation and arable land available in moderately sized "pockets." Fault-block-controlled mountain ranges and narrow gorges separate fertile, small basins and isolated communities. It makes generalizing about the landscape difficult. However, it is clear from the pre-Hispanic villages, the Spanish mission system, and the modern municipalities, that these are productive and well-watered farming areas, albeit somewhat isolated ones.

Looking cross-temporally, the Bavíspe Project, led by John E. Douglas and César Quijada, shed light on the occupational history of this subarea. The earliest ceramics in the subregion, dated minimally to the sixth century, appear to mirror early ceramic occupations from the Sonoran culture distinctly outside the Casas Grandes region (Douglas and Quijada 2004b). But by the late Viejo Period, the Bavíspe valley had been incorporated into the Casas Grandes sphere, ceramically and possibly architecturally (Douglas and Quijada 2005).

By the Medio Period, Carretas and Huerigós Polychrome become the signature ceramic styles in the western subregion, and occupations reach their greatest size and density. This best-known occupation is outlined below; it includes hundreds of sites, and indicates substantial communities and evidence of at least small polities. What follows after the Medio Period is problematic, but the presence of substantial Opata communities that were integrated into a mission system along the Río Bavíspe demonstrates a substantial post-Casas Grandes occupation (Radding 1997; Yetman and Shaul 2010). Di Peso's suggestions that settlements in the Tres Ríos area at the headwaters of the Bavíspe were Tardio Period, post-Paquimé refugia are now in doubt (Phillips and Carpenter 1999). Braniff (1986) also interpreted the site of Ojo de Agua, farther north along the Bavíspe, as a Tardio Period occupation, based on four radiocarbon dates. These assays collectively cover a broad time span and are inconclusive. The Bavíspe Project (Douglas, Quijada, and Martínez Ramírez 2003) has identified an alternative occupation pattern from this time period. The best example is El Atravesaño (CHIH C:9:9), near the town of Bacerac, where surface indicators suggest, at a minimum, dozens of rooms arranged around four plazas/clusters near the Bavíspe flood plain, and test excavations suggest a post-Casas Grandes occupation with a distinct red ware.

A more wide-ranging discussion on the settlement patterns, public architecture, and prestige goods for the Medio Period is possible. It appears certain that the Carretas Basin was the leading population center for this area. Not only did Brand (1943, 124) state in his regional summary that "altogether, in numbers and size, the ruins of the Carretas Basin are second only to those of the Casas Grandes valley proper," but a preliminary survey by Whalen and Minnis (2001, 193) confirmed that this occupation was sizable and aggregated. It exceeded the scale of settlements in the intermediate zone that they identify as part of the Casas Grandes polity. The "large number of piedmont and intramontane sites" noted by Brand (1943, 124) for the Carretas Basin suggests the largest settlements on the plains might well have incorporated smaller mountain communities focused on terraced fields within their polity, similar to what Whalen and Minnis (2001) have identified as a basic economic linkage within the Casas Grandes polity.

Farther west and south, the arable lands near the town of Bavíspe appear to have supported the largest and most complex Casas Grandes polity west of the continental divide. There, the Bavíspe flood plain is extensive, at a locality just 20 km from the Carretas Basin (straight line over the mountains). The flood plain in this area is dominated by two large sites in commanding positions on opposing sides of the river just 2.5 km apart: Bavíspe (CHIH C:9:4), and Mesa Machichi ([CHIH C:9:29] Douglas and Quijada 2004a). Recent excavations at the Bavíspe site (CHIH C:9:4) by Júpiter Martínez of the Instituto Nacional de Antropología e Historia, Centro Sonora, demonstrated a dense occupation, with adobe walls up to 40 cm thick at the base and multiple occupation layers (personal communication, 2013). In addition, both Bavíspe and Mesa Machichi have some rooms with stacked stone construction. These architectural details are important, because all other known sites along the Bavíspe appear to use the less monumental cimiento construction, which combined upright stone foundations with poles and relatively thin adobe plaster, a construction style widespread in Sonora and southeast Arizona.

In addition, Mesa Machichi has a bean-shaped, south-facing, rubble-filled masonry structure 10 m long and up to 60 cm wide, outlined by upended tabular stones rising about 60 cm above the ground surface. It is clearly public architecture, and although its function is indeterminate, the structure closely matches the end of a T-shaped ball court. It seems likely that this feature was a ball court with the side embankments that were unsubstantial, were destroyed, or that had been buried. On the west side of the river, the Bavíspe site has several small, conical cobble-covered mounds that might be public architecture. Farther south, near Bacerac, an extensive terraced field system was identified, similar to those found in the Casas Grandes inner zone, indicating, as the Carretas Basin does, that the western zone employed dispersed farming systems comparable in organization to the Casas Grandes polity.

Evidently the Carretas Basin was the largest, most complex system in the western subregion, with the area around the Bavíspe site (CHIH C:9:4) second. Higher in the mountains, smaller systems include a variety of open air and cliff dwellings with dozens of rooms; some of these occupations seem to go back to Viejo times (Bagwell 2004, 2006; Martínez 2009). The Joint Casas Grandes Expedition, as discussed above, recorded sites located at Tres Ríos, an arable highland valley. It likely exemplifies such smaller systems during the Medio Period (Di Peso, Rinaldo, and Fenner 1974:5, Figure 240–5).

Exchange items from outside the west subregion appear scarce. After examining tens of thousands of sherds from excavations and survey recording lines, the Bavíspe project found only ceramics from the Chihuahuan ceramic series at all examined Medio Period sites. For the Carretas Basin Brand (1943, 128) indicated a general lack of nonlocal wares but found that Carretas W, the largest site in the area at 2.7 ha, had a diversity of trade ceramics, comprised of "Chupadero, El Paso, Mimbres, Middle Gila, and Little Colorado trade wares." Whalen and Minnis (2001, 193) observed a distinctly low frequency of shell artifacts in the Carretas Basin as compared with outlying areas believed to be part of the Casas Grandes polity, although Lister (1939) did excavate an *Alectrion* shell necklace from a Medio Period site in the basin. Marine shell was infrequently found by the Bavíspe Valley Project as well, and intriguingly, the small excavated sample revealed that shell was more common in Viejo Period deposits than Medio Period deposits. Turquoise is also rare; the only systematic observation for the area comes from the Bavíspe Valley Project, which located six pieces on the surface of as many sites. Obsidian was common at the pre-Hispanic sites examined by the Bavíspe Valley Project, but sourcing indicates almost exclusively local exchange; no sampled obsidian was positively identified from outside the immediate area (Douglas and Quijada 2005).

The Medio Period Carretas/Huerigós ceramic zone exhibits intriguing parallels and differences with the Casas Grandes polity centered on Paquimé. On the one hand, the settlements seem to build on the same social organization/farming system/basic symbolism as the core subregion. In particular, the Carretas Basin likely repeats key characteristics of Paquimé and its surroundings, albeit on a smaller scale. These include a core of large sites, one settlement with the most trade goods and nearby highland communities that were likely critical for food production. On the other hand, the material reviewed here suggests that even the largest western subregion polities were less blatantly focused on power and ritual than the Casas Grandes core. These show fewer goods circulating, fewer ball courts, less public architecture, and none of the special symbolism, ritual, and activities that fascinate students of Paquimé. Further, this brief summary considers only the largest polities in the west zone. Bagwell's (2004, 2006) discussion of the Rio Taraises or Di Peso, Rinaldo, and Fenner's (1974: 5, 868–75) evidence from the Tres Ríos area suggest systems that are more akin, socially and politically, with the previous discussion of the southern subregion.

The western subregion was likely a series of separate polities, although trade and defensive alliances were likely. A lack of overarching coordination is implicit in the infrequent ball courts, public architecture, and evidence of feasting activities. Small polities linked by more far-flung alliance and warfare relationships fits the pattern found during the early historic period for agricultural villages in northeast Sonora.

North

Geographically, the northern zone consists of an arc from southeastern Arizona, through southwestern New Mexico and adjacent areas of Sonora and Chihuahua. This includes the Animas phase and the more northern Black Mountain phase. Some archaeologists have included the El Paso phase, found farther east, as part of "the Casas Grandes World" (Hegmon et al. 1999; Schaafsma and Riley 1999) because of what obviously was a sustained, significant interaction with the Casas Grandes region. The southern Jornada area, including the El Paso phase, is better understood as a distinct entity, although complex overlap with the Medio Period is indisputable. The Animas phase, centered on the San Bernardino valley in far southeast Arizona/northeast Sonora, and the Animas, San Luis, and Playas valleys of the New Mexico Bootheel, is generally emphasized as having the largest occupation and the most unambiguous Casas Grandes traits. The Black Mountain phase, in the southern Mimbres valley, is possibly distinguished from the Animas phase by some ceramic assemblage characteristics and burial practices. The Black Mountain phase can be interpreted as a modest revitalization after the collapse and population dispersion of the Classic Mimbres core area dating between AD 1150 and 1300 (Hegmon et al. 1999; Nelson and LeBlanc 1986; Ravesloot 1979).

The Animas phase area is examined here because of its relatively rich record, clear linkages to Medio Period characteristics, and dynamic nature. Before AD 1200, the area later defined by the Animas phase is considered within the rubric of Mimbres and/or the San Simon Mogollon branches. But even in this earlier period, there are important connections between this region and Chihuahua. Mimbres Black-on-white pottery circulates broadly in Chihuahua. There appears to be some geographical overlap in settlements, and there are other broad similarities between these contemporaneous, neighboring, and farming traditions. The piecemeal and partial adoption of Chihuahuan ceramics, trade items, and ceremonialism by the Animas phase populace after AD 1200 may build on these earlier networks, but they also represent a significant break with local traditions and perhaps a reversal in the relative power between the regions, as the population in the Casas Grandes region swelled during the Medio Period. The Animas phase can be broken into an earlier interval, about AD 1200–1300, and a post-1300 interval, indicated by the presence of Salado polychromes (Douglas 1996), similar to changes seen in the Medio Period in the core subregion. Casas Grandes influences arguably are most direct in the later interval, but are present throughout the phase.

Animas phase sites are located fairly regularly along most significant drainages with agricultural potential (Findlow and DeAtley 1974). Habitation sites consist of adobe rooms arranged around plazas, typically in the range of 30 to 80 rooms at each site. Although not subject to much study, the lower, largely Sonoran, portion of the San Bernardino valley—from the springs at the San Bernardino Ranch on the international border to where the river meets the Rio Bavíspe to the south—seems to provide examples of some of the largest and most clustered Animas phase settlements (Fish and Fish 1999), and may represent a larger and more complex pattern than the upper San Bernardino valley or the Bootheel of New Mexico.

There is no clear evidence of organization for the Animas phase area above the level of the local community. There has, however, been long-standing suspicion that piedmont settlements might be part of larger communities centered on lower elevation sites near substantial agricultural lands, suggesting the possibility of lower-level multisettlement communities (Douglas 1990; Findlow and DeAtley 1974). Another possible indicator of intercommunity organization is the presence of fairly dispersed ball courts, which possibly served multiple communities (Fish and Fish 1999). Whether they reflect integration of communities, bringing together groups for shared rituals, or competition between communities, played out in a ritual context on these courts, is unclear.

In broad terms, attributes and styles of architecture, locally produced artifacts, and exotic items—shell, nonlocal ceramics, turquoise and other minerals—indicate that the Animas phase represents an eclectic mix of local and distant influences. Not all of these influences are attributable to the Casas Grandes region. Attributes and items from outside the Casas Grandes region, attributes that are Casas Grandes region-derived but with historical roots indicating connections predating the Medio Period, artifacts and styles that are clearly derived from the Medio Period Casas Grandes region, along with uniquely local attributes and styles all can be identified as attributes in the "phase." Further, there are variations in these attributes in time and space.

This is not the place to sort through the architectural, burial, ceramic traditions, and exchange network details implicit in the previous paragraph, but consider this "tale of two villages": the Pendleton Ruin, on the western side of the New Mexico Bootheel, and the Joyce Well site, on the eastern side. The sites evidently overlapped in occupation: Pendleton probably was founded earlier, but continued into the late Animas phase, when Joyce Well was occupied. Joyce Well has a well-defined ball court, Casas Grandes-style architectural features such as raised hearths, and a ceramic assemblage featuring abundant Ramos Polychrome, the signature decorated ceramic of the Casas Grandes core subregion, apparently locally produced (Skibo, McCluney and Walker 2002). With this suite of characteristics and shorter occupation, the scenario of a settlement founded by a group from Chihuahua deserves serious consideration. The motivations of such a group are unclear; possibilities include agricultural expansion, a schism group fleeing hostile relations, or an outpost of a widespread social group involved in trade networks. Interestingly, Joyce Well appears unique;

no other known Animas phase site matches the Casas Grandes core subregion patterns so closely. At Pendleton, the site where the Animas phase was first defined (Kidder, Cosgrove, and Cosgrove 1949), a wider range of Chihuahuan polychromes is found. The excavators appear to have found an adobe platform mound built on a Classic Hohokam pattern (Douglas 2004). Thus, the Pendleton Ruin appeared to incorporate an entirely different form of public architecture that required far more labor to build compared with the efforts required for the Joyce Well ball court. The Casas Grandes region appears not to have been the only source of architectural models for integrating populations and/or marking emerging leadership in the Animas phase area. That Pendleton and Joyce Well shared many characteristics, yet seemingly had different trajectories and social connections, suggests a highly dynamic social setting for these communities.

It is useful to compare the Animas area with the previously discussed west and south subregions. Overall, when the north subregion, especially the Animas phase occupation, is compared against the occupations in the south and the west subregions, the north subregion settlements appear to be more cosmopolitan and outwardly focused. Shell, turquoise, and exotic ceramics are common when compared with the south and west zones, and are routinely found at the full range of settlement sizes. In some significant ways, the Animas phase appears closer to the core subregion than the west subregion, as most clearly demonstrated by the multiple connections at Joyce Well. And yet, the pre-AD 1200 connections in the north subregion are not as strong as found in the west or south subregions, nor does the Animas phase focus on Casas Grandes region attributes, symbolism, and exchange appear as exclusive as it does in the west or south.

One idea to explain these differences is that shorter-term settlement occupations tended to break apart local interactions in the Animas phase, and ideas, symbolism, and exchange from multiple directions were one result (Douglas 1995, 2007). This may have included migrant groups, possibly including ones from the south (Brand 1943; Carpenter 2002; Di Peso 1974, vols. 1–3; McCluney 1962). For leaders, evidently this dynamic setting made available a range of goods and ideas that were incorporated into exchange networks. This range of goods and ideas might then be consciously selected and chosen by individuals, especially leaders, looking to distinguish themselves and their communities. This scenario fits the kind of variability seen in the Animas area.

East

East of the Rio Casas Grandes and Rio Santa María, elevations drop and semi-desert grasslands cede to the "true Chihuahuan desert" (Schmidt 1992). To generalize, the east is hotter, dryer and a more difficult place to farm. The Rio Santa Clara–Rio Carmen approximates the usually ascribed eastern limit of Casas Grandes culture (Brand 1933).

Preceramic period sites are abundant in the central portion of northern Chihuahua. In many areas they are easily visible in deeply eroded interdunal exposures; artifacts and rocks from features occur as lag deposits, typically mixing materials of many ages. Vestiges of earlier ceramic period components are recognizable in these settings. Sayles (1936) defined a Medanos phase for this part of Chihuahua that in today's terminology is within the Viejo Period.

Approximately one dozen Viejo Period sites are known to exist east of the Rio Santa María, based on both professional survey coverage and nonsystematic, avocation reconnaissance. None of these sites have been excavated at all, severely limiting what can be said about the Viejo Period in the east. They are most easily distinguished by the presence of the characteristic red-on-brown pottery. Eastern Viejo Period sites, at least towards the end of the period, often have small quantities of contemporary Mimbres Black-on-white pottery and southern Jornada Mogollon pottery, identifying two other major influences on the subregion. On meager evidence, the eastern Casas Grandes area seemingly was extensively, but thinly populated during the Viejo Period. There is no record of maize from these sites, although it is generally assumed that people were farming in riverine, spring, and perhaps alluvial fan settings, where they could grow maize and other cultigens. Notably, this subregion was a participant in Casas Grandes culture as it developed. The reported sites are small and probably indicative of a ranchería lifeway. In this relatively difficult setting, people would have found advantages in living in small groups of somewhat mobile agriculturalists, whom out of necessity, were adept with using all subsistence resources.

The Medio Period extended equally far to the east. Brand (1933) described several Medio Period sites at springs in the area. Di Peso and colleagues (1974) included over one dozen Medio Period sites along the Rio Carmen on their regional settlement map (see Whalen and Pitezel, this volume, for discussion of this map). The best known of these sites is Loma de Moctezuma; it includes a sizable adobe pueblo with dimensions of 150 by 70 m, as measured by Cruz et al. (2004). These authors also provide evidence that, on architectural and ceramic criteria, Loma de Moctezuma was in the later years of occupation less of a Casas Grandes–style site and more like an El Paso phase site of the southern Jornada Mogollon tradition.

Medio Period (and El Paso phase) subsistence in the east included maize farming as evidenced by charred maize from Loma de Moctezuma and hunting, indicated by remarkable quantities of rabbit bones from the site (Cruz et al. 2004). Irrigation canals that were supplied by the low-gradient Rio Carmen are a reasonable possibility for providing food for this sizable community in a low-precipitation environment. If so, some level of authority to organize construction, maintenance, and use of canals may have existed. No public architecture features, such as ball courts or large communal roasting pits, are known from this area.

A small farmstead named Casa Chica along the Rio Santa María provides evidence of an El Paso phase presence that temporally and spatially overlapped with the Medio Period (Cruz et al. 2004). The site incorporates El Paso phase architectural characteristics and relatively abundant El Paso pottery. Brand (1933, Appendix III, 66) had long-before remarked on Ojo Calientes de Santo Domingo, a site in this eastern Casas Grandes area with abundant El Paso ceramics and turquoise, yet also noted a site farther to the north-northeast where Casas Grandes ceramics prevailed. The latter site, Salinas de la Unión, is beside a salt bed that Brand conjectured may have supplied salt to the Casas Grandes area. The apparent through-flow of turquoise from New Mexico sources into Paquimé provides a second economic link between the east subregion and Paquimé (Maxwell and Cruz 2003). The eastern Casas Grandes area was, at least during the Medio Period and contemporary El Paso phase, a broad, perhaps shifting, zone of commingling between two traditions.

In the east, organization and governance likely emphasized local, weakly developed institutions. The suite of local Chihuahuan polychromes is distinct for the subregion, as is true for other subregions of the Casas Grandes region. Archaeologists have often suggested that Loma de Moctezuma was the center of a local system, which certainly may have been true. Supporting evidence is limited to the site's size and complex ceramic assemblage.

Conclusions

Just as Di Peso did in his Casas Grandes publication 40 years ago, we find it necessary to place Paquimé in a larger regional context—but one distinct from that ground-breaking work. Di Peso viewed Paquimé as an origin point, the source of innovation, from which social and political organization spread outward—a view largely falsified by better chronological control and general growth of knowledge.

During the Viejo Period, it appears that the future Casas Grandes core, along with the south, west, and east subregions, represent the initial Casas Grandes region; at this time, the north subregion appears to be part of a separate tradition, more connected to the Mimbres and San Simon areas. It is in the south subregion where the nature of this Viejo occupation is best identified. There, small-scale agricultural villages appear politically autonomous but entrained into shared artistic traditions and presumably related values. As discussed earlier, there is no reason to believe that this large area was occupied by a single language or a "people." Something larger than an ethnographic group was forged during the Viejo Period, perhaps through the development of alliances, sharing, and exchange. One window into the dynamics of creating this region comes from the research in the upper Bavíspe valley, which indicates that sometime between the early and late Viejo Period, agricultural communities "flipped" from a characteristic Rio Sonora pattern to a characteristic Casas Grandes pattern. Whether this change was created by migration or by cultural realignments, it shows that the Viejo Period characteristics were not passively carried by a people who had occupied each valley in the region since the Late Archaic Period.

During the Medio Period, this region changed dramatically and relatively small differences between zones become larger. In the north subregion, Chihuahuan influence becomes integrated for the first time within that subregion. Later in the Medio Period, the eastern site of

Loma de Moctezuma becomes less focused on Casas Grandes patterns and more closely linked with El Paso phase patterns.

Evidence of significant population growth and aggregation are widespread. Particularly in the Casas Grandes core and the west subregion, population growth appears to be rapid, presumably fueled by a combination of moderate-scale irrigation in the river valleys and widespread expansion of run-off agricultural field systems in piedmont areas. As Minnis, Whalen, and Howell (2006) and Whalen and Minnis (2001) have discussed, this "two track" agricultural system appears to inherently create multicommunity polities, by linking dense riverine occupations with rather distant agricultural production areas. Such multisettlement, multi-ecozone "communities" are found in many places in the Americas, including other cultural traditions in the NW/SW. Yet this pattern, best defined in the core and west subregions, seems unknown in the south or the east subregion, though not necessarily for the same reasons. The north lacks the extensive upland field systems, but does have hints of small-scale, multilocal communities.

Thus, the Casas Grandes core and the west subregion were on a path of agricultural intensification not matched in the rest of the region. The contrast is drawn most sharply with the south, where higher precipitation may have made the area a leader during the Viejo Period. Without explosive population growth and large-scale collective agricultural strategies, the Medio Period in the south probably retained more resemblance to Viejo Period society and polity. The structural differences between the west subregion and the Casas Grandes core undoubtedly related partially to scale. The visible differences evidently hinged on the new Medio Period symbolism and ritual fully expressed at Paquimé, drawn in no small part (but not exclusively) from the Mesoamerican "Great Tradition" (to employ Robert Redfield's classic [1956], if imperfect, term for the urban and elite beliefs and practices of a culture area), and the hyperactive exchange and hoarding system centered on Paquimé. By comparison, the west zone appears "walled off," largely continuing the basic shared symbolism of the Viejo Period with relatively few of the ritual and prestige innovations of the core subregion and relatively limited long-distance exchange networks.

Overall, then, we view the Medio Period in the south, west and Casas Grandes core as areas with a common past that diversify during the Medio Period because of varied adaption of new agricultural systems, divergent demographic trajectories, localized social innovations, and the effects of heterogeneous long-distance exchange networks. This differentiation likely had a strongly impact on society and polity in these areas: changes in the south were limited, with the subregion retaining more of its Viejo Period social and political organization; the west built a new organization based on relatively isolated, multisettlement communities with integration based on agrarian production and land wealth, potentially linked with relatively higher rates of warfare; and the Casas Grandes core reached a crescendo of competitive acquisition, hoarding of exotic goods, ritual innovation, architectural elaboration, and complex food production.

These trajectories further contrast with the north and east subregions, neither of which had the agricultural potential found elsewhere in the region. During the Medio Period, the population in the north subregion was bought into the Casas Grandes sphere, although not completely. In the east subregion, a reverse process occurred, when late Casas Grandes influence waned, at least based on results from Loma de Moctezuma. Thus, both subregions finish as heterogeneous zones during the Medio Period, combining older local patterns, influences from other, non-Casas Grandes regions, and new Casas Grandes patterns, many of which are most clearly expressed at Paquimé (although not necessarily originating from this community). Migration out of the Casas Grandes core subregion into these areas may partially explain these changes, as discussed earlier for Joyce Well, New Mexico; such communities would have brought Casas Grandes values, styles, and exchange linkages to outlying areas, a process that fits rather closely to Di Peso's generalized view of Paquimé expansion. However, we find the amalgam of cultural influences too complex to rely on migration alone, as shown by the comparison of Joyce Well and the Pendleton Ruin. Some Casas Grandes ritual and social values probably did not have meaning in areas with more marginal farming, less social differentiation, and a smaller labor force. Elements of Casas Grandes culture probably helped legitimize local leaders by providing symbols of authority and important trade partners, facilitated aggregation, and brought other social and material benefits.

The processes and histories that created differences between the subregions are critical, but it is equally important to consider what held these areas together as a recognizable region or culture. Without a pan-regional Medio Period polity, participation may have been propelled by two primary forces, one economic and one ideological. Even if people participated in the Casas Grandes world more or less on their own terms, economic and ideological participation would engender cooperation over friction. Shared pottery styles, particularly unique and value-loaded patterns such as hooded effigy pots, the construction of ball courts, and rock art all provide evidence of widespread, although hardly uniform, ideological participation. The permeability of the north and east subregions indicates that these were important contact zones for distance resources to enter the Casas Grandes region. Long-distance exchange may have been facilitated by local partners situated to contact distant sources, and the presence of a range of localized exotic goods moving between subregions is suggestive of a wider economy that may have involved a range of perishable goods.

Although direct evidence of pilgrimage from communities across the region to Paquimé is intrinsically difficult to demonstrate, it does provide a specific mechanism that might explain both the economic and ideological interconnections within the diverse Casas Grandes region. The large quantity of public architecture and space at Paquimé, as well as its store of prestige goods and religious paraphernalia, is suggestive of a pilgrimage center (Di Peso 1974; Fish and Fish 1999; Moulard 2005; VanPool 2002). Evaluating this mechanism to explain specific distributions of goods and ideas across the region would provide a useful guide for future pan-regional studies.

Much of the data accumulated since the Casas Grandes volumes were published in 1974 brings intertwined yet distinct subregional histories to light. Along the way, these advances serve to contextualize Paquimé within a vast, variegated region. Some scholars have endorsed models that adhere more closely to Di Peso's centralized vision of the region (Lekson 1999; Mathiowetz 2011; Schaafsma and Riley 1999, 248). But the evidence reviewed here indicates that there are too many early antecedents, too much regional variation, and too little structure in society and polity to accept these models. As outlined here, historical connections and noncoercive interactions—exchange, emulation, ritual leadership, and pilgrimage—can explain most of the patterns found in the region.

Obviously, this leaves open the possibility—even the likelihood—of Paquimé employing intimidation, force or colonization at specific times and places to achieve and maintain its preeminence for perhaps three centuries. Nonetheless, we speculate that heavy investment in exchange and ritual indicates that these less violent, likely less costly, and certainly more predictable, tactics were the norm. What is critical here is the evidence of a multiplicity of dynamic relationships, at varying scales and differing times, which are beginning to come into focus. It is only through the study of these relationships that a clearer understanding of the social organization and the political landscape of the Casas Grandes region will be achieved.

7

The End of Paquimé and the Casas Grandes Culture

David A. Phillips, Jr., and Eduardo Gamboa

In 1663, the Spanish founded a village and mission near the abandoned pre-Hispanic town of Paquimé (Di Peso 1974:3, 865, 998). Based on tree-ring evidence, as late as AD 1338, Paquimé was a living settlement. Whatever happened to the Casas Grandes culture, it must have happened during the intervening 325 years. The purpose of this chapter is to once again consider when and why the culture came to an end. Whether we utilize history or archaeology, our starting point for any examination of the problem is the enduring scholarship of Charles Di Peso.

Historical Evidence

The new Spanish colony at Casas Grandes did not happen in isolation. By 1660, as Di Peso (1966, 24) and Di Peso, Rinaldo, and Fenner (1974:3, 863–64) noted, missionaries and Spanish colonists had infiltrated northwest Mexico. If the Casas Grandes culture was still present, we would have heard of it. As we move backward through protohistoric time, however, the picture quickly darkens.

Our previous look at the region comes from the Ibarra expedition, which headed north in 1565. In Sonora, Ibarra found thriving agricultural societies (see Riley 1985, 1987, 1990). He then veered east, across the Sierra Madre, and the expedition "began to discover abandoned houses of two and three stories" (Hammond and Rey [1928, 197], cited in Di Peso, Rinaldo, and Fenner 1974:4, 112). When the Spanish reached Paquimé, it too was abandoned. Using sign language, the local nomads informed the Spanish that Paquimé's occupants had moved north to a place a six-days' journey distant. The locals added that four days to the west were village dwellers. This was in the same direction as the group that forced the Paquimeños to leave—a group "from the other side of

The End of Paquimé and the Casas Grandes Culture   149

the mountains" (Hammond and Rey [1928, 207–208], cited in Di Peso, Rinaldo, and Fenner 1974:4, 114).

Back in time another generation, Spanish records shed the dimmest of light on our problem. In 1536, Cabeza de Vaca traversed the south end of the Casas Grandes area (Di Peso, Rinaldo, and Fenner 1974:4, 58), where Jane Kelley and her colleagues have worked (e.g., Kelley et al. 1999; Kelley and Searcy, this volume). Cabeza de Vaca described basin-and-range country where the local people spent a third of the year eating meal from wild grasses (*polvos de paja*). In contrast, once in Sonora he found maize-growing, cotton-wearing inhabitants (Di Peso, Rinaldo, and Fenner 1974:4, 56–57). Based on the evidence given by both Cabeza de Vaca and Ibarra, the pre-Hispanic Rio Sonora culture (Doolittle 1988; Pailes 1978) carried over into historical times. In contrast, if the Casas Grandes culture was still thriving, we should have learned of it from Cabeza de Vaca—who, after all, heard of the Pueblos, despite passing hundreds of kilometers south of them.

The reach of Native geographic knowledge was confirmed three years later when Marcos de Niza traveled up the west coast of Mexico. In southern Sonora people were aware of the western Pueblos. We may conclude that regional geographic knowledge extended at least 500 km, beyond the range of continual economic interaction. This same range of knowledge was encountered as Coronado passed through Sonora in 1540. Thus, three Spanish parties could have reported on the Casas Grandes culture, if it still existed as of the late 1530s. They did not.

The lack of Spanish reports is not irrefutable evidence that the culture ceased to exist by the 1530s. Di Peso (1974, vols. 1–3) reached the contrary conclusion, using ethnographic and archaeological data to argue that the Ibarra expedition fought with a remnant group of Casas Grandes people.

Evidence from Paquimé

Before 1536, the historical record goes completely dark, and we must turn to archaeology for answers. The debate on Casas Grandes chronology goes back many years, but much of that debate is now behind us (for a summary, see Whalen and Minnis [2001, 38–42]). If we instead focus on the archaeological evidence as it is understood today, the Casas culture must have existed at least as late as 1338—the final noncutting tree-ring date from Paquimé (Di Peso, Rinaldo, and Fenner 1974:4, 21). Sadly, Paquimé yielded no cutting dates, so we must depend on Dean and Ravesloot's (1993) computer-based estimate of the number of rings missing from Paquimé samples. Their key findings, vis-à-vis this chapter, are that Paquimé "was inhabited in the fifteenth century" and that "some construction or repair activity *may have* occurred as late as the AD 1470s" (Dean and Ravesloot 1993, 93; emphasis added).

Why "as late as the AD 1470s?" In a list of estimated felling dates, Dean and Ravesloot (1993, Table 6.2) list not only their algorithmic estimate of the felling date but that date plus two standard deviations, due to "a high probability that the actual dates fall toward the later ends of the ranges" (Dean and Ravesloot 1993, 93). In other words, Dean and Ravesloot instituted a "fix" to their dates, because the central tendencies produced by the computer algorithm appeared to be too early. One of these "plus 2-sigma" fixes corresponds to a date of AD 1473 (Table 7.1). Because of the fuzziness introduced by the algorithm, however, it is best to take precautions usually reserved for radiocarbon assays. In other words, we should look at clusters of dates rather than at single dates. As it turns out, the AD 1473 date is a statistical outlier (Table 7.2). Within the cluster of dates, the latest value is 1444. Thus, a cautious interpretation of the algorithmic data is that construction at Paquimé ended in the 1440s.

This suggestion is bolstered by the radiocarbon evidence gathered by Di Peso. Radiocarbon samples figure prominently in our effort to date the end of Casas Grandes, so a discussion of our approach is in order. We use only 2-sigma date ranges to interpret the data. The ranges were interpreted using CALIB 5.0 (Stuiver and Reimer 2005), which calculates the probabilities of single or multiple intercepts of the ranges. When patterns of dates are examined, as opposed to individual dates, ranges with less than 10 percent probability of containing the correct date are reasonably ignored. In the remaining ranges, we refer to occurrences with 10 percent or greater probability of containing the correct date, as "spikes." When newly calibrated, and eliminating a humus fraction sample, Di Peso's four radiocarbon dates from Paquimé have 2-sigma spikes no later than 1423 (Table 7.3). More recently, Christopher Casserino submitted bone collagen samples from four Paquimé burials (Casserino 2009, Table 9); applying the same protocol, the four burial-derived dates yield 2-sigma spikes no later than 1406 (Table 7.3).

Table 7.1. Estimated Tree Felling Dates for Room Construction.

Computer Estimate	Estimate plus Two Sigmas	Room, Sample
1419	1473	14-26b, CG(D) 223
1382	1436	14-28b, CG(D) 187
1376	1430	14-33b, CG(D) 180
1355	1409	14-27a, CG(D) 189
1349	1402	14-24a, CG(D) 182
1390	1444	8-21c, CG(D) 118
1384	1439	8-7a, CG(D) 20
1359	1413	8-15c, CG(D) 26
1337	1391	8-6b, CG(D) 106
1328	1382	8-18b, CG(D) 48
1326	1380	8-21b, CG(D) 103
1321	1375	13-15, CG(D) 166
1319	1373	16-3cb, CG(D) 369
1301	1355	14-30b, CG(D) 190
1299	1353	12-26, CG(D) 281
1282	1335	16-6a, CG(D) 391
1276	1330	8-9b, CG(D) 19
1272	1325	16-22b, CG(D) 342
1256	1310	14-23a, CG(D) 173
1253	1306	8-29a, CG(D) 362
1250	1303	14-36a, CG(D) 220
1245	1299	14-43b, CG(D) 321
1243	1295	16-12a, CG(D) 344
1239	1292	16-20a, CG(D) 346
1224	1277	8-27, CG(D) 361

(Source: Dean and Ravesloot 1993: Table 6.2)

Table 7.2. Computer Estimates of Felling Dates from Paquimé, by 50-Year Interval.

Interval	Number of Estimated Felling Dates	Number of Dates after Adding 2 Sigmas
1201–1250	5	0
1251–1300	6	4
1301–1350	6	6
1351–1400	7	7
1400–1450	1 (@ 1419)	7 (last @ 1436)
1450–1475	0	1 (@ 1473)

(Source: Dean and Ravesloot 1993:Table 6.2)

Paquimé also yielded imported pottery suitable for cross-dating (Di Peso, Rinaldo, and Fenner 1974:4, 29–33), suggesting an occupation that ended by 1450. Finally, an average of 70 obsidian hydration samples yielded an estimate of AD 1417 ± 70 (Di Peso, Rinaldo, and Fenner 1974:4, 25–33). While obsidian hydration samples present interpretive problems of their own, the published estimate is at least consistent with Paquimé being abandoned by 1450.

Evidence from Other Casas Grandes Sites

As Di Peso pointed out, the Casas Grandes culture could have survived the abandonment of its principal center. We therefore examined available dates from outside Paquimé. Whalen and Minnis (2003, Table 1) report 13 radiocarbon dates from the Tinaja site, not far from Paquimé, and include 2-sigma calibrated date ranges. Only 2 of the 13

Table 7.3. Di Peso's Radiocarbon Dates.

Sample	Context	Material	Uncorr.	Plus or Minus	Date Spike, 1 Sigma	Relative Area (%)	Date Spike, 2 Sigma	Relative Area (%)	Refs.
Paquimé Samples									
A-226	Room 21c-8 post	Wood	740	100	1175–1316	83	1118–1412	92	1
A-412	Pit Oven 4-1	Charcoal	640	30	1289–1319; 1351–1390	43; 57	1281–1401	100	1, 3
A-415a	Room 38-11 post	Wood	820	50	1168–1265	100	1147–1283	85	1
A-415b	Room 38-11 post	Humus fraction	560	180	1277–1524	83	1149–1694	92	1
A-612	Room 24-11 hearth	Maize cobs	470	90	1217–1321	73	1152–1423	97	1, 2
Other Samples									
A-411	Chih D:9:14 upper floor	Charcoal	710	40	1258–1305; 1364–1384	78; 22	1218–1323; 1346–1393	76; 24	1
A-609	Chih D:9:14, House No. 1, Fill No. 2, 8th floor	Charred twigs	740	115	1164–1321; 1349–1391	81; 19	1039–1414	100	1, 2
A-610	Chih G:2:3, Room 2, post.	Charred wood	300	90	1466–1665	96	1431–1697; 1725–1815	79; 14	1, 2

References: 1) Di Peso et al. 1974:4; 2) Haynes et al. 1966; 3) Damon et al. 1964. All date spikes calculated with CALIB 5.0.

date ranges extend beyond 1300: one is 1270–1400, and the other is 1300–1430. Thus, the Tinaja site probably was abandoned before 1430.

Whalen and Minnis's (2009b, 2010) reports on Site 315, across the Rio Casas Grandes from Paquimé, list 18 radiocarbon dates and their 2-sigma calibrated date ranges. Eight of the date ranges extend beyond 1300. In order of terminal date (in the range provided) these are 1160–1305, 1260–1390, 1283–1396, 1290–1399, 1296–1406, 1280–1410, and 1310–1460. Thus, Site 315 probably was abandoned before 1460.

Whalen's (2011) report on Site 565, also across the river from Paquimé, lists five radiocarbon dates and their 2-sigma calibrated date ranges. Three of the date ranges extend beyond 1300: 1390–1450, 1280–1400, and 1290–1410. It is interesting that when the Whalen and Minnis dates from this site, the Tinaja site, and Site 315 are considered together, the rapid fall-off in terminal dates takes place in the early rather than the middle 1400s.

A site fairly near Paquimé, Casa del Fuego, yielded two archaeomagnetic dates from burned rooms. Those dates suggest destruction of the rooms between 1300 and 1400 (Schaafsma, Cox, and Wolfman 2002, Figure 6.8).

The Rancho el Espía site, on the Rio Casas Grandes well north of Paquimé, is not directly dated, but Fritz (1969) reports that the associated sherds include Gila, Tonto, Tucson, El Paso Polychrome, and Rio Grande Glaze A, suggesting a date range of 1200–1450.

At the south end of the Casas Grandes range, Kelley and Stewart (Kelley et al. 1999, Table 4.1; Stewart, MacWilliams, and Kelley 2004, Table 11.1) provide a wealth of radiocarbon dates for the Medio Period. In 24 cases, the "2-sigma spikes" extend into the 1300–1350 date range. Another 24 spikes extend into the 1350–1400 date range, while 19 spikes extend into the 1400–1450 date range. In contrast, only three of the 2-sigma spikes extend into the 1450–1500 date range, and all three overlap extensively with the earlier 50 year ranges (1381–1471 [TO-4126], 1374–1514 [TO-5033], and 1395–1473 [TO-5034]). Again, the evidence suggests a precipitous decline in the culture before 1450.

For the Sierra Madre, the one published tree-ring date of 1374+x (Scott 1966) is consistent with the Medio Period ending before 1450. Breternitz (1966) considered that sample nondatable, however. Working briefly in the Sierra Madre, Di Peso, Rinaldo, and Fenner (1974) obtained a single raw radiocarbon date of 300 ± 90 BP from a post in a room at Casa de Robles. Newly calibrated, it yields 2-sigma spikes of 1431–1697 (79% probability of containing the correct date) and 1725–1815 (14% [see Table 7.3]), and it is therefore difficult to reconcile with a pre-1450 end date for the culture.

Farther west, in Sonora, Beatriz Braniff recovered materials from Ojo de Agua (Son H:2:2), a site within the greater Casas Grandes tradition. In 1992, she reported four dates from the site that provide 2-sigma spikes: 1) 1379–1891 (87%); 2) 1286–1481 (100%); 3) 1413–1523 (82%) and 1571–1630 (17%); and 4) 1453–1543 (100%).[1] In other words, two of the dates are consistent with a pre-1450 occupation; a third is consistent with such an occupation; and one is entirely inconsistent with such an occupation. Braniff also recovered sherds of U.S. origin (Babocomari Polychrome, Chupadero Black-on-white, Cloverdale Corrugated, Dragoon Red-on-brown, Gila Polychrome, Santa Cruz Polychrome, Tanque Verde Red-on-brown, and Tonto Polychrome [Braniff 1986, Table 1; 1992:2, 406]).

In her article and report, Braniff also reviewed data from San José Baviácora originally reported by Victoria Dirst and Richard Pailes (Dirst 1979; Dirst and Pailes 1976; Pailes 1980). While San José is not a Casas Grandes site, we will discuss it here, as it is consistent with Braniff's approach. She listed radiocarbon dates from San José of 1075, 1085, 1305, 1315, 1500 ± 90, and 1840 ± 60. The non-Casas intrusive sherds at San José included Babocomari Polychrome, Dragoon Red-on-brown, El Paso Polychrome, Encinas Red-on-black, Guasave Red, St. Johns Polychrome, Santa Cruz Polychrome, Tanque Verde Red-on-brown, Tucson Polychrome, Tularosa Black-on-white, and Trincheras wares (Braniff 1986, Table 3). In 1986, by combining the Ojo de Agua and San José data, Braniff concluded that "the Medio and Tardío periods . . . are contemporary and late—fourteenth century plus or minus 100 years (AD 1200–1500)" (Braniff 1986, 77). In 1992, however, Braniff concluded that Ojo de Agua dated from 1300 to 1650 (Braniff 1992, 2, Table 71).

Using information in Dirst (1979), we can take a new look at the San José radiocarbon data.[2] House B-II-1 yielded four radiocarbon dates; two predate 1300 and the other two yielded 2-sigma spikes of 1261–1421 (100%) and 1267–1422 (100%). House B-I-1 yielded three radiocarbon dates; one is clearly anomalous, but the other two bracket floor construction. The earlier, subfloor date has a 2-sigma spike of 1147–1405 (90%). The later, above-floor date has 2-sigma spikes of 1302–1367 (11%)

and 1382–1647 (89%). Both houses contained Casas Grandes pottery, some of it as part of the floor assemblage of House B-II-1. As a group, the San José dates are consistent with a pre-1450 date for Casas Grandes and fail to bolster Braniff's arguments for a late dating of Ojo de Agua.

In the Bootheel of New Mexico, the Joyce Well site yielded three dates from a pile of burned corn (Schaafsma, Cox, and Wolfman 2002, 136). DeAtley (1980, Table 3) provided a corrected, averaged date of 1340 ± 68. When newly corrected, the three dates yield 2-sigma spikes of 1155–1498, 1212–1498, and 1218–1524. The same site has yielded four archaeomagnetic dates whose ranges end at 1285, 1345, 1360, and 1400 (Schaafsma, Cox, and Wolfman 2002, Table 6.2); the 1345 end date is from the same room as the burned corn. Obsidian hydration dates extended as late as 1537 but with large sigmas (Stevenson, Scheetz, and Carpenter 1989). Reviewing the data, Carpenter (2002, 154) concludes that the Joyce Well site dates from 1200 to 1450.

DeAtley (1980, Table 3) lists additional radiocarbon dates from Hidalgo County, New Mexico, most of which do not bear on the end of the Medio Period. The three most recent yield 2-sigma spikes of 1) 1301–1367 (19%) and 1382–1517 (79%); 2) 1295–1439 (100%); and 3) 1206–1330 (77%) and 1339–1397 (22%).[3] These absolute dates are consistent with the intrusive types that according to DeAtley (1980, Table 2) are present in Animas phase sites: Tularosa Black-on-white, St. Johns Polychrome, Gila Polychrome, Tonto Polychrome, Pinedale Black-on-red, Pinedale Polychrome, Tucson Polychrome, El Paso Polychrome, and Chupadero Black-on-white.

For several other excavated Animas phase sites in New Mexico, we have no independent dates. At the Pendleton Ruin (Kidder, Cosgrove, and Cosgrove 1949), the late intrusive types include Gila, Tonto, Pinto (?), Pinedale, St. Johns, and El Paso Polychrome, and Tularosa and Chupadero Black-on-white. At Clanton Draw and Box Canyon, the late intrusive types include El Paso, Gila, Tonto, Tucson, and St. Johns Polychrome and Chupadero Black-on-white (McCluney 1962, Tables 1–2).

For the Boss Ranch site of southeastern Arizona, John Douglas (1996, 189) reports two dates that yield 2-sigma spikes of 1) 1260–1455 (100%); and 2) 1297–1378 (30%) and 1377–1483 (70%).[4] The U.S. types include (among others): Pinto Black-on-red; Gila, Tonto, Tucson, Maverick Mountain, Babocomari, Santa Cruz, St. Johns, and El Paso

Polychrome; Tanque Verde Red-on-brown; Tularosa White-on-red, and Chupadero Black-on-white. Other non-Chihuahuan wares include Trincheras Purple-on-red and Trincheras Polychrome. Small numbers of earlier wares are also present (Douglas 1990, Table 16; 1996, Table 1). Douglas dates the Animas phase from 1150 to 1450.

Myers (1985) partly reports a group of Animas phase (?) sites excavated by Cochise College (the Darnell, Price Canyon, Bernardino, Reagan, and J. Cowan sites) that yielded whole vessels of Ramos Polychrome as well as sherds of Ramos, Babicora, Carretas, Corralitos, Dublan, Huerigos, and Villa Ahumada Polychrome.

In reviewing the data from Animas phase sites in New Mexico and Arizona, Fish and Fish (1999, 29) comment that "available dates from most large sites parallel ceramic estimates." Their table indicates that the ceramic date ranges at the sites in question extend no later than 1450, except at Slaughter Ranch where the estimated end date is 1500 (Fish and Fish 1999, Table 1.2).

Finally, to the east, dates are available from the Villa Ahumada site. Rafael Cruz and Timothy Maxwell (1999) report four calibrated central values from undisturbed contexts: 1212, 1259, 1278, and 1279 along with two calibrated ranges from disturbed contexts of 1413–1436 and 1522–1648. Elsewhere, Cruz et al. (2004, 165) report "radiocarbon samples derived from carbonized maize found in Stratum III [that] yielded calibrated dates of AD 1244–1290 and AD 1255–1294 at one standard deviation. Using OxCal software, a combined date of AD 1260–1288 was calculated." Cruz and Maxwell (1999) also report three archaeomagnetic dates; one is early, but the other two are 1255–1290 and 1255–1285 (see also Cruz et al. 2004, 165). They conclude that "excepting the disturbed areas, these results fall within the revised Medio Period dates ascribed to Casas Grandes" by Dean and Ravesloot (Cruz and Maxwell 1999, 46). The pottery at Villa Ahumada includes El Paso Polychrome and Chupadero Black-on-white (Cruz et al. 2004, Table 9.1).

Evidence from Non-Casas Sites

To provide an independent line of evidence on the dating of the Medio Period, we present a list of Casas Grandes pottery from a number of non-Casas Grandes sites (Table 7.4).[5] Casas pottery occurs widely outside its area of origin (see, for example, the sources cited by Wiseman

Table 7.4. Casas Grandes Pottery as Trade Wares in Excavated Sites

Site	Casas Grandes Sherds (Counts provided where available.)	Local Dating	References p.c. = personal communication
New Mexico			
LA 120, Gran Quivira	Ramos Poly. (5)	1300–1680	Hayes et al. 1981
LA 416, Pottery Mound	Ramos Poly. (1), Ramos or Babicora Poly. (3), Villa Ahumada Poly (1).	1350–1500	Maxwell Museum, UNM, Cat. No. 69.32.1
LA 1549, Henderson Site	Babicora Poly. (16), Carretas (?) Poly. (2), Villa Ahumada Poly. (1), Ramos Poly. (3), unident. (9)	1250/1275 to ca. 1400	Wiseman 2004
LA 2113, Smokey Bear Ruin	Ramos Poly.	pre 1400	Wiseman et al. 1971
LA 2292, Pinnacle Ruin	Ramos Poly. (5)	1240–1400	Karl Laumbach and Stephen Lekson, p.c. 2007, 2008
LA 2528, Bloom Mound	Ramos Poly. jar and sherds	1400–1450 (Note)	Kelley 1984:475; Wiseman 1970:9
LA 12077, Janss Site	Chihuahuan polychrome (1)	1300–1450	Nelson and LeBlanc 1986
LA 15021, Disert Site	Chihuahuan polychromes (10)	1300–1450	Nelson and LeBlanc 1986
LA 18839, Stailey Site	Chihuahuan polychrome (1)	1300–1450	Nelson and LeBlanc 1986
LA 46326, Robinson Site	Ramos Poly. (32), Babicora Poly. (3), Villa Ahumada Poly. (1) (note)	1150–1500	Stewart et al. 1991

LA 68188, Fox Place	Babicora Poly. (4), Ramos Poly. (1)	1250–1425	Wiseman 2002
LA 71167, Tintop Cave, Lincoln Co., NM	Babicora Polychrome (9) Victoria or Anchondo Red-on-brown (2)	1100/1150–1300	Wiseman 1996
LA 97128, Meyer Pithouse Village	Chihuahuan sherds (11)	1150–1200	Peterson 2001
LA 97768 (FB 9657), Meyer Shallow Pit Village	Chihuahuan sherds (3)	1100–1400	Peterson 2001
Multiple sites of the southern San Andres Mountains		1140/1150–1350/1500	Kemrer 2007
Site near Deming			David Kirkpatrick, p.c. 2007–2008
Site near Sta. Theresa (excavated by D. Batcho)			Karl Laumbach, p.c. 2007
Phillips Site	House Unit 46: Ramos Poly. (6) (Note)	1200–1450	Kelley 1984
Fleck Draw and Cottonwood Draw site cluster, NM	Chihuahuan polychromes	1275–1400	Kemrer 2007
Texas			
41EP5 (FB6363), Hot Wells Pueblo	Chihuahuan ware (1)	1100 to 1400	Peterson 2001

(*continued*)

Table 7.4. Casas Grandes Pottery as Trade Wares in Excavated Sites (*continued*)

Site	Casas Grandes Sherds (Counts provided where available.)	Local Dating	References p.c. = personal communication
4EP499 (FB6442), Hot Wells Reservoir	Chihuahuan ware (8)	1100 to 1400 (note)	Peterson 2001
41EP823 (FB 6425)	Chihuahuan ware (4)	1200 to 1300	Church et al. 2007
41EP1647 (FB 6831)	Chihuahuan Black-on-white (1)	Pre-1100	Church et al. 2007
EPAS-60, Sgt. Doyle Site	Ramos Black, Carretas Poly, Villa Ahumada Poly, unid. plainware	1200 to 1450**	Green 1969
Tobin Ranch cache	Ramos Poly. (7 vessels.), Villa Ahumada Poly. (2 vessels)	1200 to 1450**	Moore and Wheat 1951
La Junta sites	Villa Ahumada Poly., Babicora Poly., Madera B/R (?), Ramos Black (?)	1200 to 1400 or 1450	Kelley 1958:156
Sonora			
Cerro de Trincheras	**Surface:** Babicora Poly .(3), Ramos Poly (4), Chihuahua poly. (8). **Excavation:** Ramos Poly. (ca. 300), Babicora Poly. (ca. 150), Carretas Poly. (ca. 50), Villa Ahumada (?) (few), other (50–70) (note)	1300 to 1450 or 1500	Gallaga Murrieta 1998, 2004; McGuire et al. 1999; Villalpando 2000
La Playa	Huerigos Poly. (2), Villa Ahumada (1)	**	Sánchez et al. 1998
San José Baviácora	(see text)		

Arizona

AZ CC:2:64 (ASM), Epley's Ruin	Ramos Poly. (1), Babicora Poly.? (1)		Anna Neuzil, p.c. 2007
AZ CC:8:16 (ASM), Duncan	Ramos Poly. (4), Babicora Poly (1)	Site 800 B.C. to A.D. 1450, relevant contexts post-1300	Lascaux and Montgomery 2007
Shamrock Dairy Site, Tucson	Ramos Poly.	Tucson phase, A.D. 1350 to 1500	Edgar Huber and Robby Hekcman, p.c. 2007
AZ FF:3:8, Ringo Site, Cochise Co.	Babicora Poly., Villa Ahumada Poly, Dublan Poly, Madera B/R, Playas R incised	1250 to 1350	Johnson and Thompson 1963
Babocomari Village	Ramos Poly. (3), Babicora Poly (3)	1200 to 1450	Altschul et al. 1999; Di Peso 1951
Garden Canyon	Ramos Poly. (2)	1200 to 1450	Jones 1996, cited in Altschul et al. 1999
Kuykendall Site, Cochise Co.	Ramos and Carretas Poly., ca. 104 sherds plus restorable vessels	1300 to 1450 (Fish and Fish 1999, Table 1.2)	Mills and Mills 1969a, 1969b
Reeve Ruin	Ramos Poly. (1); Chihuahua incised? (3)	1200 to 1450**	Di Peso 1958
Tres Alamos Site	Described as present; no details	1200 to 1450**	Tuthill 1947

(continued)

Table 7.4. Casas Grandes Pottery as Trade Wares in Excavated Sites (*continued*)

Bloom Mound, New Mexico: dating per Speth's (2004) comments that the site was probably occupied shortly after the final abandonment of the Henderson Site. **Robinson Site, New Mexico: sherd counts based on an examination of the Robinson Site collections at the Maxwell Museum, University of New Mexico, by M. Devitt and A. Barnes, 2008. The count shown in the table includes positive identifications and probable examples. Also found: 11 possible Ramos Polychromes, 1 possible Babicora Polychrome, 2 possible Villa Ahumada Polychromes, 62 Chihuahuan sherds not identified as to type, and one possible Mexican-made copy of Gila Polychrome (not Escondida Polychrome, Lot 1093). **Phillips Site**, New Mexico: "Another room [excavated by a private collector] was said to contain restorable Ramos and Gila Polychrome vessels" (Kelley 1984:214; see also Kelley 1984: Plate 16). **Hot Wells Reservoir**, Texas; date by association with Hot Wells Pueblo. **EPAS-60, Sgt. Doyle Site**, Texas: based on the standard dates for the El Paso phase. **Tobin Ranch cache**, Texas: date inferred from presence of El Paso Polychrome, Tucson Polychrome, and Chupadero Black-on-white. **Cerro de Trincheras**, Sonora: the surface counts are from the 1991 mapping project (O'Donovan 2002:Table 4.3). The excavation counts are preliminary and from a partial analysis of the assemblage (Gallaga 1998). The other sources listed under "References" confirm the presence of the same types in excavated contexts. Together, the various references provide the local dating for the types. **La Playa**, Son.: the radiocarbon dates reported by Sánchez et al. (1998:Figure 2) mostly relate to the Archaic period occupation; only one, A-8743, relates to the late occupation of the site. This date is presented in a graphic so cannot be newly calibrated; it falls between 1000 and 1400. Because the site had such along occupation, and because Sánchez et al. (1998:994) use the Chihuahuan pottery as part of their argument for identifying a late phase of occupation at La Playa, it is probably best not to draw temporal inferences about the age of Chihuahuan pottery from this site. **Reeve Ruin**, Arizona: based on other diagnostic types. **Tres Alamos Site**, Arizona: based on other diagnostic types.

[2006] and Woosley and Olinger [1993, 110–11]) but each site tends to yield, at most, a handful of examples. Playas Red and its variants are excluded from the list, as that type was also made by non-Casas villages (Bradley and Hoffer 1985; Wiseman 1981, 2002, 2004). Based on Table 7.4, a few non-Casas sites with Casas pottery were occupied after 1450, but none of them appears to have been founded after that year. Also, we can state that Casas Grandes pottery ceased to be an important trade ware after 1450, but we cannot state that it was never traded after 1450. Based on traded pieces alone, we cannot reach a firm conclusion about a relict (post-Paquimé) Casas Grandes population.

When?

As this chapter has shown, we can no longer bemoan the lack of dates from the Casas Grandes region. Instead, we have reached the point where compiling and interpreting dates is a bit of a chore. In order to deal with the extensive but somewhat messy data set cited in the previous pages, we will adopt terminology from the U.S. legal system. "Beyond a reasonable doubt," Paquimé was abandoned by 1450. Given the amount of work done at the site, if there was a later population we should see evidence of it. We cannot claim that the entire Casas Grandes culture ended before 1450, however, simply because the principal site lay empty (see Whalen and Pitezel, this volume). The regional data have not reached the level of redundancy attained, for example, on the Colorado Plateau, so our understanding of regional chronology could change with the next excavation. Thus, even though Phillips and Carpenter questioned Di Peso's decision to define the post-Paquimé Robles phase (Carpenter 2002; Phillips and Carpenter 1999), it is also easy to question arguments that the Robles phase does not exist.

We may instead apply a less rigorous standard, "the preponderance of the evidence." This is a standard that allows for evidence to the contrary, but understands that life requires decisions. In archaeology, it is a fallback strategy to be used only when a more rigorous approach is not possible, and it seems applicable here. Taking the combined pattern of dates rather than individual dates, the preponderance of the evidence suggests that the Casas Grandes culture collapsed between 1400 and

1450. In other words, the entire culture collapsed about the same time as its most important site was abandoned.

And yet ... even though something bad happened in the early 1400s, the Paquimeños did not vanish overnight. We should therefore not lose sight of the three most anomalous radiocarbon dates found in this review: one from Casa de Robles (1431 or later), one from Ojo de Agua (1453 or later), and one from Villa Ahumada (1522 or later). None of these dates is compelling, because each comes from a site where the evidence is otherwise consistent with a pre-1450 occupation. Nonetheless, the three dates could reflect the existence of a relict population in the Casas Grandes region. To put the matter differently, it is not yet clear whether the three dates just cited are examples of the occasional gutter ball one gets with radiocarbon dating, or the first indications of a tailing off in the local population.

What Happened?

If we know, tentatively, when the Casas Grandes culture collapsed, we also need to ask how that happened. Clearly, the survivors abandoned the outward traces of their culture and therefore became invisible to archaeologists. We also have one indigenous account: the Casas Grandes people moved north, after a conflict with people to the west. In that case, the Casas Grandes people could have fought with Sonoran peoples—specifically, the Opata—after which they could have retreated north to join the ancestors of today's Pueblos. This scenario is consistent with the sharing of cultural elements by the Casas Grandes and Pueblo peoples, for example, horned serpents, kilted dancers, and polychrome vessels with red elements outlined in black.[6]

Archaeologists have repeatedly suggested a different outcome, namely, that the Casas Grandes people became the Opata (e.g., Braniff 1992; Dirst 1979). The Opata represent a linguistic wedge in the distribution of Piman speakers (Ortiz 1979, ix; see also Wilcox 1986), and one way to derive the Opata intrusion is to have them abandon northwest Chihuahua in favor of northeast Sonora. Of course, the Opata may have been everyone's nemesis, not only intruding into Piman-speaking territory but being the western people who drove the Casas Grandes people northward.

While we cannot state exactly what happened, we do have a couple of useful hints. First, in the main Casas Grandes area, each valley tends to have a few Medio Period sites whose ceramic assemblages and middens indicate substantial time depth. (Also, once archaeologists started looking, they started finding Viejo Period remains.) At most Medio Period sites, however, the architecture is not matched by the trash deposits.[7] Perhaps the Casas Grandes culture began as a moderate number of farming hamlets and villages, then experienced explosive growth, drawing in populations who adopted Casas Grandes ways. If so, it was a boom that quickly busted. Meanwhile, on the fringes, client groups (such as those in the El Paso area and New Mexico Bootheel) may have inserted, for a few generations, a time of Casas-style sedentism and ceremony into an otherwise mobile annual round.

The second hint is that by the Pueblo IV Period, population distributions were inherently uneven; increasingly, the division was between densely occupied areas and empty ones (Cameron and Duff 2008; Clark, Lyons, and Hill 2003; Hill et al. 2004, 2012; Mills et al. 2013; Wilcox 2003). In other words, families were not just leaving certain areas, they were congregating in others—responding to a pull, as well as to a push. By 1450, Chihuahua was at the losing end of the process.

Combining the two hints, it may be that during the Medio Period, the Casas Grandes area attracted large numbers of outside people; the process of uneven regional population distributions had begun. After a few generations at most, most people in the area not only left, they walked extended distances from their homes to other, more promising communities, bypassing habitable areas. We have two obvious candidates for the attractors: the historic Pueblos to the north and the Sonoran villages to the west. The Native account collected by Ibarra suggests the former, while the linguistic evidence hints at the latter. Or possibly people went in both directions—not counting any nomadic groups who bought into Casas when times were good and who reverted to old habits as soon as things got bad.

And Why?

Di Peso (1974, vols. 1–3) tied the fall of Paquimé to turmoil in Mesoamerica, but as we now understand, the timing of events makes that scenario unlikely. Thus far, there is no consensus about the actual reason for the abandonment of that site and the disappearance (then or later) of the culture. We will take advantage of this vacuum to stake out a possible approach to the problem, and will let time (and new information) determine how well the approach holds up.

Explanations of cultural collapse by U.S. Southwesternists tend to invoke an external cause for the end of a culture. Di Peso saw Paquimé as the victim of geopolitical chaos, for example, and drought played an important (if still debated) historical role on the Colorado Plateau. We will therefore briefly present a model developed by Gamboa (2008; see also Phillips and Gamboa 2012) that describes the collapse of the Paquimé-centered social system without recourse to outside factors. Gamboa views Casas Grandes society as historically derived from the *rancherías* of the Late Archaic Period, and in many ways that rural lifeway continued even as scattered farmsteads merged into small villages. At the same time, agricultural success and trade in exotic items led to the emergence of a local elite. As the elite took form, they turned to Mesoamerica for models of ritual and social practice, and imposed those forms as an overlay on the local, rural society. In doing so, the elite also created a contrast between the traditional socioeconomic base (a majority of the people) and a veneer of Mesoamerican (and thus foreign) practice imposed by Paquimé's elite (a minority). The inherent social tensions within such a culture could boil over into internal violence and collapse, without an external cause such as an attack.

If this interpretation seems extreme, consider the end of Awatovi, in the Hopi country, which sparked its destruction by other Hopi villages through the renewed acceptance of a foreign religion. If Paquimé's elite was imposing exotic religious and social ideas, might the town not similarly invite its destruction by outraged inhabitants of the surrounding villages? Whether or not this model ever gains acceptance, it serves as a reminder that the sources of collapse do not always come from outside a society.

As we noted earlier, the collapse of the Casas Grandes culture (with or without local survivors) occurred throughout the region; populations left some areas and congregated in others (or else reverted to more nomadic, archaeologically less visible lifestyles). The process happened unevenly. Much of the north end of the region emptied before 1300 (e.g., Kohler, Varien, and Wright 2010; Ortman 2012) at a time when the south end of the region was flourishing. Later, a series of apparent cultural collapses occurred among a series of contiguous, sometimes overlapping archaeological complexes: Classic Hohokam, Salado, Trincheras, Casas Grandes, and the El Paso phase Jornada Mogollon. Strikingly, the archaeological complexes that managed to exit the stage at the same time as Casas are the almost-exclusive recipients of traded Casas pottery (Table 7.4). If all this sharing of pottery, followed by disappearance, is a coincidence, it is a big one. We need to consider whether all of these archaeological complexes were taken out by a single process. If so, any model that invokes internal social dynamics in the collapse of Paquimé must also consider whether the same dynamics were at play independently in other parts of the region, or whether the fall of Paquimé had a tsunami-like effect on other cultures of the borderlands.

The Way Forward

As we work to understand what actually happened, our best hope may be the indications of a decline before the fall. At some point in Paquimé's history, monumental suites of rooms were broken up into small living quarters, sometimes referred to as "tenements," by means of insubstantial walls. The process was common enough at Paquimé that Di Peso (1974, vols. 1–3) defined the Diablo phase to describe it. At Site 565, across the river from Paquimé, internal differences in architecture (Whalen 2011) may represent a similar shift from grandiose to shabby. Whalen and Minnis (2012) have proposed a model of regional change in which the collapse of Paquimé was accompanied by a loss of the elaborate symbolism seen on Ramos Polychrome. We can combine this model with Gamboa's reconstruction of Casas Grandes society, summarized earlier: abandonment of Paquimé was tied up with rejection of Paquimé's elite and the foreign ideas and practices that elite had instituted. What remained was rural communities that continued a lifeway started long before Paquimé was founded—and which no longer had use for the polychromes tied to discarded ritual practices.

The great attraction of Whalen and Minnis's model, with or without the social interpretation we are suggesting, is that the model is testable. Specifically, archaeologists need to dig a representative sample of small, unimpressive Casas Grandes sites—without Ramos Polychrome—the very kind they tend to avoid. If that sample includes no post-1450 Casas Grandes sites, the Whalen-Minnis model probably is incorrect. If the sample yields post-1450 Casas dates, it will be time to revive the post-Paquimé Robles phase, or at least Di Peso's notion that the culture survived the end of Paquimé.

Although Phillips has argued that the Robles phase does not exist (see Phillips and Carpenter 1999), he will be quite happy if Charlie Di Peso has the last laugh on the subject. If the Robles phase returns, in whatever form, we will gain a wider temporal window on the decline and fall of the Casas Grandes culture. Instead of dealing with brief turmoil in the 1400s, with few archaeological clues left behind, we may find an orderly body of evidence derived from a progressively failing society. In that case, we should see a trajectory of failure, greatly increasing our chances of documenting the "why" of the collapse. Let us hope that Di Peso, Whalen, and Minnis are correct in proposing that people stuck around after Paquimé fell apart—at least long enough to create a record of decline that archaeologists can interpret.

Acknowledgments

Many people responded to e-mail queries about Casas pottery in the U.S. To all of them our thanks—but especially to Patrick Lyons and Jane Bradley, whose contributions to Table 7.4 were enormous. Joe Stewart commented on an early draft of this chapter. Matt Devitt and Alicia Barnes tallied Chihuahuan sherds in the Robinson site collections. Jean Ballagh provided editorial assistance. All radiocarbon corrections and calibrations prepared for this chapter were done with CALIB 5.0.

In 1961, Ray Thompson similarly dated the Medio Period using the occurrence of Casas Grandes sherds in non-Casas Grandes sites (Thompson 1961). Given the limited information then available, Thompson's analysis was remarkably accurate. It was overshadowed, however, by the chronology deriving from the excavations at Paquimé. In preparing this chapter, we have followed in Ray Thompson's footsteps.

Notes

1. In 1986, Braniff reported two samples but one date: 1420 ± 70 ([A-1911, A-1912] Braniff 1986, 76). In 1992, she provided detailed information on four dates, including from the two samples reported earlier (Braniff 1992:2, 547). The two dates run by the University of Arizona are reported as already corrected. The two dates run by the Instituto Nacional de Antropología e Historia (INAH) were not reported as corrected, are assumed to be raw dates on wood charcoal, and were corrected accordingly.

A-1911, Cuadro 1, Capa 4, 370 ± 180 BP, 1-sigma spike of 1398–1681 (98%), 2-sigma spike of 1379–1891 (87%).

A-1912, Mont. J, Cuarto 2, Piso 2, 530 ± 70 BP, 1-sigma spikes of 1316–1354 (37%) and 1389–1442 (63%); 2-sigma spike of 1286–1481 (100%).

420-INAH, Cuadro 1, Capa 4, 428 ± 41, 1-sigma spike of 1427–1491 (93%); 2-sigma spikes of 1413–1523 (82%) and 1571–1630 (17%).

421-INAH, Cuadro 2, Capa 3, 344 ± 38, 1-sigma spikes of 1480–1527 (37%) and 1554–1533 (63%); 2-sigma spike of 1453–1643 (100%).

2. According to Doolittle (1988, 36–37), the 1075 and 1085 dates from San José calibrated to 1080–1200, while the later nonanomalous dates calibrated to about AD 1320. The San José Baviácora dates summarized by Braniff are as follows (Dirst 1979, 94–95, 99, 103, Table 3).

House in pit B-II-1, remodeled? Floor assemblage included a Carretas Polychrome jar and 15 Chihuahua polychrome sherds. Four radiocarbon dates were obtained.

UGA-1502, charcoal, 1075 = 875 BP ± 60; 1-sigma spikes of 1045–1094 (32%), 1120–1141 (13%), and 1147–1222 (56%); 2-sigma spike of 1029–1262 (100%).

UGA-1503, charcoal, 1085 = 865 BP ± 60; 1-sigma spikes of 1048–1085 (23%), 1123–1137 (8%), and 1150–1229 (60%); 2-sigma spike of 1032–1265 (100%).

UGA-1504, charcoal, 1305 = 645 BP ± 60; 2-sigma spikes of 1283–1324 (45%) and 1345–1393 (55%); 2-sigma spike of 1261–1421 (100%).

UGA-1505, charcoal, 1315 = 635 BP ± 60; 1-sigma spikes of 1287–1326 (43%) and 1343–1394 (57%); 2-sigma spikes of 1267–1422 (100%).

Surface House B-I-1. Associated sherds (not from the floor, however) include five types of Chihuahua polychrome. Three radiocarbon dates were obtained.

GaK-6243, charcoal from subfloor trash, 1200 = 750 BP ± 90; 1-sigma spikes of 1170–1306 (89%) and 1363–1385 (11%); 2-sigma spike of 1147–1405 (90%).

GaK-6242, charcoal from above floor, 1500 = 450 ± 90; 1-sigma spikes of 1400–1523 (74%) and 1572–1629 (25%); 2-sigma spikes of 1302–1367 (11%) and 1382–1647 (89%).

UGA-1610, charcoal from above floor, 1840 = 110 ± 60; 1-sigma spikes of 1684–1734 (29%) and 1806–1929 (70%); 2-sigma spikes of 1668–1782 (40%) and 1797–1954 (60%).

Rectangular Enclosure A-1. One radiocarbon date was obtained from a feature thought to predate the enclosure.

UGA-1506, charcoal, 1000 = 950 BP ± 60; 1-sigma spike of 1024–1155; 2-sigma spike of 972–1224. During the original study, the probabilities were not recorded. Applying Calib. 7.0.2, this date corresponds to a 1-sigma spike of 984–1051 (58%), 1082–1128 (31%), and 1135–1151 (11%), and to a 2-sigma spike of 940–1168 (95%).

Dirst (1979, 110) also reports on three radiocarbon samples from Ojo de Agua, a site with Chihuahua pottery but not to be confused with Braniff's Ojo de Agua. Two of the three samples from the post in a room proved too modern to date, so the third radiocarbon date (which Dirst reports as AD 1660 ± 55, UGA-1511) is best ignored.

3. DeAtley did not stipulate the material being dated, but she adjusted the maize dates from Joyce Well. She would have done so for her other dates had they been from material other than charcoal. Assuming that charcoal was being dated, the three relevant dates (DeAtley 1980, Table 3), including new calibrations, are as follows.

UCLA 2122A, Site HS-1, 490 ± 60 BP: 1-sigma spike of 1394–1458 (90%); 2-sigma spikes of 1301–1367 (19%) and 1382–1517 (79%).

UCLA 2122h, Site HS-75, 560 ± 60 BP: 1-sigma spikes of 1312–1358 (54%) and 1387–1427 (46%); 2-sigma spike of 1295–1439 (100%).

UCLA 1948a, Site HS-32, 720 ± 60 BP: 1-sigma spikes of 1237–1301 (80%) and 1367–1382 (15%); 2-sigma spikes of 1206–1330 (77%) and 1339–1397 (22%).

4. The Two Boss Ranch site dates reported by Douglas (1990, Table 26; 1996, 189) are as follows.

Beta 11283, on charred beans; 590 ± 80; 1-sigma spikes of 1298–1370 (69%) and 1379–1413 (31%); 2-sigma spike of 1260–1455 (100%).

Beta 25703, on outer rings of mesquite post; 510 ± 50; 1-sigma spikes of 1325–1344 (19%) and 1394–1447 (81%); 2-sigma spikes of 1297–1373 (30%) and 1377–1483 (70%).

5. Douglas and Quijada (2004a) report on the upper Bavispe, while valuable, serves to illustrate why Table 7.4 is largely restricted to excavated sites. Their late sites frequently include Carretas, Huerigos, and Ramos Polychrome, but their AD 1200–1500 date for those late sites are based on their estimates for the Casas Grandes polychromes (Douglas and Quijada 2004a, 98). In general, at surveyed sites where Casas pottery was found in association with other diagnostic types, the danger of creating circular arguments about pottery dates is very real.

6. There is, admittedly a problem here. The nearest Sonoran villages were roughly 100 km to the west, which divided by four days works out to 25 km per day. Thus, six-day's travel to the north would be roughly 150 km—enough to take the residents of Pacuimé to the El Paso area to the northeast, but not to the southernmost Pueblo villages of the time. Either the Paquimeños did not join the protohistoric Pueblos, the account was inaccurate, garbled in translation, or all three.

7. Consider, for example, Douglas's (1996, 186) comment that "Animas phase sites tend to be shallow and lack clear stratigraphy or extensive de facto refuse."

8

Paquimé

A Revision of Its Relations to the South and West

José Luis Punzo and M. Elisa Villalpando

There has been significant debate about the archaeology of Paquimé in the 40 years since Charles C. Di Peso and Eduardo Contreras conducted the Joint Casas Grandes Expedition (JCGE) at Paquimé and the publication of Di Peso, Rinaldo, and Fenner (1974, vols. 4–8), *Casas Grandes: A Fallen Trading Center of the Gran Chichimeca*. This extraordinary research project is still the foundation for the archaeology of northwest Chihuahua and, more broadly, far northern Mexico (Figure 8.1). Nevertheless, more research has been conducted during these 40 years, not only in the area directly influenced by Paquimé but in all of northern and central Mexico. We use this opportunity to review existing archaeological research (e.g., chronological sequences) in order to reexamine Di Peso's interpretations of Paquimé's relationships with its southern and western pre-Hispanic neighbors.

We begin by summarizing Di Peso's core interpretation of Paquimé as exemplified by the subtitle of his book *A Fallen Trading Center of the Gran Chichimeca*. Di Peso was convinced that a sophisticated group of merchants from Mesoamerica arrived at the Casas Grandes Valley and inspired the local populations, *Chichimecas*, to create the city of Paquimé during Viejo Period (Di Peso, Rinaldo, and Fenner 1974:2, 290). This theme is interwoven throughout Di Peso's interpretation. Therefore, it is important to address the ethnohistory and archaeological research available to him.

A logical first question to ask is, where did the merchants come from? Di Peso's answer is quite inaccurate, as he suggested that they came from somewhere along the Pacific Coast, bringing with them remarkable technological advancements like hydraulic systems. He posits that these merchants arrived into the valley as waves of immigrants, families, or through conquest and established themselves as coleaders

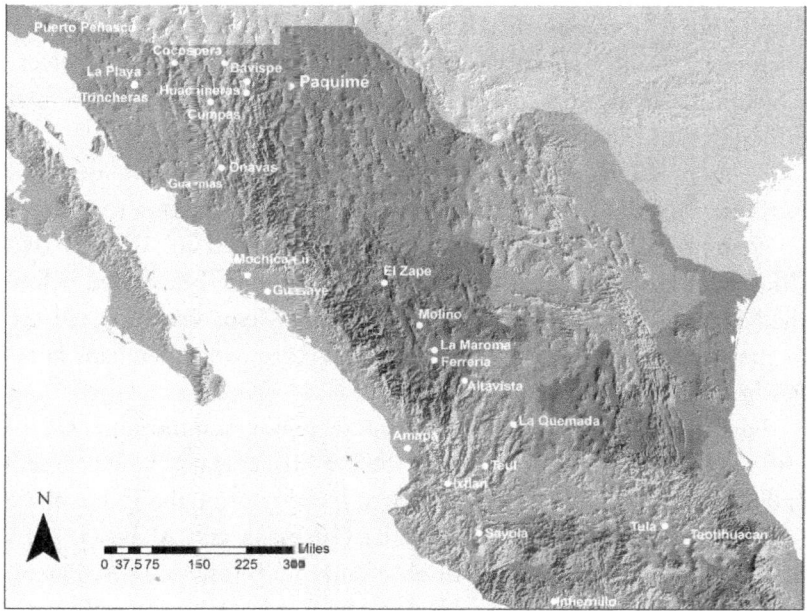

Figure 8.1. Map of Paquimé in relation to northern Mexico (José Luis Punzo).

who taught the local population (Di Peso 1974:2, 290). According to Di Peso, trade routes could have been established by informants who arrived as early as the Viejo Period and who were motivated by trade in "blue stones" and peyote (Di Peso 1974:2, 299, 301).

Di Peso also considered that the change between the Viejo and Medio periods was fast and dramatic. The merchants not only transported their products, but also brought their religious cults focused on gods such as *Tezcatlipoca, Quetzalcóatl,* and *Huitzilopochtli* (Di Peso 1974:2, 292). Di Peso was even more specific as he considered that many of the elements found in Paquimé came from Tula, a center which itself had diverse iconography from such places as the Huasteca or the Maya areas. From Tula, those elements diffused into the northern Mesoamerican border, such as the Chalchihuites and the Pacific Coast, and finally arrived at Paquimé.

It is important to note that Di Peso's interpretation of Paquime's Mesoamerican relationships focused on Tula—its emergence, end, and transition to the Mexica society. He explained the founding and developing of Paquimé through a broad analysis of sixteenth-century documents from Central Mexico, particularly the Historia Tolteca-Chichimeca as his principal source, and here is where we find the first difficulties for this interpretation.

Many of the researchers who work in the Casas Grandes area now attribute it to the Medio Period between AD 1200–1450, a revision of Di Peso's original dates. Tula's apogee is now dated to AD 950–1150 (Mastache, Cobean, and Healan 2002). As a result, Tula ended before the Medio Period began, so it is unlikely that Mesoamerican *pochtecas*, or the "southern donors" as Di Peso called them, were merchant families from or controlled by Tula.

Furthermore, Tula scholars posit that there was an important "northern" component in the structure of the pre-Hispanic city based on several indicators of relations with northern groups during the Tollan phase (ca. AD 900–1150), especially with La Quemada and Altavista, parts of the Chalchihuites culture, or the Ranas and Toluquilla in Querétaro (Mastache, Cobean, and Healan 2002). Mastache and colleagues believe that the Coyotlatelco population of central Mexico during the Epiclassic was related to its northern components. Evidence includes ideological concepts seen in the village's structure and plans, and hill top architecture—a characteristic from the Chalchihuites culture. There are also artifactual similarities, such as the fact that Coyotlatelco were part of the red-on-brown ceramic tradition, which possibly originated in the Mesoamerican northern periphery (Braniff 1974). Hers (1989, 2001b) has described the presence of *tzompantli* (trophy skulls), feathered snakes, *chacmools* (ritual tables for sacrifice), and other items as indicators of a strong relation between Tula and the Chalchihuites culture, and Braniff (2001, 109) explains them as the arrival of northern people to Tula. It is important to note that Chalchihuites culture was present from AD 200 to 1350 on the eastern flank of the Sierra Madre Occidental in the states of Zacatecas and Durango.

Regardless of whether there were Paquimé/Tula relationships, Di Peso recognized relationships between Paquimé and Mesoamerica. These include iconographic complexes, many architectural forms, settlement patterns, the exchange system, and the organization of some crafts, such as copper metallurgy and musical instruments—particularly the ceramic drums and the shell trumpets (Di Peso 1974:2, 622).

Ceramics from nonlocal sources are among the most important indicators of Paquimé's relationships with the south. Di Peso (Di Peso, Rinaldo, and Fenner 1974:8, 144) mentions a Ramos Polychrome sherd from the Tlamimilolpa phase at Teotihuacán that the Swedish academic Sigvald Linné identified. However, this artifact is very problematic because Teotihuacán is older than Paquimé.

There are several foreign sherds from Paquimé associated with ceramics reported to have been from the Guadiana Branch of the Chalchihuites culture in Durango and from Jalisco and Nayarit in West Mexico. Six different ceramic types were identified. Among them were 15 sherds of the Chalchihuites type, Mercado Red-on-Cream, recovered from floors on the west side of Paquimé. There were also 6 modeled and incised decorated spindle whorls; 4 were found in the storage room of House of the Well (Unit 8) attributed to the Diablo phase (Di Peso 1974:2, 624). It is important to note that sherds from Chalchihuites were identified by Ellen Abott in February, 1965, when she was working with J. Charles Kelley in the Guadiana Valley, Durango. The ceramic typology was published in 1971 and is still used in the Durango and Zacatecas regions. Nevertheless, Michael Foster, who worked with Kelley in Durango, has suggested that these sherds could be misidentified (Foster 1990, 1992). As a matter of fact, the senior author does not think that the sherd classified as Mercado Red-on-Cream is that type. It would be very important to have an additional ceramic analysis, since there are serious doubts about the "foreign" sherds from JCGE's work.

After decades of an intense debate about Chalchihuites archaeology and because of the series of new ^{14}C and thermoluminiscence dating, researchers have realized that the first chronology proposed by Kelley in 1971 is much more accurate than the one he proposed a decade later. Kelley's last chronology generated significant confusion because it correlated Chalchihuites artifacts from Durango with other regions. As a result, Punzo and Ramírez (2008) and Punzo (2013b) propose a new chronology for the Chalchihuites culture in Durango; it is one very close to Kelley's 1971 chronology. Based on improved dating calibration and a better chronology from the southern coast of Sinaloa and Nayarit, the Chalchihuites occupation in Durango developed between AD 600 and 1350. This means that its beginning was before the emergence of the Medio Period in Paquimé.

In this sense, Mercado sherds that Ellen Abott identified from the assemblage at Paquimé could have been produced in the area of Durango between AD 600 and 850, earlier than the Medio Period. In addition, incised button spindle whorls have been found in very diverse contexts in Durango from AD 600 to probably AD 1350. The majority are from contexts between AD 850–1250,[1] thus, temporally correlating with the end of the Viejo Period. It is also every important to mention that no Casas Grandes type sherds have been found in the Chalchihuites area.

Type 1 platform hearths are also one of the many elements common to both cultures.[2] This hearth type is exactly the same as the ones illustrated by Di Peso for Casas Grandes (Di Peso, Rinaldo, and Fenner 1974:4, 255) and has been found in Cerro de la Maroma in the rich lowland area of the Rio Sauceda at the very north of the Guadiana Valley, Durango. This hearth is associated with a sherd that was dated to AD 650, the beginning of the Ayala phase.

Ceramics types from West Mexico were found at Paquimé and were used as evidence of relationships beween the two areas. Di Peso (1974:2, 624) mentions an Amapa White-on-red sherd, that likely came from Nayarit during Amapa's Gavilán phase, and three Nayarit Polychrome sherds from the highlands. However, the Amapa White-on-red type is actually related to the Amapa phase, post-Gavilán phase, dating between AD 200 and 425, according to Meighan (1976) or AD 500–750 following Grosscup (1976). Both types correspond to dates earlier than the Medio Period at Paquimé. It is important to mention that polychrome ceramics types continue through all the Amapa phases; Di Peso relates the Nayarit Polychrome sherd to Ixtlán del Rio, although this ceramic type dates to later than AD 900. There was also a Cerro Colorado Polychrome sherd from the Sayula-Zacoalco area south of Chapala Lake, presented also as evidence of Paquimé's relationships with Mesoamerica (Di Peso, Rinaldo, and Fenner 1974:2, 624). This type is now assigned to the Sayula phase, dating between AD 550–1100 (Valdéz, Schondube, and Empoux 2005). Four fragments of a Totoate bowl were also identified from Alto Rio Bolaños (Di Peso, Rinaldo, and Fenner 1974:2, 624), although this ceramic type is no later than AD 1120 (Cabrero 2007).

Di Peso considers the presence of a ceramic drum painted in red as an important indicator of Mesoamerican relationships. He believed that it probably was from the Pacific Coast (Di Peso 1974:2, 624). More recent research indicates that similar drums have been found in many sites of western Mexico and even in Cañón del Molino in the Guatimape Valley, Durango.

The pseudo-cloisonné technique was also found at Paquimé, and Di Peso points out that it is a ceramic technology only found at central Mexico, Tula, and western Mexico (Di Peso, Rinaldo, and Fenner 1974:2, 616). We now know of multiple examples of this technique in a corridor that goes from Michoacán, to Sinaloa, and inland to Durango as its northern distributional limits.

The new data and dates gathered since the JCGE time show that many of the foreign artifacts from Paquimé were older than the Medio Period. Consequently, these data do not support the interaction model of specialized merchants as the founders of Paquimé. Either these artifacts are heirloom artifacts, or their presence suggests long-distance relationships with the south during the Viejo Period in Casas Grandes. Therefore, in order to develop a better understanding of such relationships we need a deep chronological perspective.

Ceramics are not the only artifacts from Paquimé indicative of interaction with Mesoamerica, according to Di Peso. Analysis of shell artifacts recovered in Paquimé (70 species of bivalves, univalves, and scaphopods) allowed Di Peso to differentiate between the access to these materials during the Viejo Period, when shells were used as personal paraphernalia, and the Medio Period, when the shells were socio-religious goods stored in massive quantities inside the city (Di Peso, Rinaldo, and Fenner 1974:6, 385). Di Peso also argued that most of the marine species present at Paquimé were found in the biotic district of Guaymas, Sonora, and beaches to the south, especially the millions of *Nassarius* beads. He also suggested that some species, such as the red shell oyster and black murex (*Hexaplex nigritus*), found in Paquimé can be exclusively collected south of the Tropic of Cancer (Di Peso 1974:2, 629). *Persicula bandera* shells, which are endemic to Banderas Bay in Jalisco, were used for making pendants (Di Peso, Rinaldo, and Fenner 1974:6, 403).

The supposed provenience of most of the shells from the Guaymas area, and Di Peso's own experience searching overland and by air for the routes that connected the Casas Grandes valley to the Gulf of California, allowed him to propose a route through the Tres Ríos/Chuhuichupa area. This route crosses over the mountain range to Nacori Chico, continues in Chipájora to Sahuaripa, and then moves up to the Nuri valley to descend by the Rio Cedros to the mouth of the Rio Mátape and Río Yaqui (Di Peso 1974:2, 390, 401, 628).

There are two issues about trade routes. The first are the routes used to transport raw materials from the Gulf Coast to Paquimé. Most of the 70 species identified from Paquimé are from the Panamic Province (Keen 1971); they are not only limited to the Guaymas area and can be found along the entire Gulf of California (Keen 1971; Parker 1963). Moreover, 15,000 examples of *Nassarius* sp. were excavated in a pit at Humedal Las Salinas, a shell midden situated north of Rocky Point, Sonora (Cristina García, personal communication, 2013). The second concern is that there is no archaeological evidence related to Casas Grandes in the Mátape and Yaqui coastal areas. No Casas Grandes artifacts have been found in the central coast or southern Sonora during recent archaeological surveys but only in northern Sinaloa, which will be discussed later.

It is certain that some shell present at Paquimé (especially *Persicula bandera*) could indicate strong relations with "the folk who lived along the West coast of Mexico" (Di Peso, Rinaldo, and Fenner 1974:6, 385). However, the relationships with the farming communities of the Sonoran desert, who were producers of substantial quantities of shell ornaments since early agriculture times with a considerable increase during the Medio Period of Paquimé, have gone largely unnoticed. Sonoran Desert societies had settlements on the Gulf Coast and seem to have had exchange relations with fishermen and gatherers from the central Gulf Coast. Such relations made possible the extraction of an important variety of marine species for exchange with their inland neighbors.

Very little was known about the Trincheras tradition when Di Peso proposed that there was a Hohokam supply route from the Guaymas area to the north, following the Gila and Salt rivers to the central part of Arizona. The Hohokam people, maybe including Trincheras' inhabitants (thinking of them as the rural branch of the Hohokam), would be part of another "inter-center competition in the Shell economy of the Northern Frontier" (Di Peso 1974:2, 628; Di Peso, Rinaldo, and Fenner 1974:6, 433).

Di Peso (1979, 158) considered an alternative interpretation that the main site of the Trincheras tradition was "a spectacular hillside trenched defense system" constructed by Mesoamerican merchants to protect the shell ornament industry of nearby La Playa. McGuire and Villalpando's research has demonstrated that this is erroneous, because Cerro de Trincheras has no Mesoamerican connections. As well, this site is later than La Playa, which is largely associated with the Early Agricultural Period (1500/800 BC–AD 200) and not with the Medio Period of Paquimé.

Another key element in Di Peso's model was commerce in turquoise that he argued came from New Mexico mines. Di Peso thought that turquoise extracted north of Paquimé was transported to the Toltec capital (Di Peso 1974:2, 630). Phil Weigand and collaborator have studied turquoise trade (Weigand 2008; Weigand and Harbottle 1993; Wilcox et al. 2008). Even when its transport and consumption was most important during the Postclassic Period in central Mexico, there are still many questions about turquoise provenience, and it is important to review all the past models on this. There was a broad practice in the use of green/blue stones, now called "cultural turquoise," which could come from places closer to central Mexico than the U.S. Southwest, to supply the substantial consumption of green/blue stones at that time. An example is the wide use of amazonite, another green/blue stone, in parts of west (Robles and Sánchez 2011) and northwest Mexico that substituted for the real turquoise in Mesoamerica.

Although obsidian was not especially common at Paquimé, Di Peso thought that it came from the deposits found in the Chalchihuites territory in Durango (Di Peso 1974:2, 631). Since the 1950s, Kelley knew that Llano Grande's obsidian deposits in Durango were without any doubt the most abundant in the area. However, we now know that many other smaller deposits exist along the Sierra Madre streams in Durango, where the Chalchihuites people could obtain obsidian. Therefore, the origin of obsidian at Paquimé is uncertain.

The best-known example of Paquimé's interaction with the south is the presence of exotic birds. Among the identified species is a large quantity of birds identified as scarlet or "red" macaw (*Ara macao*). This macaw is found in pre-Hispanic times as far north as the Huasteca in the Gulf of Mexico, far to the southwest of Paquimé (Di Peso 1974:2, 632).

Breeding of birds was a generalized practice in many places of northern Mexico as noted by early Spanish explorers. Di Peso presents evidence of these breeders in the Huasteca (Di Peso 1974:2, 632), but there were also some bird breeders among the Acaxées who lived at the borders of Durango, Sinaloa, and Chihuahua, in the Sierra Madre Occidental.

Figure 8.2. La Ferreria site in Durango, Mexico (José Luis Punzo).

These groups traveled during colonial times with macaws and parrots from the highlands as part of their more precious possessions (Punzo 2013a). In addition, the historic depth of this practice could be earlier in this region, as three fragments of stone rings similar to the ones identified as macaws nest doors in Paquimé were found in the Chalchihuites site of La Ferrería (Figure 8.2).[3] They could date to AD 600–1000.

Another trait noted by Di Peso as evidence of Paquime's relationship to parts of Mesoamerica is the practice of "trophy skulls," found since the Buena Fé phase. Di Peso correlates the presence of trophy skulls (*tzompantli*) at Paquimé to those found at Tula, Tenochtitlán, and the Maya area (Di Peso 1974:2, 638). However, it was not known during Di Peso's time that this practice was also common among the Chalchihuites people in Durango, Zacatecas, and northern Jalisco since the beginning of the first millennium. There are several such others from the same period discovered by Piña Chan and Kuniaki (1982) inside Tomb 1 at Tingambato, Michoacán, and Ekholm reported trophy skulls in Guasave (Zazueta Manjarrez and Guerrero Astorga 2008). Another relation to Mesoamerica is marked by the existence of special burials, as the ones found in Mound of the Offerings, where it is thought that members of the local elite were buried (Di Peso 1974:2, 637).

Metal artifacts and metallurgy have been noted as evidence of relationships between southern Mesoamerica and Paquimé. Di Peso only reports two copper objects from the Viejo Period: a conical bell and a plate (Di Peso, Rinaldo, and Fenner 1974:7, 499), so the Medio deposits contain the greatest amount of copper. Although Di Peso reports some copper artifacts unique to Paquimé, he suggested that most of the copper artifacts produced by the artists during the Medio Period at Paquimé were similar to Mesoamerican artifacts. There is a clear similarity of techniques and objects with the ones found in Amapa. The presence of copper in the form of a raw material, slag, sprue, and finished objects, as well as the chemical and spectroscopic studies available to the JCGE, allowed him to postulate that Paquimé was a locus of copper production during the Medio Period (Di Peso, Rinaldo, and Fenner 1974:8, 506).

However, researchers now working in the Casas Grandes region have not found evidence of metallurgy in the region. Di Peso's idea that copper metallurgy was common at Paquimé must be revisited. It is possible that copper was cold hammered, but there is no evidence of melting or the *cere perdue* (lost wax) process at Paquimé (Paul Minnis, personal communication, 2012). Vargas (1995, 12) indicates that techniques used by Di Peso are not conclusive, and the pieces he considered as unique have strong relations with different western Mexico areas, especially with Amapa.

The earliest dates associated with the metallurgy are from Tomatlán in Jalisco, Amapa in Nayarit, and from the Infiernillo region, in the Rio Balsas region, Michoacán (Hosler 2005), and more recently from Teúl de González Ortega in Zacatecas (Peter Jiménez, personal communication, 2012). In these sites, copper metallurgy corresponds to Hosler's phase I (AD 800–1200) with more refined production of metal objects during phase II (AD 1200–1520) in western Mexico, especially during the Postclassic in the Tarascan Señorío. There are abundant indications of copper metallurgy in the northern portion of western Mexico (Hosler 1988), in Nayarit, Sinaloa, and Durango. During phase II there were large quantities of bells, earrings, plates, tubular beads, buttons, rings, and needles.

Figure 8.3 Cerro de Trincheras site in Sonora, Mexico (Elisa Villalpando).

There are some copper artifact designs that very clearly demonstrate relationships between western Mexico and Paquimé, and even farther north to the U.S. Southwest. We are referring to the Tláloc-type effigy copper bells classified in Paquimé as 1C1a (Di Peso, Rinaldo, and Fenner 1974:8, 524), and in Amapa as 1A5a. This type is also present in the following sites from western Mexico: Amapa in Nayarit, Cañón del Molino in Durango, Tuxcacuesco in Jalisco, and Apatzingan in Michoacán. There is also one reported for the Black Falls Ruins and another one in Wupatki, Arizona (Vargas 1995). Recently, five examples were found at Cerro de Trincheras (Figure 8.3), which we discuss later.

Turtle-shaped copper bells classified in Paquimé as IIIA and in Amapa as IE2 are other important elements indicative of this interaction. These elements are present in western Mexico in El Zape, Durango, and in Naranjá and Tzintzuntzan, Michoacán. There is also one from Guerrero, although the site is not identified, and another with similar characteristics in the site of Pavón to the north of Veracruz, in the Gulf of Mexico.

Considering that the only verified copper production areas during the Postclassic Period are in western Mexico, the central plateau, and the Huasteca, more research in western Mexico should provide a better understandings of a route of interaction among the diverse Mesoamerican worlds, Paquimé, and the U.S. Southwest.

In sum, the current data allows us to refine our understanding of the relationships between Paquimé and Mesoamerica, especially with the groups who inhabited the Pacific Coast and inland in the Chalchihuites area of Durango. There is still much to do. Different models should be explored to let us refine our understanding of the interactions between both areas and not to assume a single origin, influence, or exchange route connecting the diverse pre-Hispanic communities. Probably, there was a complex interaction network that occurred in broader time lapses rather than during short periods when a long-distance exchange occurred and which is reflected in the archaeological materials recovered in both areas.

Paquimé and the West: Strong Relationships with the Trincheras Tradition

As we have pointed out, Di Peso proposed that the shell route from the Gulf of California to Casas Grandes followed the Rio Mátape and crossed the Sierra Madre in the Tres Ríos Plateau. The site of Cerro de Trincheras, west of the Sierra Madre Occidental, was one of the most important settlements of a regional polity during the late pre-Hispanic period (the fourteenth and fifteenth centuries) and was contemporary with Paquimé. Cerro de Trincheras, a site in the Trincheras core, was the result of a large and complex process of economic diversification, population concentration, and social complexity among the farming communities of the Sonoran desert's river valleys. It was not due to the sudden presence of Mesoamerican merchants.

The relatively short occupation of this community corresponds to Paquimé's apogee during the Medio Period, ca. AD 1300–1470 (Dean and Ravesloot 1993, Table 6.2). Contrary to previous interpretations (Di Peso 1979; Haury 1973) there is no evidence suggesting close interactions between Cerro de Trincheras, immediate Hohokam communities, or Mesoamerica (McGuire and Villalpando 2011; Villalpando and McGuire 2009) or with the regional system centered at Paquimé (McGuire et al. 1999, 146).

Excavations during 1995 and 1996 recovered 3 metric tons (6,600 lb.) of local monochrome ceramics, almost 1.5 metric tons (3,300 lb.) of lithics, and a little more than 6 kg (13 lb.) of shell. There were also nonlocal materials like turquoise beads and pendants and several hundred decorated sherds, especially Ramos Polychrome, Bavícora Polychrome, and Carretas Polychrome, which petrographic analysis indicated were made with nonlocal clay (Gallaga 2011, 105–9).

It is evident that relations between Paquimé and Cerro de Trincheras could have occurred as Casas Grandes–related communities are numerous on the west side of the Sierra Madre Occidental. These probably formed part of the extensive interaction sphere proposed by Whalen and Minnis (2001).

Although it is not yet possible to precisely understand these interactions, they possibly expanded west to Ojo de Agua de Corodehuachi, which according to Braniff (1986, 1992), was a village with traits from the Casas Grandes Medio Period. Such traits included Playas Red textured ceramics and a macaw (*Ara militaris*) associated with an inhumation. These materials were indicative of old, strong relations with Arizona and New Mexico as part of the Serrana tradition in Sonora.

Casas Grandes polychrome ceramics have been identified in different sites excavated in the valleys of Cocóspera, Dolores, Cumpas, Bavispe, and Huachineras (Júpiter Martínez, personal communication, 2012). Casas Grandes–style architecture (adobe houses with T-shape doors inside cliff dwellings) and Viejo Period ceramics have been found very recently. This indicates an interaction between communities on both sides of the Sierra Madre before the consolidation of Paquimé during the Medio Period.

During the last decade, archaeological study at Cerro de Trincheras (Cruz et al. 2010; Villalpando, Cruz-Guzmán, and Nava-Maldonado 2010, 2011) has recovered more than 130 vessels containing many cremated individuals. A small portion of a cemetery located at the northern extension of the hill, known now as *Loma de las Cremaciones*, was excavated. Jars, seed jars, and bowls used as funerary vessels for human cremations, similar in shape to the varieties of the diagnostic local ceramic, were recovered. There were also some unusual vessels, one with a small body and wide neck, one oval-shaped with two holes, and another cucurbit-shaped. Neither decorated vessel was from the Trincheras tradition, nor did the Casas Grandes polychromes seem to have been used as funerary urns. However, inside one of them, which contained the remains of a teenager (Cerezo-Román et al. 2011), were four type IA5a copper bells (Vargas 1995). Another one of the same type was collected from the surface.

These are not the first copper bells reported for the Trincheras tradition area. Some of them were excavated by amateurs in another pre-Hispanic cemetery in the town of Atil (Villalpando 2001, 252) and correspond to the types IA1a-I and IC2a from phase II. Two more IA1a-I copper bells were identified, one in Ojo de Agua (Braniff 1992) and one more in San José Baviácora (Vargas 1995). These remains support our proposal for an east-west interaction axis coming from Paquimé to Trincheras, in this case by the presence of bells with Tláloc icons.[4]

Further evidence for relationships between Cerro de Trincheras and Paquimé comes from the northwestern part of Cerro de Trincheras (Villalpando et al. 2012). Several funerary pyre compounds have been excavated. Of the 17 vessels found in association to the pyres, 5 are Casas Grandes vessels: 2 Ramos Polychrome, 1 Carretas Polychrome, 1 Villa Ahumada Polychrome, and 1 Villa Ahumada. There were 2 additional polychrome vessels, a Nogales Polychrome and a Gila Polychrome, that were broken and just partially reconstructed. None of these vessels contained human remains as was the case for the funerary containers from the Loma de las Cremaciones. The apparently organic and oily content is still being analyzed.

The Diverse Interaction Models

There has been much discussion about the various modes of exchange that could have occurred at Paquimé, especially its relationships with Mesoamerica. Evidence of such interactions was located in diverse contexts in the city, such as by the enormous amount of shell and other items stored in rooms excavated by JCGE.[5]

Diverse models have been offered to explain the interactions among the U.S. Southwest, northwest Mexico, Paquimé, and Mesoamerica. Almost all of them consist of variations of the world systems theory, originally proposed by Wallerstein (1974, 1979) and later used by archaeologists at the end of the 1970s (Braniff 1992; Kelley 1986; Pailes and Whitecotton 1979). Such models emphasize monumental architecture and prestige items as the indicators of the regional interaction spheres that were incorporated by villages and towns who participated in the long-distance trade networks.

Wilcox, among others (Wilcox 1986; Wilcox et al. 2008), argues in favor of a "Tepiman connection." In other words, relations with a very long temporal depth between the Uto-Aztecan speakers who lived in communities were linked through time. The Tepiman language family is divided into two subfamilies: one includes the Pima and the Lower Pima (Arizona and Sonora), and the second one is the Tepehuano (Durango and Chihuahua). The language continuum could have been broken by intrusive Opata groups (e.g., Taracahitas), separating the Pimas from the Tepehuanes and other groups from the Sierra Madre Occidental.[6] This connection with the Paquimé regional system and the U.S. Southwest would not have been with western Mexico but with northern marginal Mesoamerican societies established in the valleys of Durango and Zacatecas.

This Tepiman connection has led some authors to propose questionable proposals because they believe that a displacement occurred from the Trincheras communities to the Tepehuana area. All this is supported by the construction of terraces in hills and because of a lithic technology with place of origin that cannot be explained (Berrojalbiz 2006; Hers 2001a).[7] Nevertheless, it is important to mention recent investigations by the senior author on the Loma San Gabriel (Foster 1985), an early ceramic period antecedent of the Chalchihuites development. Radiocarbon dates suggest a range of occupation dates at the multicomponent site of Cerro del Nayar of 50 BC–AD 1000, and in different parts of the Guadiana Valley, to the contact with the Spaniards in the sixteenth century.

Kelley (1986) postulated the concept of "Aztatlán mercantile system" as an explanation for the presence of what he considered Mesoamerican traits at Paquimé and the U.S. Southwest. This view has been adopted by other researchers who argue that Guasave, in Sinaloa, was a commercial exchange center that in turn was part of a large network of sites that interconnected the Mixteca-Puebla capital of Cholula with Paquimé and with distant territories in the U.S. Southwest. Most of these models emphasize the Mesoamerican political-economic relations over the regional groups, which supposedly were incorporated into the extended Mesoamerican dominion, and minimized the identity of the local groups.

Mountjoy (2000, 95), following Kelley (2000), has considered that the Aztatlan tradition was a "Mesoamerican" expansion, which was wide and relatively uniform, with extension into the western Mexico Coast. This tradition even impacted the northwestern central plateau, at least in Durango, where a ceremonial or civic center from the Aztatlan tradition, was established near the middle part of each important coastal valley between Jalisco and Sinaloa's northern border. These centers were also located inland on strategic communication and commerce routes.[8]

Kelley sees a strong relation between the Aztatlan tradition and the Chalchihuites culture, especially in the Guadiana valley and in the Guatimapé lagoon, in the substantial quantity of ceramic sherds in La Ferrería and Cañón del Molino. As previously mentioned, recent works in the Guadiana valley have documented, through petrographic studies, a strong interaction between both regions. Evidence of this is the presence of Lolandis or Red Rim sherds—produced in the valley—in sites on the southern coast and sherds produced on the coast in Guadiana Valley sites.

Following this proposal and a lack of archaeological evidence to demonstrate such a route, most of Sonora would have been outside Aztatlan (Kelley 2000).[9] All maps of these routes generally exclude most of Sonora (Weigand 2003; Weigand and Harbottle 1993; Wilcox et al. 2008). Nevertheless, it is very probable that an interaction route from the north and south of western Mexico to Paquimé existed through the mountain range and the intermountainous valleys.

Carpenter (Carpenter et al. 2010) has termed this route "the road to Paquimé," considering that the *despoblado* (inhabited area), which many colonial documents mention and includes area from the Rio Yaqui to the Rio Sonora in its west trajectory, might have been also insignificant in pre-Hispanic communication (Pailes and Reff 1985; Pailes and Whitecotton 1979; Riley 1982, 1999). There were certainly other routes.

In this sense, the coastal interaction corridor between western Mexico and Paquimé would not have followed the entire Gulf of California coast. It may have ended at the Rio El Fuerte, and from there, it would have changed into an interior corridor, as proposed by Carpenter and colleagues (Carpenter and Sánchez 2007a; Carpenter et al. 2010; Carpenter et al. 2011). They have identified two pre-Hispanic exchange routes in this region: one would have used the Álamo stream (also known as Cuchujaqui), and the other would have followed the Janalicahui stream, which runs 20 km parallel to the west of the Alamos stream. These authors also propose the possibility that both routes would have come together in the town of Cuchujaqui, Sonora. The route which passed through the Alamos stream was probably controlled by the Tehueco. Meanwhile, the route that used the Janalicahui stream would have been controlled by the Sinaloa people. It is useful to emphasize that during the colonial period, both routes were recognized as *caminos reales*.

Prestige goods economy is another theoretical model that has been applied to explain the relation for long-distance trade among diverse archaeological traditions (Bradley 1999; Foster 1986; McGuire 1980, 1987; McGuire and Howard 1987; Nelson 1981, 1986). These models emphasize the exchange of special or exotic goods used by elites to gain status and/or power (Nelson 1981). This does not necessarily mean that all power groups would have been connected directly, because the elite from one area could have exchanged some goods with the power groups of its neighbors, using the items as symbols of ostentation to validate their domains.

This could have occurred among the farming communities of the Sonora Desert and the Casas Grandes regional system. Therefore, the presence of Paquimé's polychrome ceramics at Cerro de Trincheras would have had exceptional value for the people who possessed them. Possibly they were related to the power group in Cerro de Trincheras. Thus, when the individual who owned them passed away, these items would have been retired from circulation and incorporated into a sacred funerary context. This value was given to the rest of the offerings, such as where the copper bells were found.

Neither Di Peso (1974, vols. 1–3) nor Whalen and Minnis (2009a) considered that interaction between Paquimé and Trincheras was important. However, it is possible that a significant amount of shell from the Gulf of California would have been transported through an east-west interaction axis, associating the Trincheras economy from the coast through the valleys of Altar, Cocóspera, and Fronteras with the

Paquimé

Casas Grandes communities from the Sierra Madre Occidental. These foreign goods likely arrived in Paquimé as finished ornaments (see Rakita and Cruz, this volume).

We are able to suggest that these foreign goods would have been traded for the polychrome ceramics as part of power strategies in middle rank societies and based on the economic and ideological control of the shells as prestige items (although they are considered to have "little value" [Whalen and Minnis 2009a, 5]). The iconography of the ceramics has attributes that could have been ideologically meaningful to the power groups of both regional centers.

It is interesting to point out that production of Trincheras vessels decorated with specular hemitate apparently ceased during Cerro de Trincheras occupation. We could propose that during the exchange of these sumptuary goods among the elite groups from both communities, Paquimé demand of specular hematite (Whalen and Minnis 2009a, 248) could have caused the end of Trincheras tradition painted ceramics. In reciprocity, they would obtain polychrome vessels for specular hematite and the marine shells as finished ornaments or as raw material.

In this way, the power hierarchy of the Cerro de Trincheras elite would have been reinforced via access to some sumptuary goods (e.g., polychrome ceramics and copper bells). These are some artifacts associated with social hierarchy postulated that Lightfoot (1984) and Whalen and Minnis (2009a, 9–11) note are found at Paquimé that represent the "funds of power." These could include intensification of the subsistence products, large-volume storage ceramics, a range of prestige goods, authority and power symbols in the architecture, and funerary treatment.

Some Concluding Thoughts

There is no concrete evidence during the Medio Period of the existence of a mercantile system along a south-north axis that moved Mesoamerican items between the heart of Mesoamerica and the U.S. Southwest with Paquimé and Chalchihuites as key nodes on this network.[10]

The best indicators of long-distance trade routes during this period come from the western slope of the Sierra Madre Occidental and from the Pacific Ocean coastal fringe, where sites which would have participated in a Pacific Coast trade network can be identified. Such sites could be Amapa, Guasave, Mochicahui, and recently, Rincón de Buyubampo (Carpenter and Sánchez 2007a, 2007b; Carpenter et al. 2010; Carpenter, Sánchez, and Vicente 2011), where there has been found undeniable evidence of their participation in long-distance trade.

It is also noted that by the end of the sixteenth century, the Spaniards observed a great quantity of merchandise moving to the coastal plains, including turquoise, copper, shell, cotton cloths, feathers, maize, animal skins, and slaves (Di Peso 1974:8, 192; Riley 1982).

Although foreign objects indicate the existence of trade, these do not support the idea of a Mesoamerican mercantilism and exploitation as an explanation of the pre-Hispanic development in northern Mexico. It seems more acceptable to us that the acquisition of nonlocal goods reflect a prestige goods economy (McGuire 1987; McGuire and Howard 1987), which results from the intensification of the social relations among societies of similar rank.

This could be considered a consequence rather than the cause of the evident differentiation in the social relations of the pre-Hispanic communities established in the area. On the other hand, these are long-occupied pre-Hispanic communities based on complex networks of economic factors and reciprocal relations among social groups which comprised a very wide interaction rank and several degrees of a wide regional and interregional integration that were modified through time.

Northern Mexico was a dynamic territory during the pre-Hispanic period where human groups had much interaction and movement across the landscape, establishing possible long-distance relations that changed over time.

Notes

1. Di Peso mentions that these materials are from Chalchihuites during the Tunal/Calera phase, according to Kelley's personal communication in May, 1964 (Di Peso, Rinaldo, and Fenner 1974:2, 703).

2. Columns with disks, *atalayas* (circular structures on top of the hills), buildings with multiple-story earthen architecture, buried vessels with pendants, effigy and phytomorphic vessels, copper bells, rectangular metates, stone phallus, stone balls, *Glycymeris* bracelets, horned-snake iconography, bird men, bird snake, stepped-fret patterns, and chess motif decoration.

3. Generally known in the United States as the Schroeder site, which J. Charles Kelley named after the last name of the person who took him to the site, and who was one of the main looters of the settlement.

4. Even though the formal attributes like the big rings surrounding the eyes and the dentate mouth, that in Mesoamerica is the bow compass, are also present in the Hopi deity of earth and death, *Masau*, who controls the path to the underworld and is represented as a skull (Schaafsma 1999, 173).

5. These materials, such as the quadrangular grinding metates or the millions of *Nassarius* shells, are currently in the Museo de las Culturas del Norte at Paquimé.

6. Taking into account the linguistic data, Miller (1983) and Moctezuma Zamarrón (personal communication, 2009) have allowed Carpenter, Sánchez, and Vicente (2011, 5) to suggest that it is very probable that the Cahita speakers were already established in the coastal plains before the Christian era, and that the Tepimanos were a late intrusion around the second century, arriving possibly from the north.

7. It is not possible since there are already examples of terraces in Durango in early phases (AD 600–900).

8. Interactions among diverse areas of western Mexico and the U.S. Southwest have followed a south-north axis. This axis physiographically corresponds to the tropical lowlands, which include the Balsas-Tepalcatepec basins and the coastal plains of Nayarit and Sinaloa, as well as the Sierra Madre Occidental (Gorenstein and Foster 2000, 10). Sinaloa and Sonora, as well as Arizona, correspond to the extra-tropical dry lands.

9. Recent excavations in Ónavas, in the middle part of the Rio Yaqui have recovered more than 20 human inhumations, some of them with cranial deformation and shell ornaments with meaningfully different styles from the Sonoran and Southwestern techniques. These data could link this area to some interaction routes from western Mexico to the north. However, there is no element that suggests this bond with Paquimé because the decorated ceramics recovered in Ónavas have not been identified as Casas Grandes polychromes, and they probably have a more southern affiliation (Cristina García, personal communication, 2012).

10. It definitely did not exist in the Medio Period of Paquimé. In relation to Chalchihuites, we cannot affirm this for previous periods, and what is more important is that the Chalchihuites influences are a different matter and do not correspond to the route proposed by Carpenter and Sánchez for the Medio Period.

9

Ancient Paquimé
A View from the North
Linda S. Cordell

The impressive archaeological site of Casas Grandes in northern Chihuahua, Mexico, has been described as a manifestation of both U.S. Southwest and Mesoamerican archaeological features. The organizers of the seminar tasked me with commenting on the conference papers and Casas Grandes from my perspective, which, given my background in Rio Grande Ancestral Pueblo archaeology, is surely a view from the North. Fortunately, Punzo and Villalpando (this volume) offer their perspective from the South. Two views are appropriate because of the nature of the site itself, and because most of what we know about Casas Grandes derives from the Joint Casas Grandes Expedition ([JCGE] 1958–1961), a collaboration between Eduardo Contreras of Instituto Nacional de Antropología e Historia and Charles Di Peso of the Amerind Foundation with institutional support and intellectual guidance from *ambos lados de la frontera* ("both sides of the border").

As we have learned over the 40 years since the appearance of the JCGE publications, Di Peso's *Gran Chichimeca* is best understood as its own place separate from Mesoamerica and the Colorado Plateau's portion of the U.S. Southwest (Braniff 2001), yet interacting with both, as well as with western Mexico and the Rio Grande regions. Ideas from ambos lados in this volume are crucial. I comment briefly on older, yet highly influential interpretations of Casas Grandes and emphasize how recent research discussed in the preceding chapters requires modification of those older understandings. I recontextualize Casas Grandes in its region and time.

Di Peso's Archaeohistory of Casas Grandes

Di Peso's achievements as an archaeologist, analyst, and synthesizer of data cannot be overemphasized (see papers in Woosley and Ravesloot

1993). In the first three volumes of his Casas Grandes reports (Di Peso 1974, vols. 1–3), Di Peso wrote a vivid, engaging history of the rise and fall of the site of Casas Grandes as he thought it occurred enmeshed—as histories are—in the political landscape of northwest Mexico and the U.S. Southwest (NW/SW), the region he termed *La Gran Chichimeca*. Di Peso gave the name Paquimé to Casas Grandes specifically referring to the site as a "city," an urban center related to Tula or Tenochtitlán, the Toltec and Aztec capitals. He described Paquimé as a mercantile trading outpost of an unspecified Mesoamerican state from which goods, especially turquoise, were sent south to central Mexico, and copper bells, macaw feathers, and perhaps macaws themselves were sent north in exchange. Di Peso viewed the merchant system as having been imbedded in and facilitated by Mesoamerican ideologies that would have been attractive to people in the north. He thought the Mesoamerican traders also brought practical knowledge, such as how to construct and maintain canal irrigation systems (Di Peso 1974, vol. 2).

Di Peso was confident about his archaeohistory, because he had done careful stratigraphic excavations, worked backward through the early historic and protohistoric sequences in southern Arizona, and used both tree-ring and radiocarbon dates from his excavations at Casas Grandes. Nevertheless, Di Peso's dates for the Medio Period at Casas Grandes, when major developments at the site occurred, were off by about 250 years (Dean and Ravesloot 1993; Whalen and Minnis 2009a). Di Peso erroneously considered Casas Grandes contemporary with the eleventh-century Bonito phase in Chaco Canyon and with the Chalchuites culture site of Alta Vista in Zacatecas. Revised dates for Casas Grandes are 1250 to 1450, so Paquimé is much later than either of these (Punzo and Villalpando, this volume; Whalen and Minnis 2009a).

Di Peso chronicled the development of Paquimé over time. He thought that during the Buena Fe phase at the beginning of the Medio Period, Paquimé consisted of a series of 20 independent but associated adobe-walled houses in clusters, each with an open plaza area surrounded by an enclosing wall, rather like Late Classic Period Hohokam sites in the Phoenix Basin. Later in the Paquimé phase, still within the Medio Period, Paquimé was reorganized and rebuilt with multistory adobe complexes. About half the site was allocated for public and ceremonial use as indicated by ball courts, platform and effigy mounds, a walk-in well, a reservoir, a system of slab-covered stone drains, and an open area that Di Peso called a marketplace. These public and ceremonial areas were placed outside the residential core. The Paquimé phase was to have been a time during which Paquimé was the center of trading activities between the NW/SW and Mesoamerica, with artisan-citizens laboring in workshops to fashion desired objects for Mesoamerican elite classes from raw materials extracted from the surrounding populations, especially those to the north and west. Di Peso described the later occupation of Paquimé, which he named the Diablo phase, as a time when two and a half generations watched the magnificent city fall into disrepair. Artisan-citizens continued to produce an abundance of marketable goods, but civil construction and public maintenance nearly ceased. The total population, however, may have increased. Domestic living space was expanded by subdividing some rooms and by altering and subdividing open public space. Square-columned galleries were walled off and subdivided into rooms. Some former plaza drains became burial sites, and the well was no longer used (Di Peso 1974: 2, 319). This description of the Diablo phase is rather like the end of the Classic Period Hohokam site of Pueblo Grande, near Phoenix (Abbott 2003).

At Paquimé, architectural features include massive walls, T-shaped doorways, raised hearths, galleries fronted by square columns, and adobe stairways. This combination of architectural features was thought to have been unique to fourteenth-century Paquimé. Recent excavations at Tinaja pueblo and other sites in the Casas Grandes valley revealed thirteenth-century examples. One house compound at Paquimé contained rows of rectangular macaw breeding boxes, and remains of these (cage door stones) are also now known from some nearby earlier sites (Dean and Ravesloot 1993; Di Peso 1974, vol. 2; Whalen and Minnis 2003).

The enormous quantity of artifacts excavated from Paquimé includes utilitarian objects and materials made or obtained locally as well as items from distant sources. Imported materials included marine shell, redrock ricolite (serpentine), copper, turquoise, and scarlet macaws. Nearly 4 million shell artifacts (weighing 1,325 kg), were recovered at Paquimé, many of them from contexts that Di Peso considered workshops. Paquimé yielded almost 15 kg of copper, including 688 artifacts that were made by a variety of techniques, such as cold hammering and lost wax casting. Turquoise was less abundant than other minerals at

Paquimé, but 2.2 kg of turquoise were recovered, mostly from rooms that Di Peso thought were warehouses. Ramos Polychrome is a distinctive pottery type that was widely traded and was once thought to have been produced only at Paquimé. Compositional studies indicate that the Ramos Polychrome made at Paquimé was distributed to communities within a radius of about 75 km (50 mi.). Outside that limit, people at sites with Ramos Polychrome made the pottery locally or obtained it from other sources in the region. Di Peso and others propose that Ramos Polychrome at Paquimé was made by craft-specialists. It is argued that other specialists bred macaws, raised turkeys, processed agave, and made large basalt metates (Di Peso 1974, vol. 2; Lekson 1992; Rakita and Cruz this volume, Woosley and Olinger 1993; Whalen and Minnis 2009a).

Problems with Archaeohistory

Whalen and Minnis (2003, 2009a) knowledgeably critique the archaeohistory from the perspective of the Casas Grandes region. Punzo and Villalpando (this volume) describe substantive problems with Di Peso's scenario with data from Zacatecas and Sonora. I refer readers to their discussions. I object to archaeohistory for theoretical and practical reasons. From a theoretical perspective, archaeohistory is not explanatory (Spaulding 1968). Historical explanations are based upon common knowledge and are not sufficient because they do not specify the conditions under which what we observe is likely to occur in societies different from our own. My practical objection to archaeohistory is that if the chronology is wrong, so is the story. Narratives depend upon time lines. If one event is designated as a cause of another event, it must precede the second event in time. If an event is described as having happened because appropriate conditions came together, then those conditions also must be present at the same time. As McGuire (2011) wisely cautions, analysis needs to be historically contextualized correctly. Di Peso's archaeohistoric scenario fails these requirements.

What We have Learned

The research conducted by and reported in the contributions to this volume have been carried out since Di Peso's (Di Peso, Rinaldo, and Fenner 1974, vols. 4–8) publications on Casas Grandes and most since the first professional retrospective look at Di Peso's Casas Grandes studies (Woosley and Ravesloot 1993). The new research referenced in the preceding chapters encompasses long-term field projects that include both survey and excavation in the Casas Grandes Valley and neighboring areas in northwest Chihuahua. These include work by Kelley and MacWilliams and their colleagues (Kelley and MacWilliams 2005; Kelley, Burd-Larkin, and Hendrickson 2004; Newell and Gallaga 2001); Whalen, Minnis, and their colleagues (Whalen and Minnis 2001, 2009a); Cruz (Cruz and Maxwell 1999; Maxwell 2002; Rakita and Cruz, this volume); Pitezel (Pitezel 2007); and C. VanPool, T. VanPool and Leonard (VanPool, VanPool, and Leonard 2005). The new research also includes important laboratory analyses of collections, such as those by Rakita (2009), C. VanPool (2001, 2003), T. VanPool and Leonard (T. Van Pool and Leonard 2002), Phillips (2012), and Cruz and colleagues (see Rakita and Cruz, this volume). This book also contains summaries of and references to recent research in Zacatecas and Sonora, Mexico (Punzo and Villalpando, this volume) that reveal the contexts within which Casas Grandes developed and the likely places with which its residents were in interaction. Because so much of Di Peso's finely crafted archaeohistory is undermined by new information from the field and the laboratory, the time is right to reflect on what this new work means.

Chronology is still a major problem. An abbreviated list of talking points for future collaborative research related to chronology that emerged from the Amerind seminar would include the following problems: 1) Maize agriculture and Early Agricultural Period monumental cerros de trincheras constructions are quite well documented for Chihuahua (Fish, Fish, and Villalpando 2007). Nevertheless, the Viejo Period in northwest Chihuahua is not well dated (Kelley and Searcy, this volume). There are problems of site visibility. Viejo Period sites have been found under later, Medio Period, architecture. Remnants of Viejo Period sites have been found nearly destroyed by modern agriculture. Most authors in this volume agree that the Viejo Period occupation of the Casas Grandes region was larger than is documented, large enough to account for the early Medio Period population at Casas Grandes. Until we have dates for more Viejo Period components, this likely assumption remains unresolved. The lack of resolution is important because there is continuing debate about whether or not the founders of Casas Grandes were local or if they were migrants, and if the latter, from which direction they might have come. 2) The timing (abrupt or gradual) of the transition from the Viejo to Medio Period is largely unknown. 3) The phases Di Peso outlined for the Medio Period are not adequately dated. We do not know that Paquimé initially consisted of about 20 clustered house mounds that were suddenly transformed into an organized, multistory settlement with public architecture. We do not have confidence in construction and occupation sequences of the excavated portions of the site, and much of the site remains unexcavated (Whalen, MacWilliams, and Pitezel 2010). 4) We do not know when Paquimé met its end. We do not know over what period of time Paquimé fell into disrepair or how sudden and complete its final destruction may have been. We do not know the relative size of Paquimé over time. Finally, we do not know if there were remnant populations from Paquimé in potential areas of refuge (Phillips and Gamboa, this volume).

Problems of site size over time and of regional site distribution over time are not unique to northwest Chihuahua. Indeed they are common to the NW/SW as a whole. These problems, however, do prevent writing narrative archaeohistory. The good news is that we now know that the major occupation at Casas Grandes dates between AD 1250 and 1450, which enables meaningful comparison with most of the northern NW/SW, including the Rio Grande region. The 1250 to 1450 dating encourages evaluating Casas Grandes in the context of newer models of organization among Pueblo peoples and their contemporaries during the Protohistoric Period (Adams and Duff 2004).

Casas Grandes in the Long Fourteenth Century: From the North

The Ancestral Pueblo world and much of the NW/SW were transformed between about AD 1250 and 1475. This period was characterized by population movement, as people left vast areas of the northern and western U.S. Southwest and founded new communities, some in places where there were previously few year-round residents. New settlements were created that were larger than any previously known in the region.

Distinctive pan-regional art styles developed that are visible in painted pottery, textiles, petroglyphs, pictographs, and rare kiva murals. Perhaps most dramatic was movement of peoples across the landscape. For the region as a whole, this took place gradually, over about 250 years. In smaller geographic areas, movement could be quite rapid. Mesa Verde is the prime example, with depopulation taking place there in about two human generations (Spielmann 2004; Wilshusen 2002). By AD 1300, the Mesa Verde, San Juan Basin, and Four Corners regions were largely depopulated. By about 1400, most of the Western Pueblo region, except the Hopi, Zuni, and Acoma areas, was no longer permanently occupied. The Mogollon highlands and Mimbres Valley also saw population loss in the early fourteenth century, while population increased in northern Chihuahua and the Rio Grande, Salinas, and Jornada Mogollon regions. The revised dating of Casas Grandes to between 1250 and 1450 places it firmly within this tumultuous time (Cordell and Habicht-Mauche 2012b, 2).

In general, the population centers of the NW/SW shifted from northwest to southeast, and there is little to no agreement among archaeologists about why this happened. Following Fish, Fish, and Gumerman (1994), I argued (Cordell 1997), as does Rakita (2009), that the distribution of population after depopulation of the far north and west reflects population growth in those areas where irrigation agriculture is possible. However, there seems to be little correlation between this kind of agricultural technology and population increase, which belies simple cause and effect in linking these movements to underlying climate and rainfall patterns. For example, despite its long tradition of irrigation agriculture, the Hohokam heartland was largely unoccupied after 1450. Some areas saw unexpected expansion of upland rainfall-fed fields after 1300, for example the Rio Chama, the Galisteo Basin, the Salinas district, and the Jornada Mogollon region (Boyer et al. 2010; Graves 2004; Kelley 1984; Lekson, Bletzer, and MacWilliams 2004; Snead, Creamer, and Van Zandt 2004). The upland agricultural terraces in the Casas Grandes region (Doolittle 1993; Minnis and Whalen, this volume; Whalen and Minnis 2009a; Minnis, Whalen, and Howell 2006) along with the relatively late development of irrigation fits the larger northern pattern perfectly.

I think we need a better understanding of how immigration and agricultural intensification took place in the NW/SW, a region known for unpredictable weather patterns. A key question for me relates to understanding the circumstances under which it makes sense to claim land, intensify agricultural production, and enforce rules of land tenure when the productivity of specific plots of land is not reliable. Not only is precipitation spatially unpredictable, making dry-land farming risky, but irrigated fields may be lost to devastating floods. For example, the Rio Grande villages of Santo Domingo and San Marcial were each destroyed by flooding several times during the nineteenth and early twentieth centuries. Dry land fields must have the right amount of rainfall at appropriate times. In addition to examining upland farming as political economy (Minnis, Whalen, and Howell 2006), the Casas Grandes area, the Jornada Mogollon, Salinas, and the Rio Grande regions are places for archaeologists to investigate basic past agricultural modes of production where neither rainfall nor river flows are reliable.

In most views (Di Peso 1974, vol. 2; Lekson 2008, 208–9; Lekson, Bletzer, and MacWilliams 2004), Casas Grandes is described as planned and off the scale in size for a pueblo. A careful re-evaluation of site maps, architecture, and Di Peso's excavation strategy at Paquimé (Whalen, MacWilliams, and Pitezel 2010) provide evidence that convinces me that Paquimé had about 1,130 rooms, or about half what Di Peso originally estimated. The restudy, along with evaluation of the distribution of Ramos Polychrome at Paquimé (Whalen and Minnis 2012), do not support the integrity of distinct Buena Fe and Paquimé phase constructions at the site.

At slightly more than 1,000 rooms, Casas Grandes is not unique among Ancestral Pueblo sites of the 1400s and 1500s. In the Rio Chama, Ponsipa'akari had more than 2,000, as did Pose'ouinge. Sapawe had about 2,524 rooms and Poshuouinge 1,800 rooms. South of Santa Fe, in the Galisteo Basin, Pueblo San Marcos had an estimated 2,500 rooms, Pueblo She and Pueblo Blanco, more than 1,500 rooms apiece. The Ancestral Pueblo site of Kuaua, near Albuquerque, encompassed about 1,700 rooms, and Arroyo Hondo Pueblo, near Santa Fe, 1,100 rooms. Continuing south and east, Gran Quivira in the Salinas area contained more than 1,000 ground floor rooms as did Tenabo. Abo had an estimated 500 to 1,000 rooms. To the west, the ancestral Zuni sites of Archaeotekopa II and Heshotauthla had 1,412 and 875 rooms, respectively, although survey data of room counts are known to be inaccurate and on the low side. The ancestral Hopi site of Homol'ovi II had 1,200 rooms. It is difficult to count rooms for the Classic Period in the Hohokam area, because people lived both in pithouses and above ground rooms. Nevertheless, Classic Period Hohokam irrigation communities such as Pueblo Grande, Casa Grande, Los Muertos, and Marana are estimated to have housed about 2,400 to 3,000 residents apiece (see Cordell and McBrinn 2012, 247–48 for references). In the context of Ancestral Pueblo population aggregation of the fourteenth and fifteenth centuries, Paquimé's size is not unique. Further, Paquimé is not unique among large Ancestral Pueblo sites in very different environments in the central and southern Rio Grande or among some Classic Period Hohokam sites in the Arizona deserts.

We must all do better at estimating the numbers of people who lived at large sites at any one time. The numbers problem is recognized for many sites, such as Casas Grandes, that have public architecture that was not used as domestic space. We are also aware that some of our best examples of planned architecture, such as Pueblo Bonito, assumed their classic configurations only over many centuries. Given the lack of chronological precision for building sequences at Paquimé (Whalen and Minnis 2012), we must wonder how massive and organized the change from Buena Fe to Paquimé phases actually was.

Deriving population or occupation estimates for fourteenth-century sites, even those without public architecture, is a continuing challenge. Today, modern Rio Grande Pueblo villages, without planned multi-story structures (for example, Santa Clara, Ohkay Owingeh, Santo Domingo) often have sections or room blocks that are two stories high (Stubbs 1950). Only portions of Paquimé may have had multistories (Whalen, MacWilliams, and Pitezel 2010). Tijeras Pueblo, a smallish (250 rooms) site east of Albuquerque that both Jim Judge and I excavated, yielded 462 tree-ring dates. Both Judge and I, separately, postulated one or more complete hiatuses in the occupation of the site, until Nicholas Damp and I plotted tree-ring cutting dates and their locations. We found that there was no time between 1313 and the 1390s when there was not construction—hence presumably people living—in some part of the site (Cordell and Damp 2010).

As archeologists move to use our robust new databases (the VEP, Coalescent Community Data Base, tDAR), we need to be mindful of improving accuracy and precision in estimating the sizes of simultaneous site occupations. In an otherwise excellent recent volume (Kohler, Varien, and Wright 2010) contributors use entirely different techniques to estimate population, which leads only to confusion. It might be fruitful to explore population growth models developed by Bocquet-Appel for the Neolithic Demographic Transition (Kohler et al. 2008; Kowalewski 2003). We might compare the demographic profile of communities during various phases of growth, for example, between Buena Fe, Paquimé, and Diablo phases at Paquimé. I understand that the NTD measures must be used with caution. Nevertheless, Paquimé could serve as a case study of method because the NTD methods could be compared with the fertility measure (Buikstra, Konigsberg, and Bullington 1986) Rakita (2009) employed.

Between AD 1250 and 1475, new ceramic styles were made in the NW/SW that used color and iconic imagery in innovative ways that do not appear to have had precedents in the earlier regional corpus of decorated pottery. The pottery, polychrome and glaze-paint decorated wares, are compositionally and technologically complex. Their production, distribution, and use involved activating multiple social networks at various scales. In a recent edited volume (Cordell and Habicht-Mauche 2012a), contributors investigate these networks by using a variety of archaeological, archaeometric, ethnoarchaeological, and experimental techniques to trace patterns of raw material acquisition, to reconstruct production techniques and sequences, to define and compare local and regional technological and decorative styles, and to start to model local and regional patterns of distribution and deposition of these styles and wares. In this context, the Chihuahuan polychromes are one of a set (Phillips 2012). It should come as no surprise that these wares were produced in many different locations, were exchanged and copied, and relied upon complicated social networks that at times spanned very large geographic areas within the NW/SW. Ramos and Babicora polychromes can and should be seen in this larger context.

Fourteenth-century iconography painted on the pottery, woven in textiles, depicted in rock art, and rare kiva murals have received far more scholarly attention thus far than has production technology. The attention to design and iconography owes much to Patricia Crown's (1994) studies of the Salado Polychrome and her proposed "Southwest regional cult." Crown considered the ideology of Salado Polychrome decoration to have been essentially egalitarian, serving to integrate people from diverse ethnic backgrounds across an enormous area. She also suggested that there were other, contemporary ideologies, such as those related to katcina beliefs and rituals, that were more closely related to iconography derived from Mesoamerica—reflected in Ramos Polychrome. Pottery is seen as serving an integrating function for formerly disparate peoples—not through trade or exchange of an elite good—but as manifesting shared identity at public rituals, most particularly feasting (e.g., Mills 2007). Crown's view does not preclude a hierarchically organized system for Paquimé. Rakita (2009, 154) follows the notion that rival cults do not have to supplant one another. Rather a great number of redundant belief systems and ritual organizations coexist simultaneously. If these are not arranged in a hierarchical fashion, they would fit a definition of heterarchical complexity. I think we must allow for these possibilities for the suggested Southwestern ideological systems.

It is interesting that there is heterogeneity in the ways in which particular iconographies functioned in their respective systems. Defining a regional cult vs. an ancestor cult is a distinction that reflects dual processual models of hierarchical complexity (Mills 2000). Rakita's (2009) suggestion that the two kinds of cults could or should be found in the same community offers a productive entry to studying origins of social complexity. On the Pajarito Plateau and nearby Galisteo Basin of the northern Rio Grande, widespread iconography (on so-called biscuit ware) reflects specialized production and also exchange of enormous quantities of vessels over extensive areas (Shepard 1936). Kohler, Herr, and Root (2004) link this specialized production to market exchanges, suggesting markets without money using a Latin American model of village markets that are specialized and temporally organized. For example, a market generally occurs in a particular day of the week. Productive specialization in pottery manufacture is also documented for the Rio Grande glazes (Schleher, Huntley, and Herhahn 2012), although the ways in which the glaze wares were exchanged were likely different that those of biscuit ware.

There are other explorations of fourteenth-century iconography. Christine VanPool, especially links much Ramos iconography to shamanism, and Sikyatki iconography has been linked to the Flower World (Hays-Gilpin and LeBlanc 2007). These approaches offer insights into the possible role of iconography in integrating various peoples by exploring what the icons may have meant, and they are fascinating. For example, C. VanPool notes that the snake motifs on Ramos vessels represent snake species local to the Casas Grandes area and not those of Mesoamerica, therefore showing that this aspect of iconography was not the result of foreign Mesoamerican religious ideology. Yet it is not the intent of these studies to link the inferred meanings of icons with particular kinds of political or social formulations.

All that Stuff: Craft Production at Casas Grandes

Di Peso characterized Paquimé as a mercantile center where craftsmen labored to produce finished objects for Mesoamerican elites. In their thoughtful analysis Rakita and Cruz (this volume), examine the potential manufacture at Paquimé of shell, turquoise, agave, polychrome pottery, basalt metates, macaws, and turkeys. They note that most of the shell consists of only slightly modified gastropod beads that might have required only some coordinated acquisition, and they suggest Cerro de Trincheras of Sonora as a likely source. Punzo and Villalpando (this volume) concur regarding the source and make the important additional point that Cerro de Trincheras and Paquimé are contemporary. Rakita and Cruz further note that most of the beads from burial contexts at Casas Grandes are from the Viejo Period, rather than Medio Period, burial contexts. This observation is in accord with a general observation from the north, where the most abundant shell from Colorado Plateaus sites are in early (Late Basketmaker) contexts (Cordell and McBrinn 2012, 183). For the loci at Paquimé where there appears to be cached or stored shell, it might be possible to use accelerator mass spectrometry dating on samples to see if these were accumulated over time. In any case, there appears to have been no shell-production workshops at Paquimé. An important point made by Punzo and Villalpando is that there seems to be a negative correlation between Cerros and Paquimé in that when shell is abundant at Cerros de Trincheras, it is less so at Paquimé and vice versa.

Turquoise is not as abundant as shell at Paquimé, and Rakita and Cruz (this volume) point out that the limited evidence of manufacture of turquoise objects comes from the central part of the site where it may have been associated with ritual activities. In fact, most of the turquoise at Paquimé came from the ceremonial cache at the bottom of the reservoir. They conclude that Paquimé was a consumer of turquoise rather than a production center. Turquoise is ubiquitous though rare elsewhere in the region except for the sites of Los Patos and Villa Ahumada where there is abundant evidence of turquoise artifact production. As yet, we do not know the geological provenance of the Chihuahuan turquoise, although some is being tested (Timothy D. Maxwell, personal communication, 2013). It may be of interest that there are few finished turquoise pieces from Galisteo Basin and the Central Rio Grande sites, which are near turquoise sources in the Cerrillos Hills and date to the fourteenth and fifteenth centuries when production centers may have shifted to Chihuahua, although probably to Los Patos or Villa Ahumada and not Paquimé. The absence of turquoise in sites close to mines in New Mexico may reflect a similar negative correlation in timing to the shell exchange that Punzo and Villalpando (this volume) note between Cerro de Trincheras, Sonora, and Paquimé. As is noted for glaze-paint, decorated pottery, proximity to source, in that case lead, does not indicate place of manufacture (Cordell and Habicht-Mauche 2012b).

The authors in this volume concur with Victoria Vargas's (1995) analysis that there is no evidence of copper manufacture at Paquimé and that copper from the NW/SW in general came from western Mexico. While I have no reason to doubt this conclusion, it would be useful, I think, to develop provenance studies of copper ore. Copper in the form of malachite was widely used as a pigment among fourteenth-century Ancestral Pueblos, and it is often a constituent of fourteenth-century glaze paint (Cordell and Habicht-Mauche 2012a). Copper ore is common in the Sandia and Manzano Mountains, and in the Cerrillos Hills. The one copper bell found at Pottery Mound, south of Albuquerque, is of a type thought to have come from Paquimé (Vargas 1995).

Agave production is inferred from the large roasting pits that could have accommodated thousands of pounds of agave. While I have no reason to doubt the capacity of the roasting pits, there seems to be no evidence of what quantities (or what commodities) were being roasted at one time. Di Peso (cited in Rakita and Cruz, this volume) wrote of lenses of fire cracked stone. Roasting pits with lenses of stone, carefully excavated from Henderson Pueblo, near Roswell (Speth 2008) have been shown to represent intermittent firings. We do not know the periodicity of roasting events at Paquimé, nor do we know when or if agave was grown in the nearby upland terraced fields. Finally, there is no evidence that large, formal, basalt metates were fabricated at Paquimé. Indeed, like turquoise and copper, Paquimé may have been a consumer of basalt metates rather than a production center. Communal grinding areas are suggested for Paquimé as they are for many Ancestral Pueblo sites (Cordell and McBrinn 2012, 250–90; Rakita and Cruz, this volume). Specialist production of Ramos Polychrome at Paquimé, also unlikely, was discussed above. Interestingly, Rakita and Cruz (this volume) find more evidence for uniformity in Gila Polychrome from Paquimé, especially in a cache of 49 vessels. For a variety of reasons, I am not persuaded that uniformity is a good indicator of craft specialization. See Schleher (2010) for alternative observations for pottery. I do find the cache of vessels intriguing, perhaps suggesting objects belonging to a particular sodality.

Paquimé does seem to have been a center for aviculture, particularly of scarlet and military macaws, although one with precedents in the region (Minnis et al. 1993; Whalen and Minnis 2001). Successfully breeding macaws would require specialist knowledge and might well have been the purview of one ritual sodality. I am less impressed by an argument for similar expert knowledge regarding turkeys.

Some Last Words

In sum, I find little evidence that Paquimé was a city, nor that the site housed artisan citizens of a mercantile trading center supplying goods to Mesoamerican elites. Rather, I view Paquimé as similar in size and complexity to some Ancestral Pueblo communities of the central and southern Rio Grande, Salinas, and Zuni regions. Unlike some of the conference presenters, I am not inclined to categorize Paquimé as a particular kind of site. In an informal show of hands, most of those at the seminar agreed that Paquimé was a "pilgrimage center." I disagreed on the grounds that I do not know what such a designation means. I see a great deal of heterogeneity among Ancestral Pueblo communities of the long fourteenth century, and I recognize similar variety among modern

Pueblos. As I write this in January, I think of my recent experiences at the Pueblo of Zuni for Shalako and at Ohkay Owingeh Pueblo for the Turtle Dance. The public aspect of Shalako is a multiday ceremony held around the time of the winter solstice. The Turtle Dance is currently performed at Ohkay Owingeh on December 26. Both Zuni and Ohkay Owingeh are Pueblos with resident populations; somewhat over 6,000 at Zuni and about 3,300 at Ohkay Owingeh. People live there year round, and houses are refurbished and new housing built. They are not empty centers. Those fortunate enough to observe Shalako or the Turtle Dance, see huge amounts of ritual paraphernalia and adornment displayed and enormous numbers of people fed. The two ceremonies are very different qualitatively and in number of participants and items displayed, which many of us understand as representing linguistic and ethnic differences (Zuni vs. Tewa). Nevertheless, the number of pieces of turquoise (and now silver), feathers, loaves of bread, stews, pigments, animal skins, and so on that are stored, refurbished, and subsequently displayed are impressive by any standard, and I believe would comfortably include Paquimé at any particular point in its history, although not as the two hundred-year accumulation that the archaeologist sees. The acquisition of materials, their fabrication, use, re-use, curation and consumption are manifestations of ritual economies that are both sacred and secular (Wells and Davis-Salazar 2007).

Keith Kintigh (2007, 375) characterizes the political organization of the protohistoric/historic Zuni village of Hawikku as lineage based and ritually legitimated. I view Paquimé the same way. I interpret caches and hoards as potentially representing lineage or sodality property, an inheritance that is curated in particular places to be removed, refurbished, re-used, and returned as long as required and appropriate. There is no reason to assume that all lineages or sodalities are of equal status. There is abundant ethnographic evidence that ceremonies controlled by particular sodalities or lineages are shared across village and linguistic boundaries, and not infrequently across long distances. Some Pueblo groups specifically refer to the process of replicating sodalities in different villages as planting, or if a ritual has lapsed, as replanting.

I do not wish to imply that Paquimé or any other large fourteenth-century Pueblo is exactly like a modern Pueblo village. Pueblo territories have been sliced and diced by modern polities and an international border. Land in between Pueblo settlements is filled with other ethnic groups, their livestock, and cities. We must also remember that archaeologists see neither the longue durée nor a moment in time. We see a jumble of ruins representing different periods and events with different periodicities. I find it interesting that the potential networks visible at Paquimé do unite people over very long distances and perhaps over long periods of time—from Cerro de Trincheras in Sonora to the Cerrillos Hills of the Galisteo Basin, and wherever the breeding stock of the original scarlet macaws came from. There were linkages as well to the Southern Plains documented at Bloom Mound and Henderson Pueblo (Kelley 1984; Speth 2008) and by bison bones found at Paquimé. Some of the shift of the center of gravity in the Pueblo world to the south and east may have been influenced by access to bison.

As archaeologists, we seem caught wanting to write big picture scenarios of archaeohistory with site or local level analyses. Perhaps we need to refocus our views to a middle ground while paying attention to chronology. We are now in a much better position to do this than we were 20 years ago. Of course we need better dates, but with our current understanding, Casas Grandes becomes an important player in the demographic and social dynamics of the fourteenth-century NW/SW. I look forward to what we learn in our continuing research.

Note

Sadly, our colleague Linda Cordell died after she wrote her chapter but before review and production of the volume. As is characteristic of her work, this craft is of such high quality and useful insights that it deserves publication.

REFERENCES CITED

Abbott, David R. 2003. *Centuries of Decline during the Hohokam Classic Period at Pueblo Grande*. Tucson: University of Arizona Press.
Adams, E. Charles. 2000. "The Katsina Cult: A Western Pueblo Perspective." In *Kachinas in the Pueblo World*, edited by P. Schaafsma, 35–46. Salt Lake City: University of Utah Press.
Adams, E. Charles, and Andrew I. Duff. 2004. *The Protohistoric Pueblo World, AD 1275–1600*. Tucson: University of Arizona Press.
Adams, Karen. 2013. "Ancient Plant Use in West-Central Chihuahua." Ms. in possession of Karen Adams.
———. 2014. "Little Barley (*Hordeum pusillum* Nutt.): 'A Pre-Hispanic New World Domesticate Lost to History.'" In *New Lives for Ancient and Extinct Crops*, edited by Paul Minnis, 179–91. Tucson: University of Arizona Press.
Aldhouse-Green, M., and S. Aldhouse-Green. 2005. *The Quest for the Shaman: Shape-Shifters, Sorcerers, and Spirits*. New York: Thames.
Altschul, Jeffrey H., César A. Quijada, and Robert A. Heckman. 1999. "Villa Verde and the Late-Prehistoric Period along the San Pedro River." In *Sixty Years of Mogollon Archaeology: Papers from the Ninth Mogollon Conference, Silver City, New Mexico, 1996*, edited by Stephanie M. Whittlesey, 81–92. Tucson: SRI Press.
Amsden, Monroe. 1928. "Archaeological Reconnaissance in Sonora." *Southwest Museum Papers*, No. 1. Highland Park, CA.
Bagwell, Elizabeth A. 2004. "Architectural Patterns Along the Rio Taraises, Northern Sierra Madre Occidental." *Kiva* 7:7–30.
———. 2006. "Domestic Architectural Production in Northwest Mexico." PhD diss., Department of Anthropology, University of New Mexico, Albuquerque.
Bandelier, Adolph F. 1890. "The Ruins of Casas Grandes." *The Nation* 51:185–87.
Bartlett, John R. 1854. *Personal Narratives of Exploration and Incidents in Texas, New Mexico, California, Sonora, and Chihuahua*. New York: D. Appleton and Co.
Berrojalbiz, Fernando. 2005. "El Origen Norteño de los Tepehuanes: Elementos Arqueológicos sobre la Antigua Relación Tepima." In *Las Vias del Noroeste I: Una Macroregión Indigena Americana*, edited by C. Bonliglioli, A. Gutierrez and M. E. Olavarría, 83–112. México, D.F.: Instituto de Investigaciones Antropológicas UNAM.

Bishop, Ronald L., Daniela Triadan, M. James Blackman, and Eduardo Gamboa Carrera. 1998. "Production and Distribution of Polychrome Ceramics in the Casas Grandes Region, Chihuahua, Mexico." Paper presented at the 63rd Annual Meeting of the Society for American Archaeology, Seattle.

Blackiston, A. Hooton. 1905. "Cliff Dwellings of Northern Mexico." *Records of the Past* 4:355–61.

———. 1906a. "Ruins of the Cerro de Moctezuma." *American Anthropologist* 8:257–61.

———. 1906b. "Casas Grandes Outposts." *Records of the Past* 5:142–47.

———. 1908. "Ruins of the Tenaja and the Rio San Pedro." *Records of the Past* 7:282–90.

———. 1909. "Recently Discovered Cliff-Dwellings of the Sierra Madres." *Records of the Past* 8:20–32.

Boyer, Jeffrey L., James L. Moore, Steven A. Lakatos, Nancy J. Akins, C. Dean Wilson, and Eric Blinman. 2010. "Remodeling Immigration: A Northern Rio Grande Perspective on Depopulation, Migration, and Donation-Side Models." In *Leaving Mesa Verde, Peril and Change in the Thirteenth-Century Southwest*, edited by Timothy A. Kohler, Mark D. Varien, and Aaron M. Wright, 285–324. Amerind Studies in Archaeology, Tucson: University of Arizona Press.

Bradley, Ronna J. 1993. "Marine Shell Exchange in Northwest Mexico and the Southwest." In *The American Southwest and Mesoamerica: Systems of Prehistoric Exchange*, edited by Jonathan E. Ericson and Timothy G. Baugh, 121–51. New York: Plenum Press.

———. 1995. "A Comparison of Shell Ornament Production Strategies in the North American Southwest." Paper presented at the 60th Annual Meeting of the Society for American Archaeology, Minneapolis.

———. 1996. "The Role of Casas Grandes in Prehistoric Shell Exchange Networks within the Southwest." PhD diss., Department of Anthropology, Arizona State University, Tempe.

———. 1999. "Shell Exchange within the Southwest: The Casas Grandes Interaction Sphere." In *The Casas Grandes World*, edited by Curtis F. Schaafsma and Carroll L. Riley, 213–28. Salt Lake City: University of Utah Press.

———. 2000. "Recent Advances in Chihuahuan Archaeology." In *Greater Mesoamerica: The Archaeology of West and Northwest Mexico*, edited by Michael S. Foster and Shirley Gorenstein, 221–40. Salt Lake City: University of Utah Press.

Bradley, Ronna J., and Jerry M. Hoffer. 1985. "Playas Red: A Preliminary Study of Origins and Variability in the Jornada Mogollon." In *Proceedings of the Third Jornada-Mogollon Conference*, edited by Michael S. Foster and Thomas C. O'Laughlin, 161–77. *The Artifact* 23(1, 2).

Brand, Donald D. 1933. "The Historical Geography of Northwest Chihuahua." PhD diss., Department of Geography, University of California, Berkeley.

References Cited

———. 1935. "The Distribution of Pottery Types in Northwest Mexico." *American Anthropologist* 37(ns):287–305.

———. 1936. "Notes to Accompany a Vegetation Map of Chihuahua." *University of New Mexico Bulletin* 4(4).

———. 1943. "The Chihuahua Culture Area." *New Mexico Anthropologist* 6–7(3):115–58.

Braniff Cornejo, Beatriz. 1974. "Oscilación de la Frontera Septentrional Mesoamericana." In *The Archaeology of West Mexico*, edited by B. Bell, 40–50, Jalisco: Ajijic.

———. 1986. "Ojo de Agua, Sonora and Casas Grandes, Chihuahua: A Suggested Chronology." In *Ripples in the Chichimec Sea: New Considerations of Southwestern-Mesoamerican Interaction*, edited by Frances Joan Mathien and Randall H. McGuire, 70–80. Carbondale: Southern Illinois University Press.

———. 1992. *La Frontera Protohistórica Pima-Ópata en Sonora, México, Proposiciones Arqueológicas Preliminares*. 2 vols. México, D.F.: Instituto Nacional de Antropología e Historia.

———. 1999. Paquimé: The Roots of a New Ceramic Tradition. *Artes de México* 45:82–83.

———. 2001. *La Gran Chichimeca, el Lugar de las Rocas Secas*. México, D.F.: CONACULTA and Jaca Books, Consejo Nacional para la Cultura y las Artes.

Breternitz, David A. 1966. *An Appraisal of Tree-ring Dated Pottery in the Southwest*. Anthropological Papers of the University of Arizona 10. Tucson: University of Arizona Press.

Broda, Johanna. 1991. "Sacred Landscape of Aztec Calendar Festivals: Myth, Nature, and Society." In *To Change Place: Aztec Ceremonial Landscapes*, edited by David Carrasco, 74–112. Boulder: University Press of Colorado.

Brown, David E. 1982. *Biotic Communities: Southwestern United States and Northwestern Mexico*. Salt Lake City: University of Utah Press.

Brown, David E., and Charles H. Lowe. 1994. *Biotic Communities of the Southwest. A Supplementary Map to "Biotic Communities: Southwestern United States and Northwestern Mexico,"* edited by David E. Brown. Salt Lake City: University of Utah Press.

Buikstra, Jane E., L. W. Konigsberg, and John Bullington. 1986. "Fertility and the Development of Agriculture in the Prehistoric Midwest." *American Antiquity* 51:528–46.

Burd-Larkin, Karin. 2006. "Community Reorganization in the Southern Zone of the Casas Grandes Culture Area of Chihuahua, Mexico." PhD diss., Department of Anthropology, University of Colorado, Boulder.

Burd-Larkin, Karin, Jane H. Kelley, and Mitchel J. Hendrickson. 2004. "Ceramics as Temporal and Spatial Indicators in Chihuahua Culture." In *Surveying the Archaeology of Northwest Mexico*, edited by Gillian E. Newell and Emiliano Gallaga, 177–204. Salt Lake City: University of Utah Press.

Cabrero, María Teresa. 2007. "Un Modelo de Intercambio Comercial para la Cultura Bolaños, Jalisco, México." *Relaciones* XXVIII(111):217–45.

Cameron, Catherine M., and Andrew I. Duff. 2008. "History and Process in Village Formation: Context and Contrasts from the Northern Southwest." *American Antiquity* 73:29–57.

Carey, Henry A. 1931. "An Analysis of the Northwestern Chihuahua Culture." *American Anthropologist* 33:325–74.

Carpenter, John P. 2002. "The Animas Phase and Paquimé: Regional Differentiation and Integration at Joyce Well." In *The Joyce Well Site: On the Frontier of the Casas Grandes World*, edited by James M. Skibo, Eugene B. McCluney, and William H. Walker, 149–66. Salt Lake City: University of Utah Press.

Carpenter, John P., and Guadalupe Sánchez. 2007a. "El Rincón de Buyubampo y las Rutas de Intercambio." Paper presented at the XXVIII Mesa Redonda de la Sociedad Mexicana de Antropología, México, D.F.

———. 2007b. "Nuevos Hallazgos Arqueológicos en la Región del Valle del Río Fuerte, Norte de Sinaloa." *Diario de Campo INAH* 93(julio-agosto):18–29.

Carpenter, John. P., Guadalupe Sánchez, Ismael Sánchez, A. Abrego, V. H. García, and D. Rodriguez. 2010. *Proyecto Arqueológico Norte de Sinaloa: Rutas de Intercambio. Investigaciones en Mochicahui, Sinaloa. Informe Técnico de la Temporada 2009 Entregado al Consejo de Arqueología del INAH*. México, D.F.: Instituto Nacional de Antropología e Historia.

Carpenter, John. P., Guadalupe. Sánchez, and Julio Vicente. 2011. "El Engrane Tahue-Ópata: Un Modelo Explicativo del Intercambio de Larga Distancia entre Mesoamérica y el Norte de México/Suroeste de los EUA." Paper presented at the Seminario Nuevas Miradas sobre los Ópatas, Hermosillo, Sonora.

Carriker, Emily R. 2009. "A Morphological Analysis of Gila Polychrome from Paquimé." Poster presented at the 74th Annual Meeting of the Society for American Archaeology, Atlanta.

Casserino, Christopher M. 2009. "Bioarchaeology of Violence and Site Abandonment at Casas Grandes, Chihuahua, Mexico." PhD diss., Department of Anthropology, University of Oregon, Eugene.

Cerezo-Román, Jessica C., Carlos Cruz, Silvia Nava, and M. Elisa Villalpando Canchola. 2011. "Cremaciones de Tradición Trincheras." Paper presented at the 76th Annual Meeting of the Society for American Archaeology. Sacramento, CA.

Chang, K. C. 1983. *Art, Myth, and Ritual: The Path to Political Authority in Ancient China*. Cambridge, MA: Harvard University Press.

Chiykowski, Tanya. 2011. "Viejo Period Architecture in the Southern Zone of the Chihuahua Culture Area, Mexico." MA thesis, Department of Anthropology, State University of New York, Binghamton, New York.

Clark, Jeffery J., Patrick D. Lyons, and J. Brett Hill. 2003. "Precontact Population Decline and Coalescence in the Southern Southwest." Proposal to the National Science Foundation by the Center for Desert Archaeology, Tucson. Available online at http://www.archaeologysouthwest.org/pdf/nsf_descriptiom.pdf.

Cobb, Charles R. 2000. *From Quarry to Cornfield: The Political Economy of Mississippian Hoe Production*. Tuscaloosa: Alabama University Press.

Contreras Sánchez, Eduardo. 1982. *Guia Oficial al Zona Arqueológica de Casas Grandes, Chih*. México, D.F.: Instituto Nacional de Antropología e Historia.

———. 1985. *Antigua Ciudad de Casas Grandes Chihuahua (Paquimé): Tecnología Aplicada a la Construccion de Edificios Habitaciones*. México, D.F.: Dirección de Monumentos Prehispánicos, Cuidernos de Trabajo 1, Instituto Nacional de Antropología e Historia.

———. 1986. *Paquimé: Zona Arqueológica de Casas Grandes*. Cd. Chihuahua: Gobierno del Estado de Chihuahua.

Coon, Matthew S. 2009. "Variation in Ohio Hopewell Political Economies." *American Antiquity* 74(1):49–76.

Cordell, Linda S. 1997. *Archaeology of the Southwest*, 2nd edition. San Diego: Academic Press.

Cordell, Linda S., and Nicholas E. Damp. 2010. "Adobe Melt-Down." In *Threads, Tints, and Edification*, Papers in Honor of Glenna Dean, edited by Emily J. Brown, Karen Armtrong, David M. Brugge, and Carol J. Condie, 49–60. Papers in Honor No. 36. Albuquerque: Archaeological Society of New Mexico.

Cordell, Linda S., and Judith A. Habicht-Mauche, eds. 2012a. *Potters and Communities of Practice, Glaze Paint and Polychrome Pottery in the American Southwest, AD 1250–1700*. Anthropological Papers of the University of Arizona 75. Tucson: University of Arizona Press.

———. 2012b. "Practice, Theory, and Social Dynamics among Pre-Hispanic and Colonial Communities in the American Southwest." In *Potters and Communities of Practice, Glaze Paint and Polychrome Pottery in the American Southwest, AD 1250–1700*, edited by Linda S. Cordell and Judith A. Habicht-Mauche, 1–7. Anthropological Papers of the University of Arizona 75. Tucson: University of Arizona Press.

Cordell, Linda S., and Maxine E. McBrinn. 2012. *Archaeology of the Southwest*, 3rd edition. Walnut Creek, CA: Left Coast Press.

Costin, Cathy Lynne. 1991. "Craft Specialization: Issues in Defining, Documenting, and Explaining the Organization of Production." In *Archaeological Method and Theory*, edited by Michael B. Schiffer, 3:1–56. Tucson: University of Arizona Press.

———. 2007. "Thinking about Production: Phenomenological Classification and Lexical Semantics." *Archeological Papers of the American Anthropological Association* 17(1):143–62.

Crown, Patricia L. 1994. *Ceramics and Ideology: Salado Polychrome Pottery*. Albuquerque: University of New Mexico Press.

Crown, Patricia L., and W. James Judge. 1991. *Chaco and Hohokam: Prehistoric Regional Systems of the American Southwest*. Santa Fe, NM: School of American Research Press.

Cruz, Carlos, Silvia Nava, and M. Elisa Villalpando Canchola. 2010. "Investigaciones Recientes en Cerro de Trincheras. Patrimonio Funerario de Tradición Trincheras." Paper presented at the Sociedad Mexicana de Antropología XXIX Mesa Redonda, Puebla Pu.

Cruz Antillón, Rafael, Robert D. Leonard, Timothy D. Maxwell, Todd L. VanPool, Marcel J. Harmon, Christine S. VanPool, David A. Hyndman, and Sidney S. Brandwein. 2004. "Galeana, Villa Ahumada, and Casa Chica: Diverse Sites in the Casas Grandes Region." In *Surveying the Archaeology of Northwest Mexico*, edited by Gillian E. Newell and Emiliano Gallaga, 149–75. Salt Lake City: University of Utah Press.

Cruz Antillón, Rafael, and Timothy D. Maxwell. 1999. "The Villa Ahumada Site: Archaeological Invetigations East of Paquimé." In *The Casas Grandes World*, edited by Curtis Schaafsma and Carroll L. Riley, 43–53. Salt Lake City: University of Utah Press.

Cunningham, Jerimy J. 2009. "Water and Ritual Power in the Casas Grandes Regional System." Paper presented to Theoretical Research Group, December. Durham, UK.

Damon, Paul E., C. Vance Haynes, and Austin Long. 1964. "Arizona Radiocarbon Dates V." *Radiocarbon* 6:91–107.

Dean, Jeffrey S., and John C. Ravesloot. 1993. "The Chronology of Cultural Interaction in the Gran Chichimeca." In *Culture and Contact, Charles C. Di Peso's Gran Chichimeca*, edited by Anne I. Woosley and John C. Ravesloot, 83–103. Albuquerque: University of New Mexico Press.

DeAtley, Suzanne P. 1980. "Regional Integration of Animas Phase Settlements on the Northern Casas Grandes Frontier." PhD diss., Department of Anthropology, University of California, Los Angeles. Ann Arbor: University Microfilms.

Di Peso, Charles C. 1951. *The Babocomari Village Site on the Babocomari River, Southeastern Arizona*. Publication No. 5. Dragoon, AZ: Amerind Foundation.

———. 1966. "Archaeology and Ethnohistory of the Northern Sierra." In *Handbook of Middle American Indians*, Volume 4: *Archaeological Frontiers and External Connections*, edited by Robert Wauchope, 3–25. Austin: University of Texas Press.

———. 1974. *Casas Grandes: A Fallen Trading Center of the Gran Chichimeca*, vols. 1–3. Flagstaff: Northland Press.

———. 1979. Prehistory: The Southern Periphery. In *Handbook of North American Indians, Southwest*, vol. 9, edited by Alfonso Ortiz, 152–161. Washington, D.C.: Smithsonian Institution Press.

Di Peso, Charles C., John B. Rinaldo, and Gloria J. Fenner. 1974. *Casas Grandes: A Fallen Trading Center of the Gran Chichimeca*, vols. 4–8. Flagstaff: Northland Press.

Dirst, Victoria A. 1979. "A Prehistoric Frontier in Sonora." PhD diss., Department of Anthropology, University of Arizona, Tucson.

Dirst, Victoria A., and Richard A. Pailes. 1976. "Economic Networks: Mesoamerica and the American Southwest." Paper presented at the 41st Annual Meeting of the Society for American Archaeology, St. Louis.

Doolittle, William E. 1988. *Pre-Hispanic Occupation in the Valley of Sonora, Mexico: Archaeological Confirmation of Early Spanish Reports*. Anthropological Papers of the University of Arizona 48. Tucson: University of Arizona Press.

———. 1993. "Canal Irrigation at Casas Grandes: A Technological and Developmental Assessment of Its Origins." In *Culture and Contact, Charles C. Di Peso's Gran Chichimeca*, edited by Anne I. Woosley and John C. Ravesloot, 133–53. Albuquerque: University of New Mexico Press.

Douglas, John E. 1990. "Regional Interaction in the Northern Sierra: An Analysis Based on the Late Prehistoric Occupation of the San Bernardino Valley, Southeastern Arizona." PhD diss., Department of Anthropology, University of Arizona, Tucson.

———. 1992. "Distant Sources, Local Contexts: Interpreting Nonlocal Ceramics at Paquimé (Casas Grandes), Chihuahua." *Journal of Anthropological Research* 48(1):1–24.

———. 1995. "Autonomy and Regional Systems in the Late Prehistoric Southern Southwest." *American Antiquity*, 60(2):240–57.

———. 1996. "Distinguishing Change during the Animas Phase (AD 1150–1450) at the Boss Ranch Site, Southeastern Arizona." *North American Archaeologist* 17:183–202.

———. 2000. "Exchanges, Assumptions, and Mortuary Goods in Pre-Paquimé, Chihuahua." In *The Archaeology of Regional Interaction*, edited by Michelle Hegmon. 189–208. Niwot, CO: University of Colorado Press.

———. 2004. "A Reinterpretation of the Occupational History of the Pendleton Ruin, New Mexico." *Journal of Field Archaeology* 29:425–36.

———. 2007. "Making and Breaking Boundaries in the Hinterlands: The Social and Settlement Dynamics of Far Southeastern Arizona and Southwestern New Mexico." In *Hinterlands and Heartlands in Southwest Prehistory*, edited by Allan P. Sullivan III and James Bayman, 97–108. Tucson: University of Arizona Press.

Douglas, John, and César A. Quijada. 2003. "El Valle Bavíspe, Entre los Culturas del Rio Sonora y Casas Grandes." *Noroeste de México* 14:17–26.

———. 2004a. "Between the Casas Grandes and the Rio Sonora Valleys: Chronology and Settlement in the Upper Bavispe Drainage." In *Surveying the Archaeology of Northwest Mexico*, edited by Gillian E. Newell and Emiliano Gallaga, 93–109. Salt Lake City: University of Utah Press.

———. 2004b. "Not So Plain After All: First Millennium AD Textured Ceramics in Northeastern Sonora." *Kiva* 70:29–50.

———. 2005. "Di Peso's Concept of the Northern Sierra: Evidence from the Upper Bavispe Valley, Sonora, Mexico." *Latin American Antiquity* 16(3):275–91.

Douglas, John E., César A. Quijada, and Júpiter Martínez Ramírez. 2003. *Reconocimiento Arqueológico en los Valles Bavispe y San Bernardino, Sonora, Segunda Temporada: Excavaciones Arqueológicas del Periodo Ceramico en los Valles Bavispe y Huachinera*, México, D.F.: Technical Report on file with the Instituto Nacional de Antropologia e Historia.

Findlow, Frank J., and Suzanne P. De Atley. 1974. "Prehistoric Land Use Patterns in the Animas Valley: A First Approximation." *Anthropology UCLA* 6(2):1–57.

Fish, Paul R., and Suzanne K. Fish. 1999. "Reflections on the Casas Grandes Regional System from the Northwestern Periphery." In *The Casas Grandes World*, edited by Curtis F. Schaafsma and Carroll L. Riley, 27–42. Salt Lake City: University of Utah Press.

Fish, Paul R., Suzanne K. Fish, and George J. Gumerman. 1994. "Toward an Explanation for Southwestern Abandonments." In *Themes in Southwest Prehistory*, edited by George J. Gumerman, 135–65. Santa Fe, NM: School of American Research Press.

Fish, Suzanne K. 2004. Corn, Crops and Cultivation in the North American Southwest. In *People and Plants in Ancient Western North America*, edited by Paul E. Minnis, 115–66. Washington, D.C.: Smithsonian Books.

———. 2009. "Report on Pollen Recovered from Upland Terraced Sites in the Casas Grandes Region, Mexico." Ms. in possession of Suzanne Fish.

Fish, Suzanne K., and Paul R. Fish. 2014. "Agave (*Agave* spp.): A Crop Lost and Found in the US-Mexico Borderlands." In *New Lives for Ancient and Extinct Crops*, edited by Paul E. Minnis, 102–38. Tucson: University of Arizona Press.

Fish, Suzanne K., Paul R. Fish, and M. Elisa Villalpando Canchola. 2007. *Trincheras Sites in Time, Space, and Society*. Amerind Studies in Archaeology. Tucson: The University of Arizona Press.

Foster, Michael S. 1985. "The Loma San Gabriel Occupation at Zacatecas and Durango, Mexico." In *The Archaeology of West and Northwest Mesoamerica*, edited by Michael S. Foster and Phillip C. Weigand, 327–52. Boulder, CO: Westview Press.

———. 1986. "The Mesoamerican Connection: A View from the South." In *Ripples in the Chichimec Sea: New Considerations of Southwestern-Mesoamerican Interactions*, edited by Frances Joan Mathien and Randall H. McGuire, 55–69. Carbondale: Southern Illinois University Press.

———. 1990. "Casas Grandes as a Mesoamerican Center and Culture." In *Actas del Primer Congreso de Historia Regional Comprada*, 33–39. Juárez, CH: Universidad Autónoma de Ciudad Juárez.

———. 1992. "Arqueología del Valle de Casas Grandes: Sitio Paquimé." In *Historia General de Chihuahua I. Geología, Geografía y Arqueología*, edited by

A. Márquez-Alameda, 12–32. Cd. Juárez: Universidad Autónoma de Cd. Juárez.

Fralick, Phillip W., Peter Hollings, and Joe D. Stewart. n.d. "Geochemistry and Provenance of Archaeological Ceramics from West-Central Chihuahua." Ms on file, Department of Anthropology, University of Calgary.

Fralick, Philip W., and Joe D. Stewart. 1999. "Un Informe sobre Análisis Composicional de Pastas Cerámicas de Chihuahua Oeste Central." Una Ponencia Presentado: "La Cerámica Prehispánica de Chihuahua." II Conferencia de Arqueología de la Frontera, 25 y 26 de junio, 1999, Museo de las Culturas del Norte en la Zona Arqueologica de "Paquimé," Casas Grandes, Chihuahua, Mexico. Ms. on file at Lakehead University and University of Calgary.

Freidel, David, Linda Schele, and Joy Parker. 1993. *Maya Cosmos: Three Thousand Years on the Shaman's Path*. New York: Quill William Morrow.

Fritz, Gordon L. 1969. "Investigations at the Rancho El Espia Site, Northwestern Chihuahua." *Transactions of the Fifth Regional Archeological Symposium for Southeastern New Mexico and Western Texas*, 51–63. Portales, NM: El Llano Archaeological Society.

Gallaga Murrieta, Emiliano. 1998. "El Intercambio del Sitio Cerro de Trincheras, Sonora, y la Cerámica Polícroma Chihuahuense." In *Antropología e Historia del Occidente de México II*, edited by Rosa Brambila Paz, 1011–24. XXIV Mesa Redonda, Tepic: Sociedad Mexicana de Antropología, México.

———. 2004. "A Spatial Distribution Analysis of Shell and Polychrome Ceramics at the Cerro de Trincheras Site, Sonora, Mexico." In *Surveying the Archaeology of Northwest Mexico*, edited by Gillian E. Newell and Emiliano Gallaga, 77–92. Salt Lake City: University of Utah Press.

———. 2011. "Tepalcates Trinchereños. The Ceramic Analysis from Cerro de Trincheras." In *Excavations at Cerro de Trincheras, Sonora, México*, edited by R. McGuire and M. Elisa Villalpando Canchola, 93–109. Arizona State Museum Archaeological Series 1. Tucson: University of Arizona Press.

Gamboa Carrera, Eduardo. 2008. "Materialidad e Historicidad de Paquimé." Ms. on file at the Centro del INAH en Chihuahua, Chihuahua, México. Also on file at the Maxwell Museum of Anthropology (Catalogue No. 2012.27.3), University of New Mexico, Albuquerque.

Garber, James F., and Jennifer P. Mathews. 2004. "Models of Cosmic Order: Physical Expression of Sacred Space Among the Ancient Maya." *Ancient Mesoamerica* 15:49–59.

Gillespie, S. D. 1991. "Ballgamers and Boundaries." In *The Mesoamerican Ballgame*, edited by Vernon L. Scarborough and David R. Wilcox, 317–45. Tucson: University of Arizona Press.

Gladwin, Harold S., Emil Haury, E. B. Sayles, and Winifred Gladwin. 1936. *Excavations at Snaketown: Material Culture*. Globe, AZ: Gila Pueblo Medallion Papers 25.

Gorenstein, Shirley, and Michael S. Foster. 2000. "West and Northwest Mexico: The Ins and Outs of Mesoamerica." In *Greater Mesoamerica: The Archaeology of West and Northwest Mexico*, edited by Michael S. Foster and Shirley Gorenstein, 3–19. Salt Lake City: University of Utah Press.

de Grandpre, Pauline. 2011. "Las Ceramicas Viejas: The Creation of a Working Typology for Chihuahuan Ceramics." Honors thesis, Department of Anthropology, University of Alberta, Edmonton.

Graves, William M. 2004. "Social Identity and the Internal Organization of the Jumanos Settlement Cluster in the Salinas District, Central New Mexico." In *The Protohistoric Pueblo World, AD 1275–1600*, edited by E. Charles Adams and Andrew I. Duff, 43–52. Tucson: University of Arizona Press.

Green, John W. 1969. "Preliminary Report on Site EPAS-60: An El Paso Phase House Ruin." *Transactions of the Fifth Regional Archeological Symposium on Southeastern New Mexico and West Texas*, 1–12. Portales, NM: El Llano Archaeological Society.

Grosscup, Gordon L. 1976. "The Ceramic Sequence of Amapa." In *The Archaeology of Amapa, Nayarit*, edited by C. Meighan, 209–72. Los Angeles: University of California Press.

Guevara Sánchez, Arturo. 1984. *Las Cuarentas Casas: Un Sitio Arqueológico del Estado de Chihuahua*. México, D.F.: Cuaderno de Trabajo 27, Departmento de Prehistoria, Instituto Nacional de Antropología e Historia.

———. 1985. *Apuntes para la Arqueología de Chihuahua*. México, D.F.: Cuaderno de Trabajo 1, Departmento de Prehistoria, Instituto Nacional de Antropología e Historia.

———. 1986. *Arqueología del Area de las Cuarentas Casas*. México, D.F.: Instituto Nacional de Antropología e Historia.

———. 1988. *Arqueología del Valle de las Cuevas, Chihuahua: Reconocimiento*. México, D.F.: Cuaderno de Trabajo 5, Departmento de Prehistoria, Instituto Nacional de Antropología e Historia.

Hagstrum, Melissa. 2001. "Household Production in Chaco Canyon Society." *American Antiquity* 66(1): 47–55.

Hammond, George P., and Agapito Rey. 1928. *Obregón's History of 16th Century Explorations in Western America, 1587*. Los Angeles: Wetzel Publishing Co.

Hard, Robert J., and John R. Roney. 1998. "A Massive Terraced Village Complex in Chihuahua, Mexico, 3000 Years Before Present." *Science* 279:1661–64.

———. 2007. "Cerros de Trincheras in Northwestern Chihuahua: The Arguments for Defense." In *Trincheras Sites in Time, Space, and Society*, edited by Suzanne Fish, Paul Fish, and Elisa Villapando, 11–52. Tucson, University of Arizona Press.

Hargrave, Lyndon Lane. 1970. *Mexican Macaws: Comparative Osteology and Survey of Remains from the Southwest*. Tucson: University of Arizona Press.

Harmon, Marcel. 2005. "Centralization, Cultural Transmission, and 'The Game of Life and Death' in Northern Mexico." PhD diss., Department of Anthropology, University of New Mexico, Albuquerque.

———. 2006. "Religion and the Mesoamerican Ballgame in the Casas Grandes Region of Northern Mexico." In *Religion in the Pre-Hispanic Southwest*, edited by Christine S. VanPool, Todd L. VanPool, and David A. Phillips, Jr., 185–217. Lanham, MD: AltaMira Press.

———. 2008. "The 'Game of Life and Death' within the Casas Grandes Region of Northern Mexico." In *Touching the Past: Ritual, Religion, and Trade of Casas Grandes*, edited by Glenna Nielsen-Grimm and Paul Stavast, 5–14. Provo, UT: Brigham Young University Museum of Peoples and Cultures.

Haury, Emil. 1976. *The Hohokam: Desert Farmers and Craftmen, Excavations at Snaketown, 1964–1965*. Tucson: University of Arizona Press.

Hayes, Alden C., Jon Nathan Young, and A. H. Warren. 1981. *Excavation of Mound 7, Gran Quivira National Monument, New Mexico*. Publications in Archeology No. 16. Washington, D.C.: National Park Service.

Haynes, C. Vance, Jr., Paul E. Damon, and Donald C. Grey. 1966. "Arizona Radiocarbon Dates VI." *Radiocarbon* 8:1–21.

Hays-Gilpin, Kelley, and Steven LeBlanc. 2007. "Sikyatki Style in Regional Context." In *New Perspectives on Pottery Mound Pueblo*, edited by Polly Schaafsma, 109–36. Albuquerque: University of New Mexico Press.

Hegmon, Michelle, Margaret C. Nelson, Roger Anyon, Darrel Creel, Steven A. LeBlanc, and Harry J. Shafer. 1999. "Space and Time Systematics in the Post-AD 1100 Mimbres Region of the North American Southwest." *Kiva* 65(2):143–66.

Hendon, Julia A. 1996. "Archaeological Approaches to the Organization of Domestic Labor: Household Practice and Domestic Relations." *Annual Review of Anthropology* 25:45–61.

Herold, Laurence C. 1965. *Trincheras and Physical Environment along the Rio Gavilán, Chihuahua, Mexico*. Department of Geography Publications 65-1. Denver: University of Denver.

Hers, Marie-Areti. 1989. "¿Existió la Cultura Loma San Gabriel? El Caso de Cerro Hervideros, Durango." *Anales del Instituto de Investigaciones Estéticas UNAM* 60:33–57.

———. 2001a. "Las Grandes Rutas que Cruzaron los Confines Tolteca-Chichimecas." In *La Gran Chichimeca: El Lugar de las Rocas Secas*, edited by Beatriz Braniff, 245–48. Milan: Jaca Books.

———. 2001b. "Zacatecas y Durango. Los Confines Tolteca-Chichimecas." In *La Gran Chichimeca. El Lugar de las Rocas Secas*, edited by Beatriz Braniff, 113–54. Milan: Jaca Book.

Hill, J. Brett, Jeffery J. Clark, William H. Doelle, and Patrick D. Lyons. 2004. "Prehistoric Demography in the Southwest: Migration, Coalescence, and Hohokam Population Decline." *American Antiquity* 69:689–716.

Hill, J. Brett, David R. Wilcox, William H. Doelle, and William J. Robinson. 2012. "Coalescent Communities" GIS Database Version 2.0: Archaeology Southwest, Museum of Northern Arizona. Ms. on file at Archaeology Southwest, Tucson.

Hodgetts, Lisa M. 1996. "Faunal Evidence from El Zurdo." *Kiva* 62:149–70.

Homburg, Jeffrey A., Jonathan A. Sandor, Paul E. Minnis, Javier M. Gonzalez, Christina A. Whitbread, and Victoria Sotelo. 2010. "Anthropogenic Effects on Soil Quality in Ancient Agricultural Fields in Chihuahua, Mexico." Presentation at the Annual Meeting of the Soil Science Society of America.

Hosler, Dorothy. 1988. Ancient West Mexican Metallurgy: A Technological Chronology. *Journal of Field Archaeology* 15:191–217.

———. 2005. *Los Sonidos y Colores del Poder. La Recnología Metalúrgica Sagrada del Occidente de México*. Toluca: El Colegio Mexiquense.

Howard, William A., and Thomas M. Griffiths. 1966. *Trincheras Distribution in the Sierra Madre Occidental, Mexico*. Department of Geography Technical Papers 66–1. Denver: University of Denver.

Hubbs, Clark. 1990. "Declining Fishes of the Chihuahuan Desert." In *Papers of the Third Symposium on Resources of the Chihuahuan Desert*, edited by A. Mitchell Powell, Robert R. Hollander, Jon C. Barlow, W. Bruce McGillivary, and David Schmidly, 89–96. Alpine, TX: Chihuahua Desert Research Institute.

Humphreys, Robert R. 1987. *90 Years and 535 Miles: Vegetation Change along the Mexican Border*. Albuquerque: University of New Mexico Press.

Johnson, Alfred E., and Raymond H. Thompson. 1963. "The Ringo Site, Southeastern Arizona." *American Antiquity* 28:465–81.

Keen, Myra A. 1971. *Sea Shells of Tropical West America: Marine Mollusks from Baja California to Peru*. Stanford: Stanford University Press.

Kelley, J. Charles. 1958. "A Review of the Architectural Sequence at La Junta de los Rios." *The Artifact* 23:149–59.

———. 1986. "The Mobile Merchants of Molino." In *Ripples in the Chichimec Sea: New Considerations of Southwestern-Mesoamerican Interaction*, edited by Frances Joan Mathien and Randall H. McGuire, 81–104. Carbondale: Southern Illinois University Press.

———. 2000. "The Aztatlan Mercantile System: Mobile Traders and the Northwestward Expansion of Mesoamerican Civilization." In *Greater Mesoamerica. The Archaeology of West and Northwest Mexico*, edited by Michael S. Foster and Shirley Gorenstein, 137–54. Salt Lake City: University of Utah Press.

Kelley, Jane H. 1984. *The Archaeology of the Sierra Blanca Region of Southeastern New Mexico*. Anthropological Paper 74. Ann Arbor: University of Michigan, Museum of Anthropology.

———. 2009a. "Al Margen del Mundo Casas Grandes." In *La Arqueología en el Norte de México, Espaciotiempo Revista Latinoamericana de Ciencias Sociales y Humanidades*, Año 2(3):42–49.

———. 2009b. *El Zurdo: A Small Prehistoric Village in West-Central Chihuahua, Mexico*. Maxwell Museum Technical Series No. 9, Parts 1, 2 and 3. Albuquerque: Maxwell Museum of Anthropology, University of New Mexico.

Kelley, Jane H., and A. C. MacWilliams. 2005. "The Development of Archaeology in Northwest Mexico." In *Southwest Archaeology in the Twentieth Century*, edited by Linda S. Cordell and Don D. Fowler, 81–96. Salt Lake City: University of Utah Press.

Kelley, Jane H., Karin Burd-Larkin, and Mitchell Hendrickson. 2004. "Ceramics as Temporal and Spatial Indicators in Chihuahuan Cultures." In *Future Directions. The Archaeology of Northwest Mexico*, edited by Gillian Newell and Emiliano Gallaga M., 177–204. Salt Lake City: University of Utah Press.

Kelley, Jane H., Richard D. Garvin, and Jerimy J. Cunningham. 2012. "Proyecto Arqueológico Chihuahua. Informe de la Temporada de 2010." Informe al Consejo de Arqueología, México, D.F.: Instituto Nacional de Antropología e Historia.

Kelley, Jane H., A. C. MacWilliams, Joe D. Stewart, Karen R. Adams, Jerimy J. Cunningham, Richard D. Garvin, J. M. Maillol, Paula J. Reimer, and Danny Zborover. 2012. "The View from the Edge: The Proyecto Arqueológico Chihuahua (PAC): 1990 to 2010: An Overview." *Canadian Journal of Archaeology* 36:82–107.

Kelley, Jane H., Joe D. Stewart, A. C. MacWilliams, and Karen R. Adams. 2004. "Recent Research in West-Central Chihuahua." In *Identity, Feasting and the Archaeology of the Greater Southwest*, edited by Barbara J. Mills, 295–310. Boulder: University Press of Colorado.

Kelley, Jane H., Joe D. Stewart, A. C. MacWilliams, and Loy C. Neff. 1999. "A West Central Chihuahuan Perspective on Chihuahuan Culture." In *The Casas Grandes World*, edited by Curtis F. Schaafsma and Carroll L. Riley, 63–77. Salt Lake City: University of Utah Press.

Kemrer, Meade F. 2007. Agriculture in the Southern San Andres Mountains, AD 900–1400, South Central New Mexico. Draft. Las Cruces, NM: Meade Kemrer Archaeological Associates.

Kidder, A. V., H. S. Cosgrove, and C. B. Cosgrove. 1949. *The Pendleton Ruin, Hidalgo County, New Mexico*. Contributions to American Anthropology and History No. 50. Publication No. 585. Washington, D.C.: Carnegie Institution of Washington.

Kintigh, Keith W. 2007. "Late Prehistoric and Protohistoric Settlement Systems in the Zuni Area." In *Zuni Origins: Toward a New Synthesis of Southwestern Archaeology*, edited by David A. Gregory and David R. Wilcox, 361–77. Tucson: University of Arizona Press.

Knight, Vernon J. 1986. "Institutional Organization of Mississippian Religion." *American Antiquity* 51:675–87.

Kohler, Timothy A., Matt Pier Glaude, Jean-Pierre Bocquet Appel, and Brian M. Kemp. 2008. "The Neolithic Demographic Transition in the U. S. Southwest." *American Antiquity* 73:645–69.

Kohler, Timothy A., Sarah Herr, and Matthew J. Root. 2004. "The Rise and Fall of Towns on the Pajarito Plateau, A.D. 1250–1375." In *Archaeology of Bandelier National Monument: Village Formation on the Pajarito Plateau, New Mexico*, edited by Timothy A. Kohler, 215–65. Albuquerque: University of New Mexico Press.

Kohler, Timothy A., Mark D. Varien, and Aaron M. Wright. 2010. *Leaving Mesa Verde, Peril and Change in the Thirteenth-Century Southwest*. Amerind Studies in Archaeology. Tucson: University of Arizona Press.

Kokrda, Ken. 2005. "Approaching Casas Grandes." In *Casas Grandes and the Ceramic Art of the Ancient Southwest*, edited by Richard F. Townsend, 99–121. Chicago and New Haven, CT: Art Institute of Chicago and Yale University Press.

Kowalewski, Stephen A. 2003. "Scale and Demographic Change: 3,500 Years in the Valley of Oaxaca." *American Anthropologist* 105:313–25.

Lascaux, Annick, and Barbara K. Montgomery. 2007. *Archaeological Investigations along U.S. 70 and State Road 75 from Solomon to Apache Grove, Graham and Greenlee Counties, Southeast Arizona*, Volume I: *The Clark Site, A Farming Community in the Duncan Valley from 800 BC to AD 1450*. Tierra Archaeological Report No. 2005–94. Tucson: Tierra Right of Way.

LeBlanc, Steven. 1980. "The Dating of Casas Grandes." *American Antiquity* 45:799–806.

Lekson, Stephen H. 1984. "Dating Casas Grandes." *Kiva* 50:55–60.

———. 1992. "Salado of the East." In *Proceedings of the Second Salado Conference, Globe, Arizona*, edited by Richard C. Lange and Stephen Germick, 17–21. Phoenix: Arizona Archaeological Society.

———. 1999. *The Chaco Meridian: Center of Political Power in the American Southwest*. Walnut Creek, CA: AltaMira Press.

———. 2006. *The Archaeology of Chaco Canyon*. Santa Fe, NM: School of American Research Press.

———. 2008. *A History of the Ancient Southwest*, Santa Fe, NM: School for Advanced Research Press.

Lekson, Stephen H., Michael Bletzer, and A. C. MacWilliams. 2004. "Pueblo IV in the Chihuahuan Desert." In *The Protohistoric Pueblo World AD 1275–1600*, edited by E. Charles Adams and Andrew I. Duff, 53–61. Tucson: University of Arizona Press.

Leopold, Aldo. 1949. *A Sand County Almanac: And Sketches Here and There*. Oxford: Oxford University Press.

Lightfoot, Kent G. 1984. *Prehistoric Political Dynamics: A Case Study from the American Southwest*. DeKalb: Northern Illinois University Press.

Lister, Robert H. 1939. "A Report on the Excavations Made at Agua Zarca and La Morita in Chihuahua." *Research* 3(1): 42–54.

———. 1946. "Survey of Archeological Remains in Northwestern Chihuahua." *Southwestern Journal of Anhropology* 2:443–52.

———. 1953. "Excavations in Cave Valley, Chihuahua, Mexico." *American Antiquity* 19:166–69.

———. 1958. *Archaeological Excavations in the Northern Sierra Madre Occidental, Chihuahua*. University of Colorado Series in Anthropology 7, Boulder: University Press of Colorado.

Luebben, Ralph A., Jonathan G. Andelson, and Laurence C. Herold. 1986. "Elvino Whetten Pueblo and its Relationship to Terraces and Nearby Small Sites, Chihuahua, Mexico." *Kiva* 51:165–87.

Lumholtz, Carl. 1902. *Unknown Mexico*. New York: Charles Scribner's Sons.

Mabry, Jonathan B. 2005. "Changing Knowledge and Ideas about the First Farmers in Southeastern Arizona." In *The Late Archaic across the Borderlands: From Foraging to Farming*, edited by B. J. Vierra, 41–83. Tucson: University of Arizona Press.

MacWilliams, A. C. 2001. "The Archaeology of Laguna Bustillos Basin, Chihuahua, Mexico." PhD diss., Department of Anthropology, University of Arizona, Tucson.

MacWilliams, A. C., and Jane H. Kelley. 2008. "Mimbres in Viejo Period Chihuahua." Paper presented at the 15th Mogollon Conference, Silver City, New Mexico.

Manglesdorf, Paul C., in collaboration with E. J. Wellhausen, L. M. Roberts, and E. Hernandez. 1952. *Traces of Maize in Mexico: Their Origin, Characteristics and Distribution*. Cambridge, MA: Harvard University, The Bussey Institution.

Martínez Ramírez, Júpiter. 2009. *Proyecto Arqueológico Sierra Alta de Sonora*. México, D.F.: Technical Report on file with the Instituto Nacional de Antropología e Historia.

Mastache, Alba G., Robert Cobean, and Dan Healan. 2002. *Ancient Tollan, Tula and the Toltec Heartland*. Boulder: University Press of Colorado.

Mathien, Frances Joan. 2003. "Artifacts from Pueblo Bonito: One Hundred Years of Interpretation." In *Pueblo Bonito: Center of the Chacoan World*, edited by Jill E. Neitzel, 127–42. Washington, D.C.: Smithsonian Books.

Mathiowetz, Michael D. 2011. "The Diurnal Path of the Sun: Ideology and Interregional Interaction in Ancient Northwest Mesoamerica and the American Southwest." PhD diss., University of California, Riverside.

Maxwell, Timothy D. 2002. 'Casas Grandes Region: Prehistoric Life in the Chihuahuan Desert." *El Palacio* 107(3):12–19.

———. 2006. "The Casas Grandes Border." In *Secrets of Casas Grandes*, edited by Melissa S. Powell, 95–104. Santa Fe: Museum of New Mexico Press.

Maxwell, Timothy D., and Rafael Cruz Antillón. 2003. "Loma de Moctezuma: At the Edge of the Casas Grandes World." *Archaeology Southwest* 17:7.

———. 2008. "Production and Exchange of Turquoise in the Casas Grandes Region: A View from the East." Paper presented at the 73rd Annual Meeting of the Society for American Archaeology, Vancouver.

McCluney, Eugene B. 1962. *Clanton Draw and Box Canyon, An Interim Report on Two Prehistoric Sites in Hidalgo County, New Mexico, and Related Surveys.* Monograph No. 36. Santa Fe, NM: School of American Research.

McGuire, Randall H. 1980. "The Mesoamerican Connection in the Southwest." *Kiva* 46(1–2):3–38.

———. 1987. "The Greater Southwest as Periphery of Mesoamerica." In *Centre and Periphery: Comparative Studies in Archaeology*, edited by T. C. Champion, 40–66. London: Unwin Hyman.

———. 2011. "Pueblo Religion and the Mesoamerican Connection." In *Religious Transformation in the Late Pre-Hispanic Pueblo World*, edited by Donna M. Glowacki and Scott Van Keuren, 23–49. Amerind Studies in Archaeology. Tucson: University of Arizona Press.

McGuire, Randall H., and Ann V. Howard. 1987. "The Structure and Organization of Hohokam Shell Exchange." *Kiva* 52:113–46.

McGuire, Randall H., and M. Elisa Villalpando Canchola. 2011. *Excavations at Cerro de Trincheras*. Arizona State Museum Archaeological Series. 2 vols. Tucson: University of Arizona.

McGuire, Randall H., M. Elisa Villalpando Canchola, Victoria D. Vargas, and Emiliano Gallaga. 1999. "Cerro Trincheras and the Casas Grandes World." In *The Casas Grandes World*, edited by Curtis F. Schaafsma and Carroll L. Riley, 134–46. Salt Lake City: University of Utah Press.

McNatt, Logan. 1996. "The Archaeology of Belize." *Journal of Cave and Karst Studies* 58(2):81–99.

Meighan, Clement. 1976. *The Archaeology of Amapa, Nayarit*. Monumenta Archaeologica 21. Los Angeles: University of California Press.

Mendiola Galvan, Francisco. 2008. *La Texturas del Pasado: Una Historia del Pensamiento Arqueología en Chihuahua, México*. México, D.F.: Colección ENAH Chihuahua.

Miller, Mary, and Karl Taube. 1993. *An Illustrated Dictionary of the Gods and Symbols of Ancient Mexico and the Maya*. New York: Thames and Hudson.

Miller, R. Wick. 1983. "Uto-Aztecan Languages." In *Handbook of North American Indians, Southwest*, vol. 10, edited by Alfonso Ortiz, 113–24. Washington, D.C.: Smithsonian Institution Press.

Mills, Barbara J. 2000. *Alternative Leadership Strategies in the Pre-Hispanic Southwest*. Tucson: University of Arizona Press.

———. 2007. "Performing the Feast, Visual Display and Suprahousehold Commensalism in the Puebloan Southwest." *American Antiquity* 72:210–39.

Mills, Barbara J., John M. Roberts, Jr., Jeffery J. Clark, William R. Haas, Jr., Deborah Huntley, Matthew A. Peeples, Lewis Borck, Susan C. Ryan, Meaghan

Trowbridge, and Ronald L. Breiger. 2013. "The Dynamics of Social Networks in the Late Pre-Hispanic U.S. Southwest." In *New Approaches in Regional Network Analysis,* edited by Carl Knappet and Ray Rivers, 185–206. Oxford: Oxford University Press.

Mills, Jack P., and Vera M. Mills. 1969a. "Burned House: An Additional Excavation at the Kuykendall Site." *The Artifact* 7(3):21–32.

———. 1969b. *The Kuykendall Site: A Pre-historic Salado Village in Southeastern Arizona.* Special Report No. 6. El Paso, TX: El Paso Archaeological Society.

Minnis, Paul E. 1984. "Peeking under the Tortilla Curtain: Regional Interaction and Integration on the Northeastern Periphery of Casas Grandes." *American Archaeology* 4:181–93.

———. 1985. *Social Adaptation to Food Stress: A Prehistoric Southwestern Example.* Chicago: University of Chicago Press.

———. 1988. "Four Examples of Specialized Production at Casas Grandes, Northwestern Chihuahua." *Kiva* 53: 181–93.

———. 1989a. "The Casas Grandes Polity in the International Four Corners." In *The Sociopolitical Structure of Prehistoric Southwestern Societies,* edited by Steadman Upham, Kent Lightfoot, and Roberta Jewett, 269–305. Boulder, CO: Westview Press.

———. 1989b. "Prehistoric Diet in the Northern Southwest: Macroplant Remains from Four Corners Feces." *American Antiquity* 54:543–63.

Minnis, Paul E., and Michael E. Whalen. 2001. "An Introduction to the Archaeology of Chihuahua." In *Surveying the Archaeology of Northwest Mexico,* edited by Gillian Newell and Emiliano Gallaga, 113–26. Salt Lake City: University of Utah Press.

———. 2005. "At the Other End of the Puebloan World: Feasting at Casas Grandes, Chihuahua, Mexico." In *Engaged Anthropology: Research Essays on North American Archaeology, Ethnobotany, and Museology,* edited by Michelle Hegmon and B. Sunday Eiselt, 114–28. Ann Arbor: Museum of Anthropology, University of Michigan.

———. 2010. "The First Pre-Hispanic Chile (*Capsicum annuum*) from the U.S. Southwest/Northwest Mexico and its Changing Use." *American Antiquity* 75:245–57.

Minnis, Paul E., Michael E. Whalen, and R. Emerson Howell. 2006. "Fields of Power: Upland Farming in the Pre-Hispanic Casas Grandes Polity, Chihuahua, Mexico." *American Antiquity* 71:707–22.

Minnis, Paul E., Michael E. Whalen, Jane H. Kelley, and Joe D. Stewart. 1993. "Prehistoric Macaw Breeding in the North American Southwest." *American Antiquity* 57:270–76.

Mobley-Tanaka, Jeannette L. 1997. "Gender and Ritual Space During the Pithouse to Pueblo Transition: Subterranean Mealing Rooms in the North American Southwest." *American Antiquity* 62:437–48.

Moore, Mrs. Glenn E., and Mrs. Joe Ben Wheat. 1951. "An Archaeological Cache from the Hueco Bolson, Texas." *Bulletin of the Texas Archaeological and Paleontological Society* 22:144–63.

Morgan, Joelle. 2010. "Specialized Agricultural Production in the Prehistoric Casas Grandes Region, Chihuahua, Mexico." MA thesis. Department of Anthropology, University of Oklahoma, Norman.

Moulard, Barbara L. 2005. "Archaism and Emulation in Casas Grandes Painted Pottery." In *Casas Grandes and the Ceramic Art of the Ancient Southwest*, edited by Richard F. Townsend, 67–97. Chicago and New Haven, CT: Art Institute of Chicago and Yale University Press.

Mountjoy, John B. 2000. "Pre-Hispanic Cultural Development along the Southern Coast of West Mexico." In *Greater Mesoamerica: The Archaeology of West and Northwest Mexico*, edited by Michael Foster and Shirley Gorenstein, 81–106. Salt Lake City: University of Utah Press.

Muir, Robert J., and Jonathan C. Driver. 2002. "Scale of Analysis and Zooarchaeological Interpretation: Pueblo III Faunal Variation in the Northern San Juan Region." *Journal of Anthropological Archaeology* 21:165–99.

Myers, Dick. 1985. "The Archaeology of Southeastern Arizona." Ms. at Arizona State Museum Archives, Tucson: University of Arizona.

Neitzel, Jill E. 2003. "Artifact Distributions at Pueblo Bonito." In *Pueblo Bonito: Center of the Chacoan World*, edited by Jill E. Neitzel, 107–26. Washington, D.C.: Smithsonian Books.

Nelson, Margaret C. 1999. *Mimbres during the Twelfth Century: Abandonment, Continuity, and Reorganization.* Tucson: University of Arizona Press.

Nelson, Ben A., and Steven A. LeBlanc, with contributions by James W. Lancaster, Paul E. Minnis, and Margaret C. Nelson. 1986. *Short-Term Sedentism in the American Southwest: The Mimbres Valley Salado.* Maxwell Museum of Anthropology Publication Series, Albuquerque: Maxwell Museum of Anthropology and the University of New Mexico Press.

Nelson, Richard S. 1981. *The Role of Pochteca Systems in Hohokam Exchange.* New York Unversity, Ann Arbor: University Microfilms.

———. 1986. "Pochtecas and Prestige: Mesoamerican Artifacts in Hohokam Sites." In *Ripples in the Chichimec Sea*, edited by Frances Joan Mathien and Randall H. McGuire, 154–84. Carbondale: Southern Illinois University Press.

Newell, Gillian, and Emiliano Gallaga. 2001. *Surveying the Archaeology of Northwest Mexico.* Salt Lake City: University of Utah Press.

Noguera, Eduardo. 1930. *Ruinas Arqueológicas del Norte de México.* México, D.F.: Publicaciones de la Secretaria de Educación Pública, Tomo II No. 14.

O'Donovan, Maria. 2002. *New Perspectives on Site Function and Scale of Cerro de Trincheras, Sonora, Mexico: The 1991 Surface Survey.* Arizona State Museum Archaeological Series No. 195. Tucson: University of Arizona.

Ortiz, Alfonso. 1979. *Handbook of North American Indians*, Volume 9: *Southwest*. William C. Sturtevant, General Editor. Washington, D.C.: Smithsonian Institution.

Ortman, Scott G. 2012. *Winds from the North: Tewa Origins and Historical Anthropology*. Salt Lake City: University of Utah Press.

Pailes, Matthew C. 2012. "Resultados Preliminares del Recorrido del Valle de Moctezuma entre Cumpas y Moctezuma, Sonora." México, D.F.: Technical Report on file with the Instituto Nacional de Antropología e Historia.

Pailes, Richard A. 1978. "The Rio Sonora Culture in Prehistoric Trade Systems." In *Across the Chichimec Sea: Papers in Honor of J. Charles Kelley*, edited by Carroll L. Riley and Basil C. Hedrick, 134–43. Carbondale: Southern Illinois University Press.

———. 1980. "The Upper Rio Sonora Valley in Prehistoric Trade." *Transactions of the Illinois State Academy of Science* 72(4):20–39.

Pailes, Richard A., and Daniel T. Reff. 1985. "Colonial Exchange Systems and the Decline of Paquimé.'" In *The Archaeology of West and Northwest Mesoamerica*, edited by Michael S. Foster and Phillip C. Weigand, 353–82. Boulder, CO: Westview Press.

Pailes, Richard A., and Joseph Whitecotton. 1979 [1985, 1992]. "The Greater Southwest and the Mesoamerican 'World System': An Exploratory Model of Frontier Relationships." In *Frontier: Comparative Studies*, edited by William Savage and Stephen Thompson, 105–21. Norman: University of Oklahoma Press.

Parker, Robert H. 1864. "Zoogeography and Ecology of Some Macro-Invertebrates, Particularly Molluscs, in the Gulf of California and the Continental Slope of Western Mexico." *Marine Geology of the Gulf of California* 3:331–76.

Parsons, Elsie C. 1996 [1939]. *Pueblo Indian Religion*, 2 vols. Reprint, Lincoln: University of Nebraska Press.

Pasahow, Ellen. 1993. "Semantics of the Effigy Mounds of Casas Grandes." In *Rock Art Papers*, edited by Ken Hedges, 7–16. San Diego Museum of Papers No. 29, San Diego.

Peterson, John A. 2001. *Archaeological Investigations of the Meyer Pithouse Village, Fort Bliss, Texas*, 2 vols. El Paso, TX: Directorate of Environment, Conservation Division, U.S. Army Air Defense Artillery Center.

Phelps, Alan L. 1998. "An Inventory of Prehistoric Native American Sites in Northwestern Chihuahua." *The Artifact* 36(2).

Phillips, David A., Jr. 1980. "The Prehistory of Chihuahua and Sonora, Mexico." *Journal of World Prehistory* 3:373–89.

———. 2012. "The Northwest Mexican Polychrome Tradition." In *Potters and Communities of Practice, Glaze Paint and Polychrome Pottery in the American Southwest, AD 1250–1700*, edited by Linda S. Cordell and Judith A. Habicht-Mauche, 34–44. Anthropological Papers of the University of Arizona 75. Tucson: University of Arizona Press.

Phillips, David A., Jr., and John P. Carpenter. 1999. "The Robles Phase of the Casas Grandes Culture." In *The Casas Grandes World*, edited by Curtis F. Schaafsma and Carroll L. Riley, 78–83. Salt Lake City: University of Utah Press.

Phillips, David A., Jr., and Eduardo Gamboa Carrera. 2012. "Shifting Visions of Paquimé: A Perspective from South of the Border." Ms. on file at the Maxwell Museum of Anthropology, University of New Mexico, Albuquerque.

Phillips, David A., Jr., Todd L. VanPool, and Christine S. VanPool. 2006. "The Horned Serpent Tradition in the North American Southwest." In *Religion of the Pre-Hispanic Southwest*, edited by C. S. VanPool, T. L. VanPool and D. A. Phillips, Jr., 17–30. Lanham, MD: AltaMira Press.

Piña Chan, Román, and Oi Kuniakí. 1982. *Exploraciones Arqueológicas en Tingambato, Michoacán*. México, D.F.:INAH.

Pitezel, Todd A. 2007. "Surveying Cerro de Moctezuma, Chihuahua, Mexico." *Kiva* 72:353–69.

———. 2011. "From Archaeology to Ideology in Northwest Mexico: Cerro de Moctezuma in the Casas Grandes Ritual Landscape." PhD diss., Department of Anthropology, University of Arizona, Tucson.

Pitezel, Todd A., and Michael Searcy. 2013. "Understanding the Viejo Period: What Are the Data?" In *Collected Papers from the 17th Biennial Mogollon Archaeology Conference*, edited by Lonnie C. Ludeman, 77–81. Silver City, NM: Western New Mexico University.

Publ, H. 1985. "Pre-Hispanic Exchange Networks and the Development of Social Complexity in Western Mexico: The Aztatlan Interaction Sphere." PhD diss. Department of Anthropology, Southern Illinois University, Carbondale.

———. 1992. "Interaction Spheres, Merchants, and Trade in Pre-Hispanic West Mexico." *Research in Economic Anthropology* 12:201–42.

Punzo Díaz, José Luis. 2013a. "Los Moradores de las Casas en Acantilado de Durango. Rememorando el Mundo de la Vida de los Grupos Serranos en el Siglo XVII." PhD diss., Escuela Nacional de Antropología e Historia, México, D.F.

———. 2013b. "La Población Chalchihuiteña del Valle de Guadiana." In *Historia de Durango. Época Antigua*, vol. 1, edited by José Luis Punzo Díaz and M.-A. Hers, 190–207. Durango, México: Instituto Invesigaciones de Historia, Universidad Autónoma de Ciudad Juárez del Estado de Durango, Durango.

Punzo Díaz, José Luis, and Alfonso Ramírez. 2008. "The Chalchihuites Chronology Revisited: The Guadiana Branch." Paper presented at the 73rd Annual Meeting of the Society for American Archeology, Vancouver.

Radding, Cynthia. 1997. *Wandering Peoples: Colonialism, Ethnic Spaces, and Ecological Frontiers in Northwestern Mexico, 1700–1850*. Durham, NC: Duke University Press.

Rakita, Gordon F. M. 2009. *Ancestors and Elites: Emergent Complexity and Ritual Practices in the Casas Grandes Polity*. Lanham, MD: AltaMira Press.

———. 2012. "The Longue Durée of Mortuary Ritual in Chihuahua, Mexico." Paper Presented at the 54th International Congress of Americanists, Vienna.

Rappaport, Roy. 1999. *Ritual and Religion in the Making of Humanity*. Cambridge: Cambridge University Press.

Ravesloot, John C. 1979. "The Animas Phase: The Post-Classic Mimbres Occupation of the Mimbres Valley." MA thesis, Department of Anthropology, Southern Illinois University, Carbondale.

———. 1988. *Mortuary Practices and Social Differentiation at Casas Grandes, Chihuahua, Mexico*. Anthropological Papers of the University of Arizona 49. Tucson: University of Arizona Press.

———. 1994. "Burial Practices in the Livingston Area." In *Archaeology of the Salado in the Livingston Area of Tonto Basin, Roosevelt Platform Mound Study: Report on the Livingston Management Group, Pinto Creek Complex*, edited by David Jacobs, 833–50. Roosevelt Monograph Series No. 3, Anthropological Field Studies No. 32. OCRM, Tempe: Arizona State University.

Rawlings, Tiffany A., and Jonathan C. Driver. 2010. "Paleodiet of Domestic Turkey, Shield Pueblo (5MT3807), Colorado: Isotopic Analysis and its Implications for Care of a Household Domesticate." *Journal of Archaeological Sciences* 37 2433–41.

Redfield, Robert. 1956. *Peasant Society and Culture: An Anthropological Approach to Civilization*. Chicago: University of Chicago Press.

Reed, Paul F. 2008. "Salmon Pueblo as a Ritual and Residential Chacoan Great House." In *Chaco's Northern Prodigies: Salmon, Aztec, and the Ascendency of the Middle San Juan Region After AD 1100*, edited by Paul Reed, 42–61. Salt Lake City: University of Utah Press.

Riley, Carroll L. 1982. *The Frontier People. The Greater Southwest in the Protohistoric Period*. Center for Archeological Investigtions Occasional Paper 1. Carbondale: Southern Illinois University.

———. 1985. "Spanish Contact and the Collapse of the Sonoran Statelets." In *The Archaeology of West and Northwest Mesoamerica*, edited by Michael S. Foster and Philip C. Weigand, 419–30. Boulder, CO: Westview Press.

———. 1987. *The Frontier People*. Albuquerque: University of New Mexico Press.

———. 1999. "The Sonoran Statelets and Casas Grandes." In *The Casas Grandes World*, edited by C. S. Schaafsma and C. L. Riley, 193–200. Salt Lake City: University of Utah Press.

———. 2005. *Becoming Aztlan: Mesoamerican Influences in the Greater Southwest (AD 1200–1500)*. Salt Lake City: University of Utah Press.

Robles, Carmen Aessio. 1925. *La Region Arqueológica de Casas Grandes, Chihuahua. Mexico*, México, D.F.: Imprenta Nuñez.

Robles, Jasinto, and Ricardo Sánchez. 2011. "Presencia de Amazonita (KAlSi3O8) en la Tierra Caliente Michoacana." In *Raíces Prehispánicas en la Historia de la Tierra Caliente Michoacana*. Zamora: Colegio de Michoacán.

Romney, Thomas Cottam. 2005. *Mormon Colonies in Mexico*. Salt Lake City: University of Utah Press.

Sánchez, Guadalupe, John P. Carpenter, and M. Elisa Villalpando Canchola. 1998. "De los Tiempos y el Rio: Investigaciones Preliminares en el Sitio de La Playa, Sonora." In *Antropología e Historia del Occidente de México II*, edited by Rosa Brambila Paz, 985–1009. XXIV Mesa Redonda, Tepic: Sociedad Mexicana de Antropología.

Sandor, Jonathon A. 1990. "Prehistoric Agricultural Terraces and Soils in the Mimbres Area, New Mexico." *World Archaeology* 22:70–86.

Santley, Robert S., and Rani T. Alexander. 1992. "The Political Economy of Core-Periphery Systems." In *Resources, Power, and Interregional Integration*, edited by Edward M. Schortman and Patricia A. Urban, 23–50. New York: Plenum Press.

Sayles, E. B. 1936. *An Archaeological Survey of Chihuahua, Mexico*. Globe, AZ: Gila Pueblo Medallion Paper 22.

Schaafsma, Curtis F., J. Royce Cox, and Daniel Wolfman. 2002. "Archaeomagnetic Dating at the Joyce Well Site." In *The Joyce Well Site on the Frontier of the Casas Grandes World*, edited by James M. Skibo, Eugene B. McCluney, and William H. Walker, 129–48. Salt Lake City: University of Utah Press.

Schaafsma, Curtis F., and Carroll L. Riley. 1999. "The Casas Grandes World: Analysis and Conclusion." In *The Casas Grandes World*, edited by Curtis Schaafsma and Carroll L. Riley, 237–49. Salt Lake City: University of Utah Press.

Schaafsma, Polly. 1997. *Rock Art Sites in Chihuahua, Mexico*. Office of Archaeological Studies, Museum of New Mexico Archaeology Notes 171, Santa Fe.

———. 1998. "The Paquimé Rock Art Style, Chihuahua, Mexico." In *Rock Art of the Chihuahuan Desert Borderlands*, edited by S. Smith-Savage and R. J. Mallouf, 33–44. Alpine, TX: Center for Big Bend Studies, Sul Ross State University, and the Texas Parks and Wildlife Department.

———. 1999. "Tlálocs, Kachinas, Sacred Bundles, and Related Symbolism in the Southwest and Mesoamerica." In *The Casas Grandes World*, edited by Curtis F. Schaafsma and Carroll L. Riley, 164–92. Salt Lake City: University of Utah Press.

———. 2000. *Warrior, Shield, and Star: Imagery and Ideology of Pueblo Warfare*. Santa Fe, NM: Western Edge Press.

———. 2001. "Quatzalcoatl and the Horned and Feathered Serpent of the Southwest." In *The Road to Aztlan: Art from a Mythic Homeland*, edited by Virginia M. Fields and Victor Zamudio-Taylor, 138–49. Los Angeles: Los Angeles County Museum of Art.

Schaafsma, Polly, and Karl A. Taube. 2006. "Bringing the Rain." In *A Pre-Columbian World*, edited by Jeffrey Quilter and Mary Miller, 231–85. Washington, D.C.: Dumbarton Oaks.

Schlanger, Sarah H., and Richard Wilshusen. 1993. "Local Abandonments and Regional Conditions in the North American Southwest." In *Abandonment of Settlements and Regions, Ethnoarchaeological and Archaeological Approaches*, edited by Catherine M. Cameron and Steve A. Tompka, 85–98. Cambridge: Cambridge University Press.

Schleher, Kari L. 2010. "The Role of Standardization in Specialization of Ceramic Production at San Marcos Pueblo, New Mexico." PhD diss., Department of Anthropology, University of New Mexico, Albuquerque.

Schleher, Kari L., Deborah L. Huntley, and Cynthia L. Herhahn. 2012. "Glazed Over: Composition of Northern Rio Grande Glaze Ware Paints, from San Marcos Pueblo." In *Potters and Communities of Practice, Glaze Paint and Polychrome Pottery in the American Southwest, AD 150–1700*, edited by Linda S. Cordell and Judith A. Habicht-Mauche, 97–106, Anthropological Papers of the University of Arizona 75. Tucson: University of Arizona Press.

Schmidt, Robert H., Jr. 1973. *A Geographical Survey of Chihuahua*. Monograph No. 37. El Paso: University of Texas at El Paso.

———. 1992. "Chihuahua: Tierra de Contrastes Geográficos." In *Historia General de Chihuahua I: Geología, Geografía, y Arqueología*, edited by Arturo Márquez-Alameda, 45–101. Cd. Juárez: Universidad Autónoma de Ciudad Juárez y Gobierno del Estado de Chihuahua.

Schmidt, Robert H., Jr., and Rex E. Gerald. 1988. "The Distribution of Conservation-Type Water-Control Systems in the Northern Sierra Madre Occidental." *Kiva* 53:165–79.

Schortman, Edward M., and Patricia A. Urban. 2004. "Modeling the Roles of Craft Production in Ancient Political Economies." *Journal of Archaeological Research* 12:185–226.

Scott, S. D., Jr. 1966. "Dendrochronology in Mexico." Papers of the Laboratory of Tree-ring Research No. 2. Tucson: University of Arizona Press.

Searcy, Michael. 2011. "Decorative Renascence: Tracing Early Ceramic Designs into the Late Prehistoric Period in the U.S. Southwest/Northwest Mexico." Paper presented at the 76th Annual Meeting of the Society for American Archaeology, Sacramento, CA.

Shelley, Phillip H. 2006. "Lithic Assembly from Salmon Ruins." In *Thirty-Five Years of Archaeological Research at Salmon Ruins, New Mexico*, Volume 3: *Archaeobotanical Research and Other Analytical Studies*, 1013–55. Tucson and Bloomfield, NM: Center for Desert Archaeology & Salmon Ruins Museum.

Shepard, Anna O. 1936. "The Technology of Pecos Pottery." In *The Pottery of Pecos*, vol. 2, by Alfred V. Kidder and Anna O. Shepard, 389–587. New Haven, CT: Phillips Academy.

Skibo, James M., Eugene B. McCluney, and William H. Walker. 2002. *The Joyce Well Site on the Frontier of the Casas Grandes World.* Salt Lake City: University of Utah Press.

Smith, Carol A. 1976. "Regional Economic Systems: Linking Geographical Models and Socioeconomic Problems." In *Regional Analysis*, Volume I: *Social and Economic Systems*, edited by Carol A. Smith, 3–68. New York: Academic Press.

Snead, James E., Winifred Creamer, and Tineke Van Zandt. 2004. "'Ruins of Our Forefathers': Large Sites and Site Clusters in the Northern Rio Grande." In *The Protohistoric Pueblo World AD 1275–1600*, edited by E. Charles Adams and Andrew I. Duff, 26–34. Tucson: University of Arizona Press.

Somerville, Andrew D., Ben A. Nelson, and Kelly J. Knudson. 2010. "Isotopic Investigation of Pre-Hispanic Macaw Breeding in Northwest Mexico." *Journal of Anthropological Archaeology* 29(1):125–35.

Spaulding, Albert C. 1968. "Explanation in Archaeology." In *New Perspectives in Archaeology*, edited by Sally R. Binford and Lewis R. Binford, 33–41. Chicago: University of Chicago Press.

Speller, Camilla. 2009. "Investigating Turkey (*Meleagris gallopavo*) Domestication in the Southwest United States through Ancient DNA Analysis." PhD diss., Department of Archaeology, Simon Fraser University, Burnaby, British Columbia.

Speth, John D. 2004. *Life on the Periphery: Economic Change in Late Prehistoric Southeastern New Mexico.* University of Michigan Memoirs No. 37. Ann Arbor: Museum of Anthropology.

———. 2008. "Following in Jane Kelley's Footsteps: Bloom Mound Revisited." In *Celebrating Jane Holden Kelley and Her Work*, edited by Meade F. Kemrer, 35–48. Albuquerque: New Mexico Archaeological Council Special Publication No. 5.

Spielmann, Kathryn. 2004. "Clusters Revisited." In *The Protohistoric Pueblo World AD 1275–1600*, edited by E. Charles Adams and Andrew I. Duff, 137–44. Tucson: University of Arizona Press.

Sprehn, Maria S. 2003. "Social Complexity and the Specialist Potters of Casas Grandes in Northern Mexico." PhD diss., Department of Anthropology, University of New Mexico, Albuquerque.

Stevenson, C. M., B. E. Scheetz, and J. Carpenter. 1989. "Obsidian Dating: Recent Advances in the Experimental Determination and Application of Obsidian Hydration Dates." *Archaeometry* 32(2):193–206.

Stewart, Joe D. 1984. "Jornada Ceramics at Casas Grandes: Chronology and Interaction." *Pottery Southwest* 1(2):1–3.

Stewart, Joe D., Jonathan C. Driver, and Jane H. Kelley. 1991. "The Capitan North Project: Chronology." In *Mogollon V*, edited by Patrick H. Beckett, 177–90. COAS Publishing and Research, Las Cruces.

Stewart, Joe D., Jane H. Kelley, A. C. MacWilliams, and Paula Reimer. 2005. "The Viejo Period of Chihuahua Culture in Northwestern Mexico." *Latin American Antiquity* 16:169–92.

Stewart, Joe D., A. C. MacWilliams, and Jane H. Kelley. 2004. "Archaeological Chronology of West Central Chihuahua." In *Surveying the Archaeology of Northwest Mexico*, edited by Gillian E. Newell and Emiliano Gallaga, 247–64. Salt Lake City: University of Utah Press.

Stubbs, Stanley A. 1950. *Bird's-Eye View of the Pueblos, Ground Plans of the Indian Villages of New Mexico and Arizona with Aerial Photographs and Scale Drawings*. Norman: University of Oklahoma Press.

Stuiver, Minze, and Paula Reimer. 2005. *CALIB Manual*. Revision 5.0. www.calib.qub.ac.uk/crev50/09/02/2005.

Taube, Karl. 2006. "Climbing Flower Mountain: Concepts of Resurrection and the Afterlife in Ancient Teotihuacan." In *Arqueología e Historia del Centro de México. Homenaje a Eduardo Matos Moctezuma*, edited by Leonardo López Lujan, David Carrasco, and Lourdes Cué, 153–70. México, D.F.: Instituto Nacional de Antropología e Historia.

Teague, Lynn S. 1998. *Textiles in Southwestern Prehistory*. University of New Mexico Press, Albuquerque.

Thompson, Marc. 2006. "Pre-Columbian Venus: Celestial Twin and Icon of Duality." In *Religion in the Pre-Hispanic Southwest*, edited by Christine VanPool, Todd VanPool, and David A. Phillips, Jr., 165–84. New York: AltaMira Press.

Thompson, Raymond H. 1961. "Rasgos Diagnósticos de la Cerámica del Siglo XIV en el Suroeste de los Estados Unidos y el Noroeste de México." Paper presented to the 9th Mesa Redonda, Sociedad Mexicana de Antropología, Nuevo Casas Grandes, Chihuahua. Arizona State Museum archives, University of Arizona, Tucson.

Townsend, Richard F. 1992. "Landscape and Symbol." In *The Ancient Americas: Art from the Sacred Landscapes*, edited by Richard F. Townsend, 159–70. Chicago: The Art Institute of Chicago.

———. 2005. "Casas Grandes in the Art of the Ancient Southwest." In *Casas Grandes and the Ceramic Art of the Ancient Southwest*, edited by R. F. Townsend, 1–28. Chicago: Art Institute of Chicago.

Turner, Raymond M., Robert H. Webb, Janice E. Bowers, and James Rodney Hastings. 2003. *The Changing Mile Revisited*. Tucson: University of Arizona Press.

Tuthill, Carr. 1947. *The Tres Alamos Site on the San Pedro River, Southeastern Arizona*. Amerind Foundation Publications No. 4, Dragoon, AZ.

Valdéz, Francisco, Otto Schondube, and J. P. Empoux. 2005. *Arqueología de la Cuenca de Sayula*. Universidad de Guadalajara e Institut de Recherche pour le Developement, Guadalajara.

VanPool, Christine S. 2001. "Birds, Burials, and Belief at Paquimé, Chihuahua, Mexico." In *From Paquimé to Mata Ortiz: The Legacy of Ancient Casas Grandes*, edited by G. Johnson, 73–88. San Diego: San Diego Museum of Man.

———. 2002. "Flight of the Shaman." *Archaeology*, 55(1):40–43.

———. 2003. "The Shaman Priests of the Casas Grandes Region." *American Antiquity* 68:696–717.

———. 2009. "The Signs of the Sacred: Identifying Shamans Using Archaeological Evidence." *Journal of Anthropological Archaeology* 28:177–90.

VanPool, Christine S., and Elizabeth E. Newsome. 2012. "The Spirit in the Material: A Case Study of Animism in the American Southwest." *American Antiquity* 77:243–62.

VanPool, Christine S., and Todd L. VanPool. 2006. "Gender in Middle Range Societies: A Case Study in Casas Grandes Iconography." *American Antiquity* 71:53–75.

———. 2007. *Signs of the Casas Grandes Shamans*. University of Utah Press, Salt Lake City.

———. 2009. "The Semantics of Local Knowledge: Using Ethnosemantics to Study Folk Taxonomy Represented in the Archaeological Record." *Journal of Anthropological Research* 65:529–54.

———. 2012. "Breath and Being: Contextualizing Object Persons at Paquimé, Chihuahua, Mexico." In *Archaeology of Spiritualities*, edited by K. Rountree, C. Morris, and A. Peatfield, 87–106. New York: Springer.

VanPool, Todd L., Christine S. VanPool, Gordon F. M. Rakita, and Robert D. Leonard. 2008. "Birds, Bells, and Shells: The Long Reach of the Aztlatlán Trading Tradition." In *Touching the Past: Traditions of Casas Grandes*, edited by Glenna Nielsen, 5–14. Provo, UT: Brigham Young University Press.

VanPool, Todd L., and Robert D. Leonard. 2002. "Specialized Ground Stone Production in the Casas Grandes Region of Northern Chihuahua, Mexico." *American Antiquity* 67:710–30.

VanPool, Todd L., Christine S. Van Pool, and Robert D. Leonard. 2005. "The Casas Grandes Core and Periphery." In *Archaeology between the Borders: Proceedings from the 13th Biennial Jornada Mogollon Conference*, edited by Marc Thompson, J. Jurgena, and L. Jackson, 25–35. El Paso, TX: El Paso Museum of Archaeology.

Vargas, Victoria D. 1995. *Copper Bell Trade Patterns in the Pre-Hispanic U.S. Southwest and Northwest Mexico*. Tucson: Arizona State Museum Archaeological Series 187. Tucson: Arizona State Museum, University of Arizona.

———. 2001. "Mesoamerican Copper Bells in the Pre-Hispanic Southwestern United States and Northwestern Mexico." In *The Road to Aztlan: Art from a Mythic Homeland*, edited by Virginia M. Fields and Victor Zamudio-Taylor, 196–211. Los Angeles: Los Angeles County Museum of Art.

Varien, Mark D. 2010. "Depopulation of the Northern San Juan Region: Historical Review and Archaeological Context." In *Leaving Mesa Verde: Peril and Change in the Thirteenth Century Southwest*, edited by T. Kohler, M. Varien, and A. Wright, 1–34. Amerind Studies in Archaeology. Tucson: University of Arizona Press.

Villalpando Canchola, M. Elisa 2000. "The Archaeological Traditions of Sonora." In *Greater Mesoamerica: The Archaeology of West and Northwest Mexico*, edited by Michael S. Foster and Shirley Gorenstein, 241–53. Salt Lake City: University of Utah Press.

———. 2001. "Las Rutas de Intercambio en Sonora." In *La Gran Chichimeca, el Lugar de las Rocas Secas*, edited by Beatriz Braniff, 250–54. México, D.F.: CONACULTA/Jaca Books.

Villalpando Canchola, M. Elisa, Carlos Cruz-Guzmán, and Silvia I. Nava-Maldonado. 2010. *Informe de las Excavaciones Extensivas en el Predio Centro de Visitantes SON:F:10:2. Proyecto Institucional Trincheras*. Hermosillo, SON: Centro INAH Sonora, Instituto Nacional de Antropología e Historia.

———. 2011. *Proyecto Institucional Trincheras. Informe de la Temporada de Campo 2010 y Análisis de Materiales*. Hermosillo, SON: Centro INAH Sonora, Instituto Nacional de Antropología e Historia.

Villalpando Canchola, M. Elisa, Carlos Cruz-Guzmán, Silvia I. Nava-Maldonado, and Adrián López-Dávila. 2012. *Proyecto Institucional Trincheras. Informe de las Excavaciones en SON:F:10:151 "Los Crematorios."* Hermosillo, SON: Centro INAH Sonora Instituto Nacional de Antropología e Historia.

Villalpando Canchola, M. Elisa, and Randall H. McGuire. 2009. *Entre Muros de Piedras. La Arqueología de Cerro de Trincheras*. Hermosillo, SON: Instituto Sonorense de Cultura/Instituto Nacional de Antropología e Historia.

Walker, William H. 2002. "Stratigraphy and Practical Reason." *American Anthropologist* 104:159–77.

Walker, William H., and Gaea McGahee. 2001. "Animated Waters: The Ritualized Life History of Wells, Reservoirs, and Springs at Casas Grandes, Chihuahua." Paper presented at 66th Annual Society of American Archaeology meetings, New Orleans.

Wallerstein, Immanuel. 1974. *The Modern World System*. New York: Academic Press.

———. 1979. *The Modern World System II*. New York: Academic Press.

Webb, Robert H., Stanley A. Leake, and Raymond M. Turner. 2007. *The Ribbon of Green: Change in Riparian Vegetation in the Southwestern United States*. Tucson: University of Arizona Press.

Webster, Monica. 2001. "Prehistoric Diet and Human Adaptation in West Central Chihuahua, Mexico." MA thesis, Department of Archaeology, The University of Calgary, Calgary.

Webster, Grady L., and Conrad J. Bahre. 2001. *Changing Plant Life of La Frontera*. Albuquerque: University of New Mexico Press.

Webster, Monica, and M. Annie Katzenberg. 2008. "Dietary Reconstruction and Human Adaptation in West Central Chihuahua." In *Celebrating Jane Holden Kelley and Her Work*, edited by Meade Kemrer, 71–102. New Mexico Archeological Council Special Publication No. 5. Albuquerque: New Mexico Archaeological Council.

Weigand, Phillip C. 2008. "Turquoise: Formal Economic Interrelationships between Mesoamerica and the North American Southwest." In *Archaeology without Borders: Contact, Commerce, and Change in the U. S. Southwest and Northwestern Mexico*, edited by Laurie Webster, Maxine McBrinn, and Eduardo Gamboa Carrera, 343–53. Boulder: University Press of Colorado.

Weigand, Phillip C., and Garmon Harbottle. 1993. "The Role of Turquoise in the Ancient Mesoamerican Trade Structure." In *The American Southwest and Mesoamerica: Systems of Prehistoric Exchange*, edited by Jonathan E. Erickson and Timothy G. Baugh, 159–78. New York: Plenum Press.

Wells, E. Christian, and Karla A. Davis-Salazar. 2007. "Mesoamerican Ritual Economy, Materialization as Ritual and Economic Process." In *Mesoamerican Ritual Economy: Archaeological Perspectives*, edited by E. Christian Wells and Karla A. Davis-Salazar, 1–26. Boulder: University Press of Colorado.

Wesche, Alice. 1981. *Runs Far, Son of the Chichimeca*. Santa Fe: Museum of New Mexico Press.

Whalen, Michael E. 1994. *Turquoise Ridge and Late Prehistoric Mobility in the Desert Mogollon Region*. Anthropological Paper No. 118. Salt Lake City: University of Utah Press.

———. 2011. "Informe Técnico Parcial al Consejo de Arqueología, Instituto Nacional de Antropología e Historia de la Segunda Temporada del Proyecto: Excavaciones en el Sitio 565, Casas Grandes, Chihuahua." Ms on file with the University of Tulsa, Tulsa.

———. 2013. "Wealth, Status, Ritual, and Marine Shell at Casas Grandes, Chihuahua, Mexico." *American Antiquity* 78:624–39.

Whalen, Michael E., and Paul E. Minnis. 1996. "Ball Courts and Political Centralization in the Casas Grandes Region." *American Antiquity* 61:732–46.

———. 2000. "Leadership at Casas Grandes, Chihuahua, Mexico." In *Alternative Leadership Strategies in the Pre-Hispanic Southwest*, edited by Barbara J. Mills, 168–79. Tucson: University of Arizona Press.

———. 2001. *Casas Grandes and Its Hinterland: Prehistoric Regional Organization in Northwest Mexico*. Tucson: University of Arizona Press.

———. 2003. "The Local and the Distant in the Origin of Casas Grandes, Chihuahua, Mexico." *American Antiquity* 68:314–32.

———. 2009a. *The Neighbors of Casas Grandes, Excavating Medio Period Communities of Northwest Chihuahua, Mexico*. Tucson: University of Arizona Press.

———. 2009b. "Informe Técnico Parcial al Consejo de Arqueología, Instituto Nacional de Antropología e Historia de la Primera Temporada del Proyecto:

Excavaciones en el Sitio 315: Investigaciones del Sistema Regional Paquimé, Chihuahua, México." Ms on file with the University of Tulsa, Tulsa and University of Oklahoma, Norman.

———. 2010. "Informe Técnico Parcial al Consejo de Arqueología, Instituto Nacional de Antropología e Historia del Proyecto: Excavaciones en el Sitio 315, Casas Grandes, Chihuahua: Segunda Temporada." Ms on file with University of Tulsa, Tulsa and University of Oklahoma, Norman.

———. 2012. "Ceramics and Polity in the Casas Grandes Area, Chihuahua, Mexico." *American Antiquity* 77:403–24.

Whalen, Michael E., A. C. MacWilliams, and Todd Pitezel. 2010. "Reconsidering the Size and Structure of Casas Grandes, Chihuahua, Mexico." *American Antiquity* 75:527–51.

Wilcox, David R. 1986. "The Tepiman Connection: A Model of Mesoamerican-Southwestern Interaction." In *Ripples in the Chichimec Sea: New Considerations of Southwestern-Mesoamerican Interactions*, edited by Frances Joan Mathien and Randall H. McGuire, 135–54. Carbondale: Southern Illinois University Press.

———. 1996. "Pueblo III People and Polity in Relational Context." In *The Prehistoric Pueblo World, A.D. 1150–1350*, edited by M. Adler, 241–54. Tucson: University of Arizona Press.

———. 2003. "Coalescent Communities GIS database Version 1.0: Museum of Northern Arizona, Archaeology Southwest, Western Mapping Company." Ms. on file at Archaeology Southwest, Tucson.

Wilcox, David R., P. C. Weigand, John S. Wood, and Jerry B. Howard. 2008. "Ancient Cultural Interplay of the American Southwest in the Mexican Northwest." *Journal of the Southwest* 50(2):103–206.

Wilshusen, Richard H. 2002. "Estimating Population in the Central Mesa Verde Region." In *Seeking the Center Place: Archeology and Ancient Communities in the Mesa Verde Region*, edited by Mark D. Varien and Richard Wilshusen, 101–20. Salt Lake City: University of Utah Press.

Wilshusen, Richard H., and Ruth M. Van Dyke. 2006. "Chaco's Beginnings." In *The Archaeology of Chaco Canyon*, edited by Stephen H. Lekson, 211–59. Santa Fe, NM: School of American Research Press.

Wiseman, Regge N. 1970. "Artifacts of Interest from the Bloom Mound, Southeastern New Mexico." *The Artifact* 8(2):1–10.

———. 1981. "Playas Incised, Sierra Blanca Variety: A New Pottery Type in the Jornada Mogollon." In *Transactions of the 16th Regional Archeological Symposium for Southeastern New Mexico and Western Texas*, 21–27. El Paso Archaeological Society, El Paso, TX.

———. 1996. *The Land in Between: Archaic and Formative Occupations along the Upper Rio Hondo of Southeastern New Mexico*. Archaeology Note 125. Office of Archaeological Studies, Museum of New Mexico, Santa Fe.

———. 2002. *The Fox Place: A Late Prehistoric Hunter-Gatherer Pithouse Village near Roswell, New Mexico*. Archaeology Notes No. 234. Office of Archaeological Studies, Museum of New Mexico, Santa Fe.

———. 2004. "The Pottery of the Henderson Site: The 1980–1981 Seasons." In *Life on the Periphery: Economic Change in Late Prehistoric Southeastern New Mexico*, edited by John D. Speth, 67–95. Museum of Anthropology, University of Michigan Memoirs No. 37, Ann Arbor.

———. 2006. "Advances in Prehistoric Pottery Studies Related to Southeastern New Mexico: An Annotated Bibliography of Selected Titles, 1976 through 2005." *The Artifact* 44:105–42.

Wiseman, Regge N., Robert H. Cobean, and Clark C. Pfingsten. 1971. "Preliminary Report of Salvage Excavations at LA2112, Lincoln County, New Mexico." *The Artifact* 9(3):1–11.

Woosley, Anne I., and Bart Olinger. 1993. "The Casas Grandes Ceramic Tradition: Production and Interregional Exchange of Ramos Polychrome." In *Culture and Contact: Charles C. Di Peso's Gran Chichimeca*, edited by Anne I. Woosley and John Ravesloot, 105–32. Albuquerque: University of New Mexico Press.

Woosley, Anne I., and John C. Ravesloot. 1993. *Culture and Contact: Charles C. Di Peso's Gran Chichimeca*. Albuquerque: University of New Mexico Press.

Wright, Barton. 1973. *Kachinas: A Hopi Artist's Documentary*. Flagstaff: Northland Press.

Yetman, David, and David L. Shaul. 2010. *The Ópatas: In Search of a Sonoran People*. Tucson: University of Arizona Press.

Zazueta Manjarrez, Carlos, and Cecilia Guerrero Astorga. 2008. *Gordon F. Ekholm Excavaciones en Guasave, México*. Culicán, SIN: Once Ríos, Colegio de Sinaloa e Instituto Nacional de Antropología e Historia.

CONTRIBUTORS

Linda S. Cordell (PhD, University of California, Santa Barbara) was director emerita of the Natural History Museum of the University of Colorado, Boulder. A leading scholar of archaeology of the U.S. Southwest and northern Mexico, she was elected to the National Academy of Science and was the author of the authoritative summary of southwestern prehistory. She passed away, spring, 2013.

Rafael Cruz (graduate in archaeology of the Escuela Nacional de Antropología e Historia) is an investigator with the Chihuahuan center of the Instituto Nacional de Antropología e Historia. He has conducted numerous research projects in the Casas Grandes region during the past two decades and has presented numerous presentations and publications on this research.

John E. Douglas (PhD, University of Arizona) is professor of anthropology at the University of Montana. He has conducted excavations and surveys in the Animas region of southeastern Arizona and the Sierra region of eastern Sonora. He is interested in social interactions at the regional scale, the interpretation of areas viewed as peripheral, and ceramic analysis. In addition to publications and research in the "International Four Corners" of NW Mexico and SW United States, he maintains research in the Neotropics, in the Amazon Basin, and the Maya region.

Eduardo Gamboa (graduate in archaeology of the Escuela Nacional de Antropología e Historia) was director of the Museo de las Culturas del Norte and is an investigator with Instituto Nacional de Antropología e Historia in Chihuahua. He has worked in the Casas Grandes region for many years, specializing on understanding communities in the Sierra Madre of Chihuahua. He has authored and edited numerous publications on Paquimé and its region.

Jane H. Kelley (PhD, Harvard University) is a professor emerita of archaeology at the University of Calgary with research experience in New Mexico, El Salvador, and the Sudan. She has been involved in west-central Chihuahuan archaeology as codirector of a long-term project since 1990. She has served as past president of the Canadian Archaeological Society, treasurer of the Society of American Archaeology, and director of the Humanities Institute at the University of Calgary.

A. C. MacWilliams (PhD, University of Arizona) is currently an adjunct professor of archaeology with the University of Calgary. He has been involved in Chihuahua archaeology since 1990. His primary interests are mid-Holocene through Ceramic Period archaeology in Chihuahua, flaked-stone technology, and boundary areas. Recent publication topics include flaked-stone technology in Chihuahua, the history of looting in Chihuahua, the northward spread of maize agriculture, and the scale of Paquimé (Casas Grandes).

Paul E. Minnis (PhD, University of Michigan) is a professor emeritus of anthropology at the University of Oklahoma. He conducts research on the pre-Hispanic ethnobotany and archaeology of the U.S. Southwest and northwest Mexico. He has studied Paquimé since 1984 and codirected research projects on Casas Grandes/Paquimé in northwest Chihuahua since 1989. He is the author or editor of twelve books and numerous articles. He is a past president of the Society of Ethnobiology, treasurer and press editor for the Society for American Archaeology, and cofounder of the Southwest Symposium.

David A. Phillips, Jr. (PhD, University of Arizona) is curator of archaeology at the Maxwell Museum of Anthropology, University of New Mexico, and a research associate professor of Anthropology at the university. His research focus on the North American Southwest extends to the prehistoric cultures of northwest Mexico. Since 1990, he has participated in fieldwork in central and west-central Chihuahua.

Todd Pitezel (PhD, University of Arizona) is assistant curator of archaeology and the *Arizona Antiquities Act* administrator at the Arizona

State Museum. He has conducted archaeological research in the Casas Grandes area since 1998. His research interests include ritual landscape with a focus on hilltop sites in the Medio Period Casas Grandes world, the roots of the Medio Period, and protohistoric times in the international borderlands.

José Luis Punzo (PhD, Escuela Nacional de Antropología) is currently a titular researcher for the INAH in the state of Michoacán. He has been involved in northern and western Mexico archaeology since 1994. He directed several research projects, especially in the state of Durango. His primary interests are in Chalchihuites culture, the transition of the societies among the Classic and Postclassic periods of western and northwestern Mesoamerica, and the relations between the U.S. Southwest and Mesoamerica. He is the author or editor of numerous books and articles about Durango and western and northwestern México. He was the director of the Museo de las Culturas del Norte in Paquimé, Chihuahua, and is a past president of the Southwest Symposium.

Gordon Rakita (PhD, University of New Mexico) is professor of anthropology at the University of North Florida (UNF). As a bioarchaeologist, his research interests include prehistoric mortuary and ritual practices, physical anthropology, evolutionary theory, and emergent social inequality and complexity. Most of his research has focused on the Casas Grandes culture area, though he also has published on archaeological materials from the U.S. Southwest and Peru. He currently serves as Director of Academic Technology at UNF and holds an adjunct faculty appointment with the Department of Anthropology at the University of New Mexico.

Michael T. Searcy (PhD, University of Oklahoma) is an assistant professor of anthropology at Brigham Young University. His research includes the dynamics of sociopolitical organization, long-distance interaction, and iconographic analysis. In addition to his primary research focus on the Casas Grandes region, he has worked on the Fremont of Utah and among Mayan communities in Guatemala. He has authored a book and many articles, and is editor of the *Utah Archaeology*.

Christine S. VanPool (PhD, University of New Mexico) is an associate professor of anthropology at the University of Missouri. For the past 18 years her main research focuses on archaeological method and theory as it pertains to ritual and pottery symbolism in the Casas Grandes world. Since 2007, she has codirected field projects with Gordon F. M. Rakita and Todd L. VanPool in northern Mexico and southern New Mexico. She is the author or editor of five books and numerous articles.

Todd L. VanPool (PhD, University of New Mexico) is an associate professor of anthropology at the University of Missouri. His research focuses on archaeological method and theory, quantitative analysis of archaeological data, and the economic and political organization of the late pre-Hispanic cultures of the North American Southwest. His most recent field research has focused on 76 Draw, a Medio Period Casas Grandes settlement in southern New Mexico. His publications include two books, three edited volumes, and numerous book chapters and articles.

M. Elisa Villalpando (graduate of the archaeology program at the Escuela Nacional de Antropología, and Centro de Estudios Historicos of El Colegio de México). A researcher with the Centro INAH Sonora since 1979, she has directed and participated in archaeological projects on hunter-gatherers and fishermen on the central coast of Sonora and binational projects on early farmers and complex societies of the Sonoran Desert. For the past seven years, she has been in charge of Proyecto Institucional Trincheras and general coordinator of the public opening of the Cerro de Trincheras archeological site. She is author and editor of numerous books and articles about the archaeology of northern Mexico and is currently Archaeology Coordinator for Centro INAH Sonora and alternate for the Presidency of the Council of Archaeology.

John A. Ware (PhD, University of Colorado) was executive director of the Amerind Foundation and former director of the Laboratory of Anthropology in Santa Fe. His recent research focuses on the intersection of archaeology and ethnography, the topic of a forthcoming volume. Ware is also vitally interested in the role of private research institutions in knowledge synthesis and the dissemination of anthropological information to a broad public audience.

Michael E. Whalen (PhD, University of Michigan) is a professor in the department of anthropology at the University of Tulsa. His research interests include complex societies, processes of sociocultural evolution, prehistoric social structure, and ceramic analysis. Before coming to the Casas Grandes area in 1989, he worked in southern Mesoamerica and in the U.S. Southwest. He has published a series of books, monographs, chapters, and journal articles on Oaxaca, western Texas, and northwestern Chihuahua. His research has been supported by the National Science Foundation and the National Geographic Society.

INDEX

abandonment: of Casas Grandes area, 122, 126; of Paquimé, 129, 167, 169; of U.S. Southwest, 201
Acoma, 203
acorns (*Quercus*), 56
agave (*Agave*), 47, 54, 56, 63, 100, 197, 204, 206, 208; at Paquimé, 62, 80–82, 91, 208; production, in Casas Grandes area, 50
agricultural intensification: in NW/SW, 204; in the western subregion, 146
alcoholic beverage production, in Paquimé, 80
Altavista site, 175
Amapa phase: in Nayarit, 179; polychrome ceramics, 179; White-on-red, 179
amaranth, 45, 104
Amerind Foundation, 3–4, 5, 12, 16, 56, 192, 196; founded by W. Fulton, 6, 18
Amerindian Cosmology and Society, 102, 111
ancestor worship, 92, 94, 98, 105
Ancestral Pueblo archaeology, 18, 56, 90, 192, 197, 199, 200, 204, 205; large sites, 205
Animas area, 120, 141; ball courts, 120, 121; ceramic assemblages in, 121
Animas phase, 137, 138–40, 157; sites, 156, 157, 171
animate objects, 74
antelope, 32, 51, 52
anthropogenic ecology, 45, 56
anthropomorphs, 92, 94, 95; macaw-headed, 95
archaeohistory, 193, 197, 199, 201; critiques of, 197
archaemagnetic dates, 154
Archaic Period, 20, 45, 89, 104, 105, 106, 107, 108, 132, 144, 166, 168
architecture of power, 82
Arroyo de Los Monos, 107
Arroyo la Tinaja, 54
artiodactyls, 34
atalayas, 99, 100, 196
Awatovi, 168

Aztatlán, 89, 95, 190; prestige goods at, 109
Aztec, 12, 91, 92, 98, 111, 193

Babícora Basin, 23, 24, 26, 30, 34, 36, 40, 44, 52, 129, 132
Bacerac, 136
ball courts, 9, 12, 44, 52, 63, 84, 87, 89, 94, 100, 119, 121, 123, 124, 127, 129, 138, 142, 148, 150, 194; Ball Court I, at Paquimé, 15; Ball Court II, at Casas Grandes, 96, 98; at Cienega Apache site (Ch-315), 44; at Joyce Well site, 146; at Paquimé, 12, 15, 96; I-shaped, 44, 90, 105; southern subregion, 132; symbolism of, 98; T-shaped, 105
ball game, 90, 94, 120; ancestor worship, 98
basin-and-range, 132, 149
Bavispe, 138, 144; and Chihuahuan ceramics, 140; exotica in, 140; project, 136; valley, 134
Bavispe site (CHIH C:9:4), 138; architecture, 138; excavations, 138
beads, 39, 63, 72, 76, 102, 181, 186, 204; copper, 82
beans, 28, 34, 35, 36, 45, 46, 50, 173; *Phaseolus acutifolius*, 49; *Phaseolus* cf. *vulgaris*, 49
bear, 34, 56, 102
beer, 54
bells, copper, 37, 58, 78, 185, 189, 193, 204; found at Wupatki, 182; Gulf of Mexico, 182; type IA5a, 182, 188; type IIIA, 182
Bernardino site, 160
bird cages, 119, 123
bison, 32, 34, 51, 52, 54, 102, 103
Black Mountain phase, 142
black wares, 35, 44, 122, 125
Blackiston, E. H., 4
Black-on-red pottery: Madera, 67; Pinedale, 158; Pinto, 159
Black-on-white pottery, 28, 35, 36, 108, 150, 158; Chupadero, 140, 156, 158, 159, 160, 161; Mimbres, 22, 46, 144. *See also* Tularosa

bobcat, 102
Boss Ranch site: dates, 159, 173; pottery types, 159
Box Canyon site: pottery tyles, 159
Brand, D., 4, 106, 112, 114, 116, 136, 138, 140, 142, 148, 150, 151; early survey by, 110, 129
brown ware pottery, 20, 24, 32; Viejo Period, 20
Buena Fe, 47, 193, 207; construction of, 205
bulrush (*Scirpus*), 46

Cabeza de Vaca, 149
caches, shamanic, 92
caciques, 90, 96, 100
Calderon site, 26, 32; infant burial in, 44; medallion at, 39; size of, 33; skeletal remains in, 28
cannibalism, 86
Carey, H., 4, 112
Carretas Basin, 127, 134, 136, 138, 140, 141
cartouches, 107
Casa Chica site: architecture in, 142; and El Paso phase, 142; location of, 142; turquoise in, 142
Casa del Fuego site: archaeomagnetic dates of, 154
Casa de Robles site: late date of, 164
Casas Grandes area: ceramic production in, 66; communities in, 186; core of, 52, 123, 127, 142, 146, 148; dates from, 167; definition, 129; early survey of and work in, 4, 129; eastern subregion, 150–54; excavations at, 49; food economy of, 49; heterogeneity of, 129; in Gran Chichimeca, 104; integrative facilities in, 119; interaction sphere of, 115, 117, 127, 129, 136, 150; kachinas in, 107; Mesoamerican ideas in, 111; migrants in, 148, 166; militarism in, 121; neighbors of, 119; nomadic groups in, 166; and Opata people, 164; organization of, 151; peripheries of, 123, 125, 127; polity of, 117, 138, 140; population, 58, 113, 128, 146, 148; recent surveys in, 108; refugee population in, 164; relict population in, 164; regional survey of Middle Zone, 115; regional survey of Outer Zone, 115; ritual landscape of, 98; river and river valley in, 18, 22, 125, 132, 137; rock art style of, 107; salt supply at, 143; settlement system in, 117; shared Pueblo elements of, 164; sites, 112, 129; size of, 110; southern subregion, 132; Spanish colony in, 152; subregions of, 127, 129; terraces in, 49, 203; tradition in, 18, 156; Viejo Period, 134, 199; western edge of, in Sonora, 134; western subregion, 142; watershed in, 132
Casas Grandes culture, 129; beginning of, 166; collapse of, 152, 168, 170; eastern limit of, 150; end date of, 167; in eastern subregion, 150; and "hearth area," 129; iconography in, 111; in outlying areas, 148; participants in, 133; and pottery, 67, 167, 186; and survival, 153; tradition of, 49
Casas Grandes site: archaeohistory of, 197–99; architecture in, 96; and ceramics/pottery, 68, 124, 162; Di Peso's view of, 199; drainage in, 44; effigies at, 84; extensive control by, 123; as historic town, 18; horned/plumed serpent and, 91, 92; iconography of, 95; influence of, 144; interaction sphere of, 3, 15, 47, 49, 51, 52, 54, 58; occupation dates of, 201; on pueblo scale, 205; Paquimé, 13, 18, 193; population estimate for, 207; and raised hearths, 146; religion of, 92, 94, 111; river, 18; shared Pueblo elements, 164; size of, 116, 129, 130; society derivation in, 168; and symbolism, 148; tree-ring dates, 193; as UNESCO site, 12
Casas Grandes volumes, 144, 175, 182, 193, 199; children's book, 12; and John Rinaldo and Gloria Fenner, 10
Central Mexico, 175, 193; Postclassic Period in, 185
ceramic: drums, 176, 180; effigies, 101; typology, 33
ceramics, Paquimé: Design Horizon A, 122, 124, 126; Design Horizon B, 122, 123, 124; Medio Period, 113, 122; nonlocal, 177–79; pseudo-cloisonné, 181
Cerro de Moctezuma, 52, 84, 98, 100, 119; ritual landscape of, 98
Cerro de Trincheras, 184, 199, 206; artifacts, 185–86; and Casas Grandes vessels, 188; cremations in, 186; and elite goods exchange, 194; interactions with, 184; and Loma de las Cremaciones, 186; and Paquimé, 184; petrographic analysis of, 186; and shells, 72, 74, 182, 184, 204, 205; and Sonora, 185; and specular hematite, 194

Index

Cerro Juanaqueña site, 20, 45, 52, 104
Cerros de Trincheras, 104
C4 plants, 28, 36, 86
chacmools, 175
Chaco Canyon, 6, 17, 60, 77, 80, 92, 129, 134, 193, 248; regional system, 24
Chalchihuites culture, 98, 173, 175, 177, 184, 190, 191, 194, 196, 197; Alta Vista site, 193; artifacts of, 178; Cerro de la Maroma site, 179; dates/dating of, 175, 177, 178, 187; and macaw nest box doors, 187; and platform hearths, 179; and trophy skulls 187; Tunal/Calera phase, 196
check dams, 56, 132
chia (*Salvia*), 46
Chichén Itzá, 84
Chichimecas, 175
chief's field, 53
Chihuahua, 14, 17, 30, 45, 51; bird breeders in, 186; current work in, 16; early pithouse period in, 20; ideology in, 69; imported goods in, 40; paucity of work in, 6; Plainware Period in, 20; and pottery, 173; precipitation in, 132; research in, 17; Santa Maria valley, 24
cholla (*Opuntia*), 56
cimientos, 129
Clanton Draw site: pottery types, 159
cliff dwellings, 140, 186
Cloverdale Corrugated pottery, 156
Clovis, 104
Coalescent Community Data Base, 208
cold-hammer technique. *See* copper
colonnades: architectural, 63; at Paquimé, 14
Colorado Plateau, 106, 167, 168, 199; shell sites at, 204
communal activity, 54, 74
community houses, 26, 33, 37, 42, 44, 46
Contreras Sánchez, E., 6, 18, 199; reconnaissance of, 14; Spanish publications of, 8
Convento phase (Viejo Period), 16, 26, 27, 28; architecture, 38; communal house, 38; houses, 26; metates, 70; palisades, 40; site, 12, 16, 26, 28, 32, 38, 45, 76, 134
copper, 42, 47, 60, 62, 63; axe head, 82; backed shield, 84; beads, 82; *cere perdue* (lost wax), 189; ceremonial uses of, 84; cold-hammer technique, 82, 189; and craft guild at Paquimé, 81; and malachite pigment, 206; and metallurgy in West Mexico, 183, 188, 190; mold technique, 82; nuggets, 82; ore in the Southwest, 206; at Paquimé, 41, 81–84, 180, 188, 189, 206; pendants, 82; plaques, 82; production, 81; slag, 82; smelting, 82; smelting critique, 82; spru, 189; tinklers, 82, 101; wire, 82. *See also* bells, copper
Core Zone, Casas Grandes, 119, 123, 125, 127; ceramics, 123; features, 119; Inner, 119; organization, 119, 121–23; Outer, 121; settlement sizes, 117; site count, 115; system center, 123
corn, 29, 30, 34, 36, 45, 54, 56, 76, 86, 111, 158; *criollo* races, 30
Coronado, 149
cotton (*Gossypium hirsutum*), 36, 46, 49, 50, 149, 196
cottontail rabbits, 58
Coyotlatelco, 174
crafts: guilds, 89; production, 59, 60, 89, 134
cranial deformation, 197
cruciforms, stone, 104
Cuarenta Casas site, 14
cults, 84, 86, 89, 90, 92, 98, 100, 107, 134; ancestor, 94, 202; Earth Fertility, 96; fertility, 94, 96; Medio Period, 109; Mesoamerican, 86, 96, 98, 107; Mimbres/Mogollon, 98; *Quetzalcóatl*, 84, 94; regional, 202; Southwestern, 123; *Xiuhtecutli*, 84

Darnell site, 160
deforestation, 58
Diablo phase, 169, 177, 195
Di Peso, Charles C.: archaeohistory and, 12, 193, 197, 199, 201; and Amerind Foundation, 10; and Casas Grandes volumes, 10; dates for Casas Grandes, 106, 193; description of Casas Grandes, 11; and Joint Casas Grandes Expedition, 10; legacy of, 14; phases for Casas Grandes, 201; population estimate by, 115; post-Paquimé area abandonment model of, 122; retrospective, 12; view of Casas Grandes, 127, 199; and Viejo Period, 24, 106; work at Casas Grandes, 10, 106
Di Peso map, 112–15, 117, 128; Medio Period settlement pattern, 115; Medio site

count, 115; Medio site size estimates, 113; overestimations, 113; regional population estimate, 115

Durango: Acaxée bird breeders in, 186; Cañón del Molino, 181; Guadiana Valley, 179; Guatimape Valley, 181; La Ferreria site, 187; Llano Grande obsidian in, 185; Mercado sherds in, 179; Rio Sauceda, 179; Sierra Madre obsidian in, 185; spindle whorls in, 179; terraces in, 197

Early Agricultural Period, 104, 105, 185, 199
Early Pithouse Period, 105
effigy: ceramic, 102; mound, 9; pregnant female, 111; smoker, 92, 95; stone, 109
Ehécatl, 84, 94
El Atravesaño site (CHIH C:9:9), 136
El Paso: area, 166, 174; phase, 142, 146, 169
El Zurdo site, 34, 36, 46, 52
Encinas Red-on-black, 156
entrepôts, 126
Escuela Nacional de Antropología e Historia, 16
ethnohistory, 175
exotic goods, 120, 148, 150, 192

farming: lowland river valley, in Medio Period, 47; upland, in Casas Grandes area, 20; upland, in Medio Period, 51, 53; Viejo Period, 28, 40
faunal remains, 52, 56
feasting, 54, 82, 89, 119, 121, 142, 202
feathers, 89, 91, 193, 196
Fenner, G., 6, 8, 45, 47, 85, 92
field houses, 109
Florentine Codex, 87

Galeana site, 40
gastropod, 74, 204
Gavilán phase: Nayarit, 179
Gila Polychrome, 70, 127, 140, 154, 156, 158, 159, 166; Cerro de Trincheras, 188; at Paquimé, 76, 208; standardization, 67
Gila Pueblo, 4, 127
goosefoot (*Chenopodium*), 56
gourd (*Lagenaria siceraria*), 49
Gran Chichimeca, 8, 104, 175, 193, 199; illustration, 16
grinding stones, 54, 65, 72

Ground Penetrating Radar (GPR), 26
ground stone production, specialization in, 74
Guadiana Valley, 177
Guasave Red, 156
Gulf of California, 183, 184, 194

Hawikuh, 77
hilltop shrines. See *atalayas*
Historia Tolteca-Chichimeca, 175
Hohokam, 51, 60, 129, 148, 169, 185, 194, 195, 203; large communities, 207; shell supply and trade, 22, 183
Homol'ovi site, 206
Hopi, 168, 203, 206; Masau diety, 197
House of the Dead: Unit 13, 14
House of the Pillars: Unit 14, 14
House of the Skulls: Unit 16, 14
House of the Well: Unit 8, 13
Huasteca, 173, 183, 185; bird breeders, 186
Huitzilopochtli, 173
hunting and gathering, 60, 106

Ibarra expedition, 17, 149, 152, 166
iconography: Mesoamerican, 202; of northern Rio Grande, 202; religious concepts in, 107
INAH. *See* Instituto Nacional de Antropología e Historia
Instituto Nacional de Antropología e Historia (INAH), 6, 13, 14, 18, 171, 199
International Four Corners, 17, 64
irrigation, 30, 44, 47, 49, 51, 53, 92, 94, 96, 106, 203, 207; canal, 193; of Casas Grandes area, 146; Medio Period, 32

J. Cowan site, 160
jacal, 13, 32
jackrabbits, 32
Jalisco, 177, 182, 187, 189, 191
Joint Casas Grandes Expedition (JCGE), 6, 10, 18, 45, 47, 49, 52, 54, 56, 57, 60, 140, 175, 177, 181, 188, 199; beginning of, 17; early survey work by, 104; end of fieldwork, 14; publications by, 199; reconnaissance survey of, 12; survey in Casas Grandes area, 112
Jornada Mogollon, 142, 150, 169, 203; rock art style in, 107
Joyce Well site, 148; architectural features of, 146; dates of, 158, 173. *See also* ball courts
juniper (*Juniperus*), 46

Index

kachinas, 92, 102, 107, 109, 202
kiln, 60, 66
kiva, 98, 105, 203
Ko'loowisi, Hopi, 92, 105

La Ferrería site: macaw cage doors at, 187
Laguna Bustillos, 34
La Playa dating, 185
La Quemada site, 175
Late Archaic Period, 16, 45
lithic pottery, 23, 24, 32, 50, 184, 186
little barley (*Hordeum pusillum*), 51
Loma de Moctezuma, 142, 144, 146, 148; charred maize, 142; irrigation canals, 142; rabbit bone, 142. *See also* Villa Ahumada
Los Metates, 74
Los Patos site, 78, 80, 206
Los Reyes sites, 22, 32, 45

macaw, 34, 62; bones, 85, 87; breeding, 87, 208; burials, 14; cage door stones, 34; ceremonial use of, 89; eggshells, 85; feces, at Paquimé, 85, 87; Gulf of Mexico, 185; House of the (Unit 12), 14, 85; husbandry, 85; isotope analysis of, 87; and military, 85; nesting boxes, at Paquimé, 14, 76, 85; production, at Paquimé, 84, 85, 89; sacrifice, at Paquimé, 84, 87; scarlet, 49, 56, 60, 63, 84, 85, 87; specialists, at Paquimé, 87; at Southwest sites, 85; in Viejo Period, 33, 34
Madrean Evergreen Woodland, 24, 42
maiz de ocho, 28
maize, 20, 28, 35, 36, 45, 49, 50, 54, 87, 104, 111, 134, 142, 149, 150, 155, 160, 173, 196, 199
manos, 56, 70, 197. *See also* grinding stones
Mata Ortiz, 22, 41, 52, 54, 68
Maya, 84, 92, 173, 187
Medanos phase, 150
Medio Period: agricultural practices, 32; architecture, 32; beginning and end of, 17; burials, 204; caciques, 96; chronological critiques of, 26; complexity of, 40; cults, 86, 109; cultural diversity, 148; dates/dating, 9, 16, 26, 106, 175, 193; definition, 126; Di Peso's phases of, 201; early surveys, 112; eastern extent, 151; growth, 22; imagery, 90; immigrants, 127; kachinas, 109; late part of, 124; leadership, 95; cieties, 90, 94; Mesoamerican influence, 107;
metate production, 74; middens, 166; migrants, 166; northern subregion, 148; outside influences during, 17; population, 113; pottery production, 68; priests, 94; processes, 20; pueblo adaption, 112; *Quetzalcóatl* cult, 84; regional differences, 40; religion, 90, 95, 109, 109; research focus, 24; ritual, 100, 146; roasting pits, 82; room blocks, 115; settlement location, 108, 110; settlement sizes, 115; settlement system, 112, 128; shamanism, 87; shells, 40, 42, 76; sites, 22, 24, 108, 110, 113, 115–16; small mounds, 112; southern subregion, 132, 134; symbolism, 146; trade, 39; transition to, 20; water ritual, 100
Mercado Red-on-Cream, 177
mercantile system, 194
Mesa Machichi site (CHIH C:9:29), 138; ball court, 138; public architecture, 138
Mesa Verde, 127, 247; depopulation of, 203
mescal, 47, 54
Mesoamerican influence, 92, 107
Mesoamerican merchants, 173, 175, 184
metallurgy, 176
metates, 56, 63, 70, 89, 196, 197, 204, 208; production debris of, 72; at Salmon Ruin site, 70; type 1A, 70, 72, 74; type 1B, 70, 72, 89. *See also* grinding stones
Mexica, 173
Mexico: archaeology in, 14; central, 181; western, 181
Michoacán, 181; Infiernillo region, 189; Rio Balsas region, 189
Middle Zone, Casas Grandes, 123, 125, 127; ceramics, 123; features, 119; organization, 127–29; settlement sizes, 117; site count, 115; system periphery, 123. *See also* Casas Grandes site
Mimbres, 20, 22, 30, 34, 35, 36, 58, 124, 127, 129, 140, 143, 144, 203; horned/plumed serpent, 92; metates, 72; migration from, 22; sites, 37
minerals, 14
mission, 135, 136, 152
modes of production, 60
Mogollon, 24, 98, 105, 129, 144, 203, 205
Mormons, 53
mound size, as predictor of room count, 112
Mound of the Bird: Unit 10, 14

Mound of the Cross, 105; Unit 2, 12, 39, 95, 96
Mound of the Heroes: Unit 9, 14
Mound of the Offerings, 105, 189; Unit 4, 12
Mound of the Pit Ovens: Unit 1, 12
Museo de las Culturas del Norte, 12

Nassarius shell, 72, 181, 183, 197; beads, 74; vast cache, 76. *See also* shell
Nayarit, 177, 182, 189; Alto Rio Bolaños site, 180; Amapa phase dates, 179; Balsas-Tepalcatepec basins, 197; Chapala Lake, 179; Gavilan Lake, 179; Ixtlán del Rio site, 179; polychrome ceramics at, 179; Sayula phase dates, 180; Sayula-Zacoalco area, 179
New Mexico: Galisteo Basin, 202, 203; Henderson Pueblo, 208; Pajarito Plateau, 202; Rio Chama, 203; Salinas district, 203; and turquoise, 185, 206
Noguera, 4, 112
non–Casas Grandes sites: Chihuahuan pottery at, 161–67
northwest Chihuahua, 45, 49, 51, 115, 127; early pithouse period, 108
Nuevo Casas Grandes, 14, 47
Northwest/Southwest (NW/SW): as copper source, 206; population centers, 203; population movement, 201

Obregón, Balthazar de, 4, 17, 51, 129
obsidian hydration dating, 153
Ojo de Agua de Corodehuachi site, 156, 158, 173; chronology, 157; dating, 156, 164; Medio Period traits of, 186
Ojo Varaleño, 16
Olmec, 87
Opata, 136, 164, 190
ovens, 9, 12, 54, 80, 81, 82, 100, 119, 121, 125; domestic use, 81; pit, 80; ritual use, 80

Pacific coast, 173, 175, 184, 195
Palanganas River, 22, 108
Paquimé: aerial view of, 9; apogee, 184; aviculture in, 208; bone collagen dates of, 150; canals in, 16, 102; and Casas Grandes, 18; ceremonial architecture in, 87, 109; and Cerro de Moctezuma, 99; and Cerro de Trincheras, 186, 188, 192; and Chalchihuites pottery, 177; and Chalchihuites obsidian, 185; children's book about, 12; collapse of, 9, 16, 122, 126, 166, 168, 169, 201; core of, 131; crafts in, 60, 89; cults in, 84; current work in, 16; dates/dating of, 150, 153; development of, 175; Diablo phase in, 169; and Di Peso, 11, 106, 115, 127; early description of, 17; early visitors to, 4; excavation of, 8, 9, 12, 112; exotica from, 40, 185; feasting in, 82; and foreign artifacts/goods, 177, 181, 194; heterarchical complexity of, 202; human sacrifice in, 98; local impulses in, 17; and long-distance trade, 9; as mercantile center or outpost, 193, 204, 208; and Mesoamerica, 12, 176, 184, 188; metal artifacts in, 189; metate production in, 70–74, 208; and Mexica, 173; mortuary data from, 94; multistory construction in, 207; museum, 14; neighbors, 117; new directions in, 16; and organization of production, 62; and ovens, 80, 82; and *pochteca*, 17; population of, 11, 201; and pottery, 64–70, 74, 153; and primate center, 117; public architecture in, 121; and *puchteca*, 92; and regional context, 112, 150; relations to south and west, 175, 177; religious significance of, 105; and reservoir, 16; revised room count for, 205; and rituals, 87, 111; settlement system of, 112; shared ideology in, 124; and shells, 72, 73, 74, 76, 82, 181, 183, 188, 204; as source of innovation, 144; specular hematite in, 194; spindle whorls in, 177; and stone pipes, 92; storage rooms in, 177; "tenements" in, 169; *Tláloc* rituals in, 100, 107; and Tula, 173; and trophy skulls, 187; and turkeys, 62, 74–80, 86; and Unit 16, 64; and water, 100, 102, 107; and West Mexican copper artifact designs, 190; and West Mexican sherds, 179
Pendleton Ruin site, 146, 158; platform mound, 148; roosting pens, 76
periphery, of Casas Grandes, 24, 59, 123, 125, 127
Perros Bravos: architecture, 42; burial, 41
Petran Montane Conifer Forest, 24
petroglyphs, 132, 203
peyote, 173
Picacho drainage, 26
pigweed (*Amaranthus*), 56
pilgrimage, 150, 208
Piman speakers, 164
piñon, 46, 50, 56

Index

pithouse, 12, 20, 26, 106, 134, 140; Viejo Period, 22, 30, 108, 112
Pithouse Period, 20, 106, 107, 108, 110; Early, 106; Late, 106; settlement system of, 106–10
pithouse-to-pueblo transition, 42, 106
plainware, 37
platform hearths, 179
platform mounds, 9, 52, 54, 63, 81, 105, 148, 194
Playas Red, 102, 167, 186
Playas valley, 142
pochteca, 17, 127, 175; Aztec, 12. See also *puchteca*
political economy, 47, 51, 56, 60, 127, 128, 129, 205
pollen, 54, 111
polvos de paja, 149
polychrome pottery and wares, 40, 63, 76, 89, 126, 128, 144, 148, 163, 164, 169, 194, 204; Babícora (Bavícora), 66, 160; Babocomari, 156, 159; Carretas, 134, 160, 171, 174, 186, 188; in Casas Grandes culture, 174, 176, 186; at Casas Grandes site, 197; at Cerro de Trincheras, 188, 192; of Chihuahua, 68, 162, 171; Corralitos, 160; Dublan, 160; El Paso, 129, 140, 142, 143, 146, 154, 156, 158, 161, 166; Escondito, 67; Huerigos, 134, 174; Maverick Mountain, 159; Medio Period, 64; Nayarit, 179; at Paquimé, 62, 74; Pinedale, 158; Pinto, 158; Salado, 70; Santa Cruz, 156, 159; St. Johns, 156, 158, 159; Tonto, 154, 156, 158, 159; Trincheras, 160; Tucson, 106, 154, 156, 158, 159, 165, 166; Viejo Period, 28, 35; Villa Ahumada, 66, 160. See also Gila Polychrome; Ramos Polychrome
Postclassic Period, 183
post-Paquimé, 112, 122, 167, 170; ceramics, 128; occupation, 128, 136; population dispersal, 126; Robles phase, 170; settlement systems, 122–28; sites, 122
pound sign, 92, 95
Preceramic sites, 104, 112; in northern Chihuahua, 150; settlement patterns of, 104–6
prestige goods, 109, 125, 127, 136, 150, 192, 194, 196
Price Canyon site, 160
priests, 87, 90, 92, 94, 95, 96, 111; and priesthoods, 86

primate settlement systems, 115, 117, 119, 121, 125, 126, 127, 128
primate centers, 59, 115, 117, 119, 121, 122, 125, 126, 127
pronghorn antelope, 32
protohistoric/historic Zuni: Hawikkiu village
Protohistoric Period, 201
Proyecto Arqueológico Chihuahua (PAC), 26, 49
public architecture, 60, 87, 121, 132, 136, 138, 142, 148, 150, 201, 207
puchteca, 86, 89, 92; turquoise, 76
Pueblo, 78, 82, 163, 164, 174, 195, 201, 207; Pueblo IV Period, 166; rainmaking ideology, 104; Rio Grande villages, 207; settlement systems, 110–12
Pueblo Bonito: copper objects in, 82; metates in, 70; shell quantity in, 72; turquoise in, 78
puma, 34
purslane (*Portulaca*), 56

Querétaro, 175
Quetzalcóatl, 84, 89, 90, 93, 94, 100, 105, 173

rabbits, 34, 51, 52
radiocarbon dating, 30, 132, 150, 164, 190; of Casas Grandes site, 193; of Convento site, 27; of Hidalgo County, 158; of Paquimé, 155; of San José Bavícora, 155, 156; of Site 315, 154; of Site 565, 154; and Viejo Period, 26; of Villa Ahumada, 160
rainmaking ideology, 104
Ramos Black, 67, 164
Ramos Polychrome: analysis, 66; at Casas Grandes site, 68; design element standardization, 70; at Joyce Well site, 146; macaw imagery in, 70; Neutron Activation Analysis of, 66; in other areas, 66; production, 66, 208; and shamanism, 202; and snake motifs, 204
Las Ranas, 175
rancherías, 134, 150, 168
Rancho el Espía site, 154
Raspadura drainage, 26, 27
Raspadura site (Ch-011), 45
red-on-brown pottery, 150, 175; Anchondo, 35, 163; Dragoon, 156; Mata, 35; Tanque Verde, 156, 160; Viejo Period, 37
red-slipped ware, 35, 37, 44, 125

red ware, 136
religious ideology, Mesoamerican, 204
reservoirs, 2, 12, 63, 80, 195, 206
Resilience Theory, 61
Reyes sites, 26, 40; pithouses, 40
Rio Bavíspe, 136
Rio Carmen, 78, 150; Medio sites, 142
Rio Casas Grandes, 18, 22, 28, 40, 45, 47, 49, 51, 53, 54, 58, 102, 104, 106, 108, 128, 150, 154
Rio Gavilán, 51, 56
Rio Grande, 154, 199, 201, 203, 207, 208; biscuit ware, 202; flood destruction, 205; Glaze A pottery, 154; glaze wares, 202; Pueblo villages, 207; turquoise, 206
Rio Mátape, 184
Rio Papagochi, 132
Rio Sonora, 144; culture, 149
ritual architecture, 132
ritual landscape, 98
roasting pits, 80, 82, 89, 132, 142, 106. *See also* ovens
Robles, 4, 112, 170; phase, 167, 170
rock art, 84, 90, 104, 107, 109, 150
rock mulch, 53
room block mound, 112, 113, 115, 117; area, 110, 116; simulated size of, 117; categories in the Casas Grandes area, 115; median size of, in Medio Period, 117
room blocks, 9, 11, 12, 13, 14, 16, 22, 26, 32, 33, 40, 115, 132, 207
room count, population estimates from, 112

sacred leaders, 92, 96
sacrifice: human, 98; of macaws, 89; of turkeys, 86
Sahagún, Bernardino de, 86; ethnohistorical records of, 87
Salado area, 70; ceramics, 124, 144
Salinas, 143, 183, 203, 205, 208; Salinas de la Unión site, 143
Samalayuca dunes, 22
San Antonio de Padua Church, 11
San Bernardino valley, 142, 144
Sand Canyon Almanac, 56
San José Bavicora, 156, 158, 164, 171
San Juan Basin, 203
San Luis valley, 142
San Pedro area, 108
San Simon area, 144

Santa Clara: Pueblo, 24; River, 23, 24, 26, 36, 40, 44, 132, 150
Santa Fe Institute, 111
Santa María River, 22, 23, 24, 25, 26, 28, 36, 40, 42, 44, 127, 128, 129, 132, 142, 150
Sayles, Edwin B., 4, 106, 112, 129; early survey by, 111
Schroeder site, 197
sedentism, 30, 166
Semidesert Grassland, 51
serpent: and Casas Grandes site, 91, 92; feathered, 94, 175; Fire, 92; flowered, 92, 94; horned, 84, 92, 105; horned/plumed, 91, 92, 95, 108; House of the (Unit 11), 14; icons, 90; Medio Period, 90, 91; Mimbres, 92; Mound of the, 90, 105, 151; pan-American water, 93; plumed, 90, 92, 94, 105; traditions, 94; Turquoise, 92; Zuni Water, 92
settlement patterns, 108, 112, 115, 123, 125, 127, 128
shamans, 86, 90, 92; and shamanism, 87, 94, 95, 111; and shaman-priests, 94, 95
shell, 10, 89, 102, 103, 140, 146, 186, 192, 195, 196, 197, 206; Archaic Period sites, 40; artisans, 72; beads, 72, 74; burial offerings, 76; in Casas Grandes area, 74; in Cerro de Trincheras, 72, 74, 205; economy, 183; freshwater, 82; Guaymas as, source, 181; Gulf of California, 74; La Playa, production, 184; marine, 36, 37, 38, 82; Medio Period, 40, 76; midden, 183; objects, ideological value of, 74, 76; Panamic Province, 183; at Paquimé, 41, 56, 58, 61, 71–74, 82, 188, 204; *Strombus*, 84; supply routes, 183; trumpets, 176; unfinished objects, 72; unworked, 82; Viejo Period, 38, 39, 44, 76, 204; and West Mexico, 22, 82, 181, 183; worked, 82. See also *Nassarius* shell
shell trade: in Cerro de Trincheras, 192, 204; coastal route of, 42; Gulf of California, with Casas Grandes site, 182, 184; Hohokam, 18, 22; Medio Period, 42; southern routes, 38
Sierra Madre, 4, 20, 42, 47, 49, 51, 53, 56, 115, 127, 128, 129, 134, 152, 155, 175, 184, 185, 190, 194, 195; bird breeders, 186; current work in, 16; excavations in, by E. Guevara, 14; and Paquimé, 186; in Sinaloa, 197; in Sonora, 197; Viejo Period, 24

Sikyatki site, 203
Sinaloa, 181; bird breeders, 186; Casas Grandes artifacts, 183; coastal plains, 197 *See also* Sierra Madre
Site 204, 113
Site 242, 52
Site 315, 51, 154
Site 317, 117
Site 565, 169
slaves, at Paquimé, 82, 196
smelting. *See* copper
smoking, 92, 94
Snaketown project, 8
Society for American Archaeology, 13
Sonora, 22, 129, 134, 142, 149, 152, 156, 165, 166, 190, 191, 192, 199, 204, 206; Casas Grandes–style architecture in, 186; cliff dwellings in, 186; culture of, 136; Las Trincheras site, 182; Ónavas site, 197; Rio Yaqui, 197; Trincheras tradition in, 183; Viejo Period ceramics in, 186
Sonoran Desert, 45, 53, 183; farming communities in, 183 184, 192
Sonora Serrana tradition, 186
sotol (*Dasylirion*), 47, 48, 56, 80
Southwest, U.S.: early pithouses in, 106; kivas in, 98, 105, 203; kachinas in, 92, 102, 107, 109, 202; Mesoamerican religious principles in, 111; metates in, 72; relations with Mexico, 6; religious images from, 123
Spanish colonists, 152
spindle whorls, 177, 179
squashes (*Cucurbita*), 28, 34, 35, 36, 46, 47, 49
stone pipes, 92
storage, 30, 49, 194; vessels, 35
survey, 4, 17, 60, 113, 115, 117, 122, 128, 137, 150, 199; 1994–95 regional, 112, 113, 115–19, 122, 128
Swartz Ruin site, 37

Tardio Period, 136
temporal agriculture, 30
Tenochtitlán, 187, 193
Teotihuacán, 92, 177
terraced fields, 51, 54, 58, 138, 139, 208
terraces, 49, 51, 53, 54, 56, 104, 107, 108, 119, 123, 125, 190, 197
tesserae, 80
Texas, 13, 106, 163, 166
textured ware, 34, 35, 37, 122, 125, 186

Tezcatlipoca, 173
thermoluminiscence dating, 177
Tinaja site, 153, 154, 207
Tláloc cult, 84, 94, 100, 182, 188; kachinas, 107; and turkey sacrifice, 86
Tlamimilolpa phase, 177
tobacco, 94
Tollan phase, 175
Toltecs, 12, 89, 98, 185, 193
Toluquilla, 175
Totoate, 180
trade: routes, 129, 173, 183, 195; wares, 140
transformations, animal, 94
tree-ring date, 150, 155
Tres Ríos area, 136, 182, 184
Trincheras: ceramic wares, 156; copper bells, 188; Purple-on-red, 160; region, 74; sites, 105; tradition, 184. *See also* polychrome pottery and wares
Tropic of Cancer, 181
T-shaped doors, 63
Tula, 84, 173, 175, 176, 181, 187, 193
Tularosa: Black-on-white, 156, 158, 159; White-on-red, 160
turkey, 33, 49, 52, 56, 63, 89, 90, 197, 204, 208; at Villa Ahumada, 78; aviculture, 85; beads, 80, 102; breeding, 76; burials, 14, 78; consumption, 80; DNA study, 34; domestication, 74, 77; feathers, 75, 78; husbandry, 87; pens, 14, 76; production, at Paquimé, 78; remains, 76, 78, 82, 84, 87; sacrifice, 75, 86; use at Paquimé, 78
turquoise, 12, 62, 63, 82, 89, 92, 103, 142, 146, 148, 186, 196, 197, 204, 208; in Casas Grandes area, 80; Cerrillos Hills, NM, as source of, 206; different uses of, 76; finished pieces, 78; mosaic work, 80; at Paquimé, 78, 79, 80, 185, 205, 206; production waste, 78; *puchteca* attraction and, 76; as raw material, 78; and relation to water, 104; and specialization, 80; standardization of products, 80; use as personal ornaments, 80; working, 72, 79
turtles, 102
tzompantli (trophy skulls), 14, 85, 86, 175; at Mesoamerican sites, 187

Unit 1, 3, 14, 20, 21; and turkey remains, 76
Unit 4: burials, 67

Unit 8, 66, 74, 87, 177; and copper, 82; and metates, 72; and turkey remains, 76
Unit 9, 47, 54, 80, 82
Unit 14, 82; and metates, 70, 72, 74
Unit 16, 66, 76, 82; and metates, 72
Uto-Aztecan, 134

vesicular basalt, 74
Viejo Period: architecture, 37; broader context, 22; Bustillos Basin, 36; Calderon site, 26; ceramic production, 35; chronology, 28, 108; copper, 40, 41, 189; corrugated wares, 35; crops, 28; dating, 199; and Di Peso, 24, 106; eastern subregion, 150; extent, 20; foreign artifacts, 181; house types, by phase, 26; ideology, 37; imported goods, 40; large site locations, 22; northern/southern divergence, 20, 26, 44; original phase dates, 26; paucity of data in, 22; Perros Bravos phase, 26, 27, 28, 38, 40; phases of, 28, 44; Pilón phase, 26, 27, 36, 40; pithouse sizes, 32; pithouse-to-pueblo transition, 106; population, 17, 22, 150; pottery trade and assemblage, 33, 35; redefinition of, 107; regional differences, 40; sedentism, 20, 30; settlement systems, 106–10; shamans, 94; sites, 22, 33, 37, 108, 110, 134, 150, 199; social hierarchy, 37; Southwest orientation, 42; storage strategies, 36; subregional traditions, 144; subsistence practices, 32; surface rooms, 38; trade, 35, 173; trait retention, 148; transition to Medio Period, 16, 33, 201; variability, 24; vessel sizes, 35; zone similarities, 40, 42
Viejo zone, northern, 22, 24; architecture, 40; animal use, 32; plant remains, 34; site clustering, 28; sites, 22; trade sherds, 27; Viejo-to-Medio transition, 33
Viejo zone, southern, 23, 26, 28, 30, 36, 132, 134; architecture, 33, 40; crops, 34, 36; community house, 32; faunal remains, 34; isotopic skeletal analyses, 28; organization, 134; pithouses, 32, 33; population growth, 146; pottery types, 35; rich burial, 39; sites, 24, 28; storage, 36; temporal agriculture, 28, 30; trade, 42; wild plant use, 36
Villa Ahumada, 40; excavations, 78; late date, 164; site, 52, 78, 80, 129, 160, 162, 164, 165, 166, 188, 206; turquoise piece count, 78. *See also* polychrome pottery and wares

walk-in well, at Paquimé, 14, 92, 100, 102, 195
warfare, 104, 129, 132, 142, 148
water: city, 100; distribution system, 9, 16; fowl, 34; management, 132, 134; ritual, 92, 100; shrine, 14; symbolism, 100, 102
weavers, at Paquimé, 91
Western Pueblo region, 203
woodworking, at Paquimé, 91
World Systems theory, 189

Xipe Tótec, 84, 85, 87, 94
Xiucóatl, 84
Xiuhtecutli, 84, 92, 94

yucca (*Yucca*), 56

Zacatecas, 98, 175, 177, 187, 190, 193, 197, 199; Teúl de González Ortega, 189
Zaragoza Basin, 40
Zuni, 77, 203, 208

AMERIND STUDIES IN ANTHROPOLOGY

SERIES EDITOR **JOHN A. WARE**

Trincheras Sites in Time, Space, and Society
Edited by Suzanne K. Fish, Paul R. Fish, and M. Elisa Villalpando

Collaborating at the Trowel's Edge: Teaching and Learning in Indigenous Archaeology
Edited by Stephen W. Silliman

Warfare in Cultural Context: Practice, Agency, and the Archaeology of Violence
Edited by Axel E. Nielsen and William H. Walker

Across a Great Divide: Continuity and Change in Native North American Societies, 1400–1900
Edited by Laura L. Scheiber and Mark D. Mitchell

Leaving Mesa Verde: Peril and Change in the Thirteenth-Century Southwest
Edited by Timothy A. Kohler, Mark D. Varien, and Aaron M. Wright

Becoming Villagers: Comparing Early Village Societies
Edited by Matthew S. Bandy and Jake R. Fox

Hunter-Gatherer Archaeology as Historical Process
Edited by Kenneth E. Sassaman and Donald H. Holly, Jr.

Religious Transformation in the Late Pre-Hispanic Pueblo World
Edited by Donna M. Glowacki and Scott Van Keuren

Crow-Omaha: New Light on a Classic Problem of Kinship Analysis
Edited by Thomas R. Trautmann and Peter M. Whiteley

Native and Spanish New Worlds: Sixteenth-Century Entradas in the American Southwest and Southeast
Edited by Clay Mathers, Jeffrey M. Mitchem, and Charles M. Haecker

Transformation by Fire: The Archaeology of Cremation in Cultural Context
Edited by Ian Kuijt, Colin P. Quinn, and Gabriel Cooney

Chaco Revisited: New Research on the Prehistory of Chaco Canyon, New Mexico
Edited by Carrie C. Heitman and Stephen Plog

Ancient Paquimé and the Casas Grandes World
Edited by Paul E. Minnis and Michael E. Whalen